ROMAN ROADS IN BRITAIN

THOMAS CODRINGTON

M. INST.C. E., F. G S.

*WITH LARGE CHART OF THE ROMAN ROADS
AND SMALL MAPS IN THE TEXT*

REPRINT OF THIRD EDITION

LONDON
THE SHELDON PRESS
NORTHUMBERLAND AVENUE, W.C. 2
NEW YORK: THE MACMILLAN COMPANY

First Edition	.	.	.	1903
Second Edition, Revised			.	1905
Third Edition, Revised		.	.	1918
,,	,,	(Reprint)	.	1919
,,	,,	,,	.	1928

PRINTED IN GREAT BRITAIN BY RICHARD CLAY & SONS, LIMITED,
BUNGAY, SUFFOLK.

PREFACE

THE following attempt to describe the Roman roads of Britain originated in observations made in all parts of the country as opportunities presented themselves to me from time to time. On turning to other sources of information, the curious fact appeared that for a century past the literature of the subject has been widely influenced by the spurious Itinerary attributed to Richard of Cirencester. Though that was long ago shown to be a forgery, statements derived from it, and suppositions founded upon them, are continually repeated, casting suspicion sometimes undeserved on accounts which prove to be otherwise accurate. A wide publicity, and some semblance of authority, have been given to imaginary roads and stations by the new Ordnance maps.

Those who early in the last century, under the influence of the new Itinerary, traced the Roman roads, unfortunately left but scanty accounts of the remains which came under their notice, many of which have since been destroyed or covered up in the making of modern roads; and with the evidence now available few Roman roads can be traced continuously. The gaps can often be filled with reasonable certainty, but more often the precise course is doubtful, and the entire course of some roads connecting known stations of the Itinerary of Antonine can only be guessed at. All vestiges may have been destroyed, but chance discoveries show that much may yet be learned from remains buried beneath the soil.

The network of roads might easily be made more complete, as a glance at the map will show; but it seems best to refrain from conjecture as much as possible, and to follow the roads only so far as there is evidence available for tracing them. Where routes of the Itinerary of Antonine can be identified, the position of the stations will be fixed by distances, or other evidence, and the dimensions of camps and walled stations on the courses of the roads will be given; but no attempt will be made to describe the remains of towns and stations.

To no one can the imperfection of this attempt to describe the Roman roads of the country be more evident than it is to myself. The materials available are incomplete, and though I am indebted for information to many under whose notice remains have come in recent years, it must happen that, in so wide a field, vestiges known locally, and perhaps described, have been overlooked.

My acknowledgments are due for the facilities for reference which have been afforded me in the library of the Society of Antiquaries with the ready help of Mr. George Clinch. My thanks are also due to the Rev. E. McClure for his valuable advice, and especially to the Rev. George Herbert for undertaking much troublesome work in looking through the proofs, and aiding in the preparation of the map.

T. C

PREFACE TO THE THIRD EDITION

A SECOND edition, issued in 1905, was a reprint of the first with an appendix containing some additional particulars which had come under my notice. These have now been embodied in the text with others matters, which have been since published, or have been courteously communicated by correspondents, or are the result of my own observation. Very few roads have been added. Claims of others to be considered Roman roads have been made, and further examination may strengthen these claims, but at present they do not seem to me to be conclusive.

While fresh remains and traces of Roman roads have been brought to light, some of those which were visible fourteen years ago may be so no longer. I am unable to verify how far that is the case, and it seems best to leave the record of traces as it was in 1903.

T. C.

Twickenham, 1918.

CONTENTS

MAPS

ROMAN ROADS IN BRITAIN

CHAPTER I

INTRODUCTION

THE roads constructed during the Roman occupation
do not appeal to the imagination like such remains as the
Wall of Hadrian, or the ruins of an ancient city; but when
the extent and the permanent nature and effect of them
are considered, they may claim a foremost place among
the remains of Roman work in the country. They were
part of the network of roads that covered the Roman world;
for many centuries they continued to be the chief means
of communication within the island; and while some of
them are still to be seen in almost perfect condition, portions
of many more form part of the foundations of roads now
in use.

The course of the roads was evidently planned with skill,
and laid out with a complete grasp of the general features
of the country to be passed through; the work of construction, however, was probably carried out under many
masters, and perhaps not at the same time.

The method of construction followed by the Roman
road-makers has unfortunately not been investigated with
any thoroughness in this country. What we do know of
it has generally been learned from sections made by chance,
and too often not carefully described, and in the absence
of ascertained facts writers have fallen back on the descriptions of ancient authors, as given by Nicholas Bergier in
1622.[1] Vitruvius, who wrote about the time of the Christian

---

[1] *Histoire des Grands Chemins de l'Empire Romain,* 1622.

era, is often cited as having described the manner in which the Romans made their roads, but he was really describing the making of pavements in connexion with architectural works.[1] Bergier states that as he found no ancient author who had described clearly the interior parts of paved Roman roads, he was led to go to descriptions of the manner of constructing pavements in connexion with buildings, and he opened Roman roads near Rheims to see how far they corresponded with Vitruvius' description. He gives the results, which show that neither the number of the layers which he found, nor their order, agreed with this description, or with each other. He however adopted Vitruvius' names for the several layers, and this is the only authority from which later writers give those names, *Stratum, Rudus, Nucleus,* and *Pavimentum,* to layers found in Roman roads.

A quotation from the poet Statius [2] (A.D. 81–96), with the explanation given by Bergier, has often been made use of since. It relates to the making of the *Via Domitiana,* but Statius was more concerned with flattering Domitian than with precise description, and he affords only a very general and poetical sketch of marking out the road, excavating the ground, and filling in other material to form a bed for the pavement or other surface layer.

Palladio [3] (1570) gives an account of two methods of making Roman roads in Italy. One is described as simply a mound of sand or gravel raised somewhat in the middle; the description of the other seems to have been based on remains of roads then existing, and a plan is given in illustration. The road consisted of three divisions, the middle

---

[1] *De Architectura,* lib. vii. cap. i.
[2] *Silvarum,* lib. iv. iii.

>Hic primus labor inchoare sulcos,
>Et rescindere limites; et alto
>Egestu penitus cavare terras.
>Mox haustas aliter replere fossas,
>Et summo gremium parare dorso;
>Ne nutent sola, ne maligna sedes,
>Et pressis dubium cubile saxis.
>Tunc umbonibus hinc et hinc coactis,
>Et crebris iter alligare gomphis.

[3] *I quattro libri dell' Architectura,* lib. iii. cap. iii.

paved with flat stones of irregular shape, closely jointed; and two sides somewhat lower separated from the middle by stones set on edge. The sides, which were half the width of the middle, were covered with sand and small gravel. According to Palladio those on foot travelled on the paved road, and horses on the side roads, and he does not mention wheeled traffic.

In France remains of Roman roads with a middle and two side spaces have been found. Bergier unfortunately tells us nothing about the transverse section of the roads which he opened near Rheims, but Gautier, a century later, describes [1] such roads, of which he had seen many remains. The materials composing the middle portion of the road were in a trench as much as three feet deep, from which the earth had been taken to form the side roads. At the bottom of the trench was a pavement of stones on edge, five or six inches thick, and a little rounded, over which was a bed two or three feet thick of stones of about the size of eggs. The middle road was separated from the side roads by flat stones set on edge, and appeared to have been used by wheeled vehicles The side roads, which were made much in the same manner, might, he thought, have served for foot passengers and perhaps for horsemen, and were wide enough to allow a horseman and a man on foot to pass easily. No mention is made of a paved surface.

Of such roads there are still remains, which are called Chaussées de Brunhaut, and the middle and side roads seem to survive in the *chaussées* and *accotements* of modern French roads. The evidences of similar roads in Britain are few and doubtful.

It is evident from remains which have been described, and others which still exist, that the Romans followed no hard-and-fast rule, but made their roads according to the situation and to the materials available, and perhaps in a different manner at different times.

In Britain we find considerable variation in the Roman method of construction. An embankment is a very usual feature, and, constructed with the utmost care on a solid foundation with suitable materials, it constitutes the ridge of the road, which often remains almost unchanged by time when man has not disturbed it.

[1] *Traité de la construction des Chemins*, p. 7, 1721.

The height of the embankment or ridge was sometimes considerable, not only where a low place had to be crossed, but on high ground. Perhaps the most striking example remaining is the embankment called Atchling Ditch or Dyke to the south-west of Salisbury, which for four miles runs across the high open down almost unchanged in profile, five yards across the top and five to six feet high. Another example may be seen between Doncaster and Pontefract, where for several miles there is an embankment four, six, and eight feet high, and six yards wide, on high ground with a rock subsoil. In some places the Roman road has been removed for the sake of the materials, so that instead of a ridge, a wide shallow trench remains. In other places the paved foundation is found a foot or more below the level of the ground without a trace of the road on the surface. This has arisen from the removal of the upper part in the interests of cultivation, the portion beyond the reach of the plough having been left; deeper ploughing has caused this process to be repeated in recent years. It is, however, difficult to suppose that the roads were in all cases raised. On the Foss Way, between Bath and Cirencester, where it is a wide, grass-grown, deserted road on a high oolitic plateau, there is, to the south of Jackments Bottom, a ridge in the middle four to six feet high; but not much further south there are no traces of a ridge for miles. The same thing is to be observed on the deserted part of Watling Street north of Watford Gap, where the green road shows no sign of a ridge for several miles until low ground is crossed, and then the ridge appears as much as five feet high, where it has not been removed for the sake of the materials.

The width of the embankment appears to have varied from six or seven feet, as at Radstock, to six or seven yards south of Jackments Bottom, both of these places being on the Foss Way. Deep trenches were commonly dug on the sides of the road, the material from which, when suitable, went to raise the ridge, but in soft places it appears to have been cast outwards. The side ditches can now generally only be traced by digging, but they sometimes remain, as on the chalk down between Vernditch Chase and Woodyates. Where Roman roads have been modernized the side ditches have become the natural receptacles of mud, etc., from the road surface, with which they are filled up.

Perhaps in this country the surface of the roads was more generally made of gravel or stone, sometimes grouted with lime or coarse mortar, and of a considerable thickness. Camden describes roads which in his time were of gravel, as in the case of Kind Street between Middlewich and Northwich, made of gravel brought from a distance. The Sussex Stane Street when it was cut through early in the last century, in a situation where previous disturbance was unlikely, was found to consist of " four and a half feet thick of flints and other stones laid alternately and bedded in sand or fine gravel." [1] The Roman road near Woodyates, between Old Sarum and Dorchester, appears to have been of gravel. The ridge on the chalk down is as much as six or seven feet high, and where it is away from a modern road appears to be in its original state. Where it has been cut through for a drove-way, a coating of tertiary gravel two and a half to three feet thick is exposed that must have been brought four or five miles, and any material for a paving was probably not to be got. Evidence of the same sort is to be seen for several miles further on.

The original structure of Watling Street may be seen near Kilsby, where no modern road has taken its place, and a brook on one side has cut into it. The ridge across the low ground close by is five feet high where it has not been dug away, but there is little or no ridge where the stream has made a section of the grass-grown road, and there is a thickness of about a yard of gravel with a layer of pebbles or cobbles at the base on a clayey subsoil.

The surface was certainly sometimes paved. Camden describes the Kentish Stone Street as being paved with stone.[2] Stukeley found part of Erming Street north of Huntingdon still paved, and describes the paving of the Foss Road south of Ilchester as consisting of the flat quarry stone of the country, of a good breadth, laid edgeways, and so close that it looked like the side of a wall fallen down,[3] and the road remained much in its original state up to the beginning of the last century. Near Radstock the

---

[1] Manning's *History of Surrey* vol. iii. p. xlv.
[2] *Britannia*, vol. i. p. 321. (Gough's edition.)
[3] *Itinerarium Curiosum*, p. 155.

paving of the Foss Road still remains on the top of a hill
where it has been deserted. Stukeley saw a paving for
several miles on the Foss near Willoughby-in-the-Wolds [1]
—some of which still remains near Six Hills; and he
described Leeming Lane [2] on Erming Street as paved with
large coggles which were being taken away for building,
and they are still to be seen in adjacent walls and buildings.
The original paving of Watling Street has been discovered
of late years in Rochester, Stroud, Dartford, and in London.
Wade's causeway remains paved on the Yorkshire moors,
where the stones have not been removed for building fence
walls. Maiden Way still retains its paved surface on the
Cumberland Fells, and part of Dean road remains paved.

The destruction of the Roman roads for the sake of their
materials began long ago, as Camden, Stukeley, and others
testify, but their wholesale obliteration took place when
turnpike roads were constructed along them or near them,
in the latter part of the eighteenth, and the beginning of
the nineteenth century. It would appear that the more
usual plan was to use the materials of the old embankment
to make a wider road, the height being reduced to insignifi-
cance in the process, and in time still further reduced by
wear. Thus, the Salisbury and Blandford road, where it
takes the line of the Roman road near Woodyates, is not
sensibly raised above the surface of the ground, while
beyond, in both directions, where it has not been destroyed
for the sake of the materials, the narrower embankment
of the Roman road remains five or six feet high. Sometimes the Roman embankment was widened, generally on
one side, and if it was reduced in height at all it was still
elevated considerably above the ground at the sides. This
is well seen along the Erming Street between Castleford and
Aberford.

The so-called milliaries afford very little information
about the roads. With very few exceptions those that have
been preserved only bear inscriptions to emperors, and it
may be doubted if many can properly be called milestones.
They consisted of a short column on a square base, or of a
flat stone set upright, and their fate has been to be used
for garden-rollers, posts, grottoes, gravestones, building,

[1] *Itinerarium Curiosum*, p. 106.
[2] *Iter Boreale*, p. 72.

and the like purposes. The inscriptions are nearly always of too late a date to be evidence for that of the roads, and the original position of the stones, which might sometimes determine the course of a road, is often unknown.

Almost the only contemporary information of the Roman roads of this country is furnished by the Itinerary of Antonine (*Itinerarium Antonini Augusti*). This work is generally considered to date from the end of the second, or the beginning of the third century ; it embraces the whole Roman Empire, giving routes from one place to another, and the total distances, with the names and distances apart of intermediate stations. It was first printed in 1512, and not long after a part of it was brought to notice with annotations by Talbot, and was afterwards printed by Hearne in Leland's Itinerary. Camden's many references to Antonine show that the Itinerary was well known to him. Roger Gale in 1709 published at length that part of it relating to Britain, with a commentary, in which, taking Iter by Iter, he suggested localities for the stations, and proposed emendations in the distances in the Itinerary to suit those localities. Horsley in 1732 [1] followed Gale in the text of the Itinerary as printed by him at length, and also in most of his alterations of the numerals, and added others of his own to suit his localities. Unfortunately in his essay, taking Iter by Iter, and localizing the stations, he prints the numerals as if the proposed emendations were of equal authority with the originals in the Itinerary. Thus he prints " XIII. al. XVI. & XVIII.," " XX. al. XXX.," " XVIII. al. XIII.," and so forth, and Gough, in his edition of Camden's *Britannia*, prints the Itinerary consecutively with Horsley's emendations in this manner. Reynolds, in a commentary published in 1799, with far less information or local knowledge than Gale or Horsley, makes much more free with the distances to suit his localities, and then prints his version of the Itinerary, " with the numerals in their corrected state, and in words to secure them from alteration." It seems to have been considered that the Itinerary had been so much corrupted by copyists that any emendation that fitted a writer's speculations was allowable.

In 1735 an edition of the Itinerary by Wesseling was

[1] *Britannia Romana.*

B

published,[1] giving the result of a comparison of various
MSS., but without reference to the localities of the stations,
except that supposed sites are given in the notes.   Another
edition by Parthey and Pinder was published at Berlin in
1848.   These authors state that out of a large number of
codices they selected twenty for comparison.   On compar-
ing the text of the *Iter Britanniarum* thus arrived at with
that of Wesseling, and with that used by Gale and Horsley,
it is found that with some variations of spelling, the
differences in the distances are few.   Thus out of 176
distances in the *Iter Britanniarum*, there are 16 differences
between the text of Parthey and Pinder and that of Wesseling, of which 10 are of one and two miles; 12 differences
between Parthey and Pinder's text and that used by Gale
and Horsley, of which seven are of one and two miles;
and eight differences between Wesseling's text and that
used by Gale and Horsley, of which four are of one and two
miles.   There are no doubt errors in all three texts, but
there is no indication of such general corruption by copyists
as to warrant the alteration of the numerals to suit mere
guesses as to the sites of stations

The *Iter Britanniarum* is here given from Parthey and
Pinder's edition.   It is prefaced by a statement of the
distance from *Gessoriacum* (Boulogne) to *Portus Ritupis*
(Richborough), which was apparently the place to which
the sea was generally crossed.   At *Gessoriacum* an Iter of
Antonine ends which begins at *Lugdunum* (Lyons) and
communicated thence with Rome by a road over the
Cottian Alps.   The *Iter Britanniarum* contains fifteen
Itinera, which are not numbered in the original, but they
have been so long known as Iter I. to Iter XV., that they
have been here so numbered.   The word " Item " which
appears at the beginning of Iter II. and each succeeding
Iter is printed by Wesseling and others " Iter," and the
" mpm " before the numbers is printed by Wesseling M. P.
In the first entry of the Itinerary " *milia plus minus* " in
Parthey and Pinder's edition is printed at length, with a
note to the effect that " mpm " is so explained in several
codices.   There can be no doubt that the figures signify
Roman miles (*milia passuum*), and they are conveniently
indicated by the abbreviation M. P.

[1] *Antonini Augusti Itinerarium.*   Amsterdam, 1735.

ITINERARIUM ANTONINI AUGUSTI.
ITER BRITANNIARUM.

A Gessoriaco de Galliis Ritupis in portu Britanniarum.
Stadia numero CCCCL.

(ITER I.)

A limite, id est a vallo, Prætorio usque mpm.	clvi
A Bremenio Corstopitum	xx
Vindomora	viiii
Vinovia	xviiii
Cataractoni	xxii
Isurium	xxiiii
Eburacum, leg. vi victrix. . . .	xvii
Derventione	vii
Delgovicia	xiii
Prætorio	xxv
	(Total 156)

(ITER II.)

Item a vallo ad portum Ritupis. . mpm.	cccclxxxi sic
A Blato Bulgio Castra exploratorum . .	xii
Luguvallo	xii
Voreda	xiiii
Brovonacis.	xiii
Verteris	xiii
Lavatris	xiiii
Cataractone	xvi
Isurium	xxiiii
Eburacum	xvii
Calcaria	viiii
Camboduno	xx
Mamucio	xviii
Condate	xviii
Deva, leg. xx vict.	xx
Bovio	x
Mediolano	xx
Rutunio	xii
Urioconio	xi
Uxacona	xi
Pennocrucio	xii
Etoceto	xii
Manduesedo	xvi
Venonis	xii
Bannaventa	xvii
Lactodoro	xii
Magiovinto	xvii

(Iter II.)—*continued.*

Durocobrivis	. . . . . .	xii
Verolamio .	. . . . . .	xii
Sulloniacis .	. . . . . .	viiii
Londinio .	. . . . . .	xii
Noviomago	. . . . . .	x
Vagniacis .	. . . . . .	xviii
Durobrivis	. . . . . .	viiii
Durolevo .	. . . . . .	xiii
Duroverno	. . . . . .	xii
Ad portum Ritupis	. . . . .	xii

(Total 501)

(Iter III.)

Item a Londinio ad portum Dubris	mpm.	lxvi sic
Durobrivis	. . . . . .	xxvii
Duroverno	. . . . . .	xxv
Ad portum Dubris	. . . . .	xiiii

(Total 66)

(Iter IV.)

Item a Londinio ad portum Lemanis	mpm.	lxviii sic
Durobrivis	. . . . . .	xxvii
Duroverno	. . . . . .	xxv
Ad portum Lemanis	. . . . .	xvii

(Total 68)

(Iter V.)

Item a Londinio Luguvalio ad vallum	mpm.	ccccxliii sic
Cæsaromago	. . . . .	xxviii
Colonia .	. . . . .	xxiiii
Villa Faustini	. . . . .	xxxv
Icinos .	. . . . .	xviii
Camborico	. . . . .	xxxv
Duroliponte	. . . . .	xxv
Durobrivas	. . . . .	xxxv
Causennis .	. . . . .	xxx
Lindo .	. . . . .	xxvi
Segeloci .	. . . . .	xiiii
Dano .	. . . . .	xxi
Legeolio .	. . . . .	xvi
Eburaco .	. . . . .	xxi
Isubrigantum	. . . . .	xvii
Cataractone	. . . . .	xxiiii
Levatris .	. . . . .	xviii
Verteris .	. . . . .	xiiii
Brocavo	. . . . .	xx
Luguvalio .	. . . . .	xxii

(Total 443)

(Iter VI.)

Item a Londinio Lindo		.	.	mpm. clvi sic
Verolami	.	.	.	. . xxi
Durocobrivis	.	.	.	. . xii
Magiovinio	.	.	.	. . xii
Lactodoro	.	.	.	. . xvi
Isannavantia	.	.	.	. . xii
Tripontio	.	.	.	. . xii
Venonis	.	.	.	. . viii
Ratas	.	.	.	. . xii
Verometo	.	.	.	. . xiii
Margiduno	.	.	.	. . xii
Ad Pontem	.	.	.	. . vii
Crococalana	.	.	.	. . vii
Lindo	.	.	.	. . xii

(Total 156)

(Iter VII.)

Item a Regno Londinio		.	.	mpm. xcvi sic
Clausentum	.	.	.	. . xx
Venta Belgarum	.	.	.	. . x
Calleva Atrebatum	.	.	.	. . xxii
Pontibus	.	.	.	. . xxii
Londinio	.	.	.	. . xxii

(Total 96)

(Iter VIII.)

Item ab Eburaco Londinium		.		mpm. ccxxvii sic
Lagecio	.	.	.	. . xxi
Dano	.	.	.	. . xvi
Ageloco	.	.	.	. . xxi
Lindo	.	.	.	. . xiiii
Crococalana	.	.	.	. . xiiii
Margiduno	.	.	.	. . xiiii
Vernemeto	.	.	.	. . xii
Ratis	.	.	.	. . xii
Venonis	.	.	.	. . xii
Bannavento	.	.	.	. . xviii
Magiovinio	.	.	.	. . xxviii
Durocobrivis	.	.	.	. . xii
Verolamo	.	.	.	. . xii
Londinio	.	.	.	. . xxi

(Total 227)

(Iter IX.)

Item a Venta Icinorum Londinio		.		mpm. cxxviii sic
Sitomago	.	.	.	. . xxxii
Combretonio	.	.	.	. . xxii
Ad Ansam	.	.	.	. . xv
Camoloduno	.	.	.	. . vi
Canonio	.	.	.	. . viiii
Cæsaromago	.	.	.	. . xii
Durolito	.	.	.	. . xvi
Londinio	.	.	.	. . xv

(Total 127)

(ITER X.)

Item a Clanoventa Mediolano	mpm .	cl sic
Galava	.	xviii
Alone	.	xii
Calacum	.	xviiii
Bremetonaci	.	xxvii
Coccio	.	xx
Mancunio	.	xvii
Condate	.	xviii
Mediolano	.	xviiii

(Total 150)

(ITER XI.)

Item a Segontio Devam	. .	mpm. lxxiiii sic
Conovio	.	xxiiii
Varis	.	xviii
Deva	.	xxxii

(Total 74)

(ITER XII.)

Item a Muriduno Viroconium	. mpm.	clxxxvi sic (Wesseling
[Vindomi	.	xv *per*
Venta Belgarum . . .	.	xxi Muridunum)
Brige	.	xi
Sorvioduni	.	viii
Vindogladia	.	xii
Durnonovaria	.	viii
Muridono	.	xxxvi
Isca Dumnuniorum . . .	.	xv]
Leucaro	.	xv
Nido	.	xv
Bomio	.	xv
Iscae leg. ii. Augusta . . .	.	xxvii
Burrio	.	viiii
Gobannio	.	xii
Magnis	.	xxii
Bravonio	.	xxiiii
Viroconio	.	xxvii

(Total 272)

(ITER XIII.)

Item ab Isca Calleva . . .	mpm.	cviiii sic
Burrio	.	viiii
Blestio	.	xi
Ariconio	.	xi
Clevo	.	xv
Durocornovio	.	xiiii
Spinis	.	xv
Calleva	.	xv

(Total 90)

(ITER XIV.)

					mpm.	
Item alio itinere ab Isca Calleva	.			.		ciii sic
Venta Silurum	.	.	.	.	.	.	viiii
Abone	.	.	.	.	.	.	xiiii
Traiectus	.	.	.	.	.	.	viiii
Aquis Solis	.	.	.	.	.	.	vi
Verlucione	.	.	.	.	.	.	xv
Cunetione	.	.	.	.	.	.	xx
Spinis	.	.	.	.	.	.	xv
Calleva	.	.	.	.	.	.	xv

(Total 103)

(ITER XV.)

					mpm.	
Item a Calleva Isca Dumnuniorum						cxxxvi sic
Vindomi	.	.	.	.	.	.	xv
Venta Belgarum		.	.	.	.	xxi
Brige.	.		.	.	.	.	xi
Sorbiodoni	.	.	.	.	.	viii
Vindogladia	.	.	.	.	.	xii
Durnonovaria	.	.	.	.	.	viii
Muriduno	.	.	.	.	.	xxxvi
Isca Dumnuniorum	.	.	.	.	.	xv

(Total 126)

The text of the Itinerary (Parthey and Pinder's edition) has been followed in the spelling of the names of the stations in preference to choosing between different forms that have been given to them. They are generally presented in the locative case, but sometimes in the nominative or accusative, and the name of the same place is in some instances differently spelt. Hence the proper form of the name is not always certain.

Another record of a somewhat similar nature is the *Tabula Peutingeriana*, a Roman Itinerary in the form of a rude map supposed to date from the third century, though the actual copy is not older than the thirteenth.[1] Four places on the south coast of England are marked as *Ysca dumnoniorum*, *Lemanio*, *Dubris*, and *Ratupis*, all of which are known; and two on the east coast, *Ad ansam*, and *Ad taum*, the former a station in Antonine's Iter IX., of uncertain position, and the latter unknown. From these, perhaps seaports, red lines are drawn inland marking roads,

---

[1] It has been reproduced in facsimile by Desjardins (Paris). There are eight " segments," a foot wide to the margin line, and the first of them containing part of England is discoloured and imperfect.

against which the names of 10 places and numerals are written. Most of the names have been identified with names in the Itinerary of Antonine, and the numerals seem to indicate the distances between the places. The map, though a mere sketch, throws some light on the relative positions of stations.

Other ancient authorities for the names and positions of places are the geographer Ptolemy, the *Notitia Dignitatum*, and the Ravenna list of place-names, said to have been compiled in the seventh century. Ptolemy gives the positions of places by degrees of latitude and longitude, but it is very unlikely that the positions of places in this country, with a few possible exceptions, were fixed otherwise than by distances obtained from Itineraries or from travellers. His degrees are five-sixths of true degrees in magnitude, and when allowance has been made for that, the relative positions of some well-known places in the south of England are tolerably correct; while others are so much out as to throw doubt upon the accuracy of some of the degrees as we have them—*Verulamium*, for instance, is placed more than four times as far from London as it ought to be. In the north the errors are more general and greater.

The *Notitia* [1] is a list of civil and military officers with the names of their stations in the beginning of the fifth century, methodically arranged.

The position of many places named in the list of the anonymous geographer of Ravenna is uncertain.

The spurious Itinerary attributed to Richard of Cirencester requires more notice.

This Itinerary, purporting to have been collected from fragments left by a Roman general, was published by Stukeley with an analysis of the treatise containing it (*De Situ Britanniæ*) in 1757, from a copy furnished him from Copenhagen by Bertram, who afterwards printed it but never produced the original.

Stukeley accepted this Itinerary as genuine, fortunately after the publication of his *Itinerarium Curiosum*, as did Whitaker (who gave a copy of it in his *History of Manchester*), R. Gough, General Roy, Sir Richard Colt Hoare,

---

[1] Notitia utraque dignitatum cum orientis tum occidentis ultra Arcadii Honoriique tempora.

Bennet Bishop of Cloyne, and others, though doubts were expressed about it from the first.

In 1809 an English translation of the treatise by Hatcher was published, with the text of the Itinerary and a commentary upon it by the Rev. T. Leman, aided by Archdeacon Coxe, Sir R. C. Hoare, and Bennet Bishop of Cloyne, and with these sponsors the Itinerary of Richard of Cirencester was generally looked upon as authentic in spite of the doubts of the more critical. Dr. Guest in 1850 [1] spoke of it as " Bertram's clever fabrication " and as a " patent forgery."

In 1869 the spuriousness of the whole treatise was completely demonstrated by Professor Mayor, in the preface to an authentic work by Richard of Cirencester,[2] edited for the Master of the Rolls. Of the Itinerary attributed to Richard, he says that it is in the main from Antonine's Itinerary, the routes broken, combined, and reversed; nine-tenths of the names in Antonine reappearing with additions from Ptolemy, the *Notitia*, the Ravenna list, the *Tabula Peutingeriana*, and from Camden's, Baxter's, and Bertram's imaginations.

Unfortunately the effects of a fabrication believed in by antiquarians for so many years have been lasting. An editor's preface to a genuine treatise is not the best means of making generally known the spuriousness of another work attributed to the same author, and the fictitious names, stations, and roads of the so-called Itinerary of Richard continue to be given without a hint of the authority for them, which probably is often not known. Those responsible for the new Ordnance maps must presumably have been ignorant that it was proved nearly fifty years ago to be a forgery, as they have engraved on them names of stations for which there is no other authority than that of those who, like Stukeley, Gough, Hoare, and others, took the names from the supposed Itinerary of Richard and found sites for them.

The first historical mention of a Roman road after Roman times is in the treaty of Wedmore, A.D. 878, in which Watling Street is named in defining the boundary between the dominions of Alfred and Guthrum. This was four and a

[1] *Archæological Journal*, vol. viii.
[2] *Speculum Historiale de Gestis Regum Angliæ*, pp. 447–1066.

half centuries after the departure of the Romans from Britain.[1]

In the Laws of Edward the Confessor [2] four ways which are undoubtedly Roman roads are given by name as protected by the King's peace : Watling Strete, Fosse, Hikenild Strete, and Erming Strete, of which it is said that two run lengthways and two across the kingdom. In the Laws of William the Conqueror, which in the preamble are stated to be the same as those of Edward, only three ways are named, viz. " Watling Strete, and Erming Strete, and Fosse," Hikenild Strete being omitted.

These names are still borne by Roman roads, but there is some doubt as to what roads they properly apply, and the uncertainty dates from early times. Henry of Huntingdon, who wrote in the first part of the twelfth century, and Ranulphus Higden, monk of Chester, who wrote about 1344, described the course of the Four Ways, and while agreeing generally about Watling Street and the Foss, they differ altogether about the other two. Higden, in his *Polychronicon*, repeats a fable of Geoffrey of Monmouth, that the four ways were made by an imaginary King Belinus, and he describes the course of them. He gives the course of Watling Street with a fulness which seems to result from a personal knowledge. According to him it begins at Dover, goes through Kent, crosses the Thames on the west of Westminster, and passes by St. Albans, Dunstable, Stretford, Towcester, Weedon, south of Lilleburne, by Atherstone, and thence to the Wrekin, crosses the Severn near Wroxeter, and goes by Stretton through the middle of Wales to Cardigan. As Dr. Guest observes, the King's peace could not have run into Cardiganshire in the time of Edward, but as far as Stretton, Higden describes accurately the course of a Roman road, which he extended without particulars through Wales to complete King Belinus's road from sea to sea. Henry of Huntingdon takes

---

[1] Dr. Guest. *Archæological Journal*, vol. xiv., says that the Foss is mentioned in Anglo-Saxon Charters as early as the eighth century, and the Rev. Edmund McClure cites charters in which the Foss is a boundary near Baltonborough, Somerset, *dated* 744; near Evenlode, *dated* 779; near Malmesbury, *dated* 931.

[2] *Leges Edwardi Regis*, David Wilkin, p. 190.

Watling Street to Chester, which Higden the monk of Chester does not.

Higden at first appears to identify the Foss with one of Geoffrey's roads, supposed to have been made by Belinus, beginning at Totnes and ending in Caithness; but he adds that according to others it begins in Cornwall, going through Devon and Somerset, near Tetbury and Coventry to Leicester, through a great plain towards Newark, and ends at Lincoln.[1] The latter description from Devon to Lincoln is generally correct.

Erming Street, according to Henry of Huntingdon, runs from south to north through Huntingdon, for which there are other ancient authorities. Camden [2] says the Roman road through Royston to Huntingdon was called Erming Street in the *Book of Ely*, and that near Stilton the road was called Erming Street in an ancient Saxon charter.[3] Higden, following another of King Belinus's roads in Geoffrey of Monmouth's account, says that Erming Street tends from west to east, beginning at St. David's, and goes to Southampton, that is, roughly parallel to Watling Street, and extending from sea to sea. There can be little doubt that he referred to the line of Roman roads through Gloucester, Cirencester, Cricklade, to near Wanborough, and then south by Marlborough to Winchester and near Southampton, a route which in Gloucestershire and North Wiltshire still bears the name of the Ermin Way.

The fourth road, called in the Laws of Edward Hikenild Strete, is generally supposed to be connected with the country of the Iceni. Dr. Guest [4] says that the earliest forms of the name in Anglo-Saxon charters are Icenhilde Weg or Icenilde Weg, that it is mentioned in an ancient parchment quoted by Dugdale probably not later than the fourteenth century as Icknild at Dunstable, and that Icenilde Weg is mentioned in a charter of the tenth century relating to estates between Blewbury and Weyland Smithy in the west of Berks, and that it is certain that in the tenth and eleventh centuries Icenilde Street was the name of the road leading on to Avebury, and also that an old charter describes

---

[1] *Polychronicon.*
[2] *Britannia*, ii. 211. (Gough's edition.)
[3] *Ibid.* ii. 249.
[4] " The Four Roman Ways," *Archæological Journal*, vol. xiv. p. 99.

an estate near Andover as bounded by Ickeneld Way. The name not long since survived in descriptions of boundaries of estates on the Roman road from Winchester to *Cunetio*. The Rev. E. McClure gives Ican-gæt as the name in a charter A.D. 779; Icenhylte as a boundary near Great Kemble, and Icenhilde weg near Hardwaela (? Wherwell), Hants, in charters of A.D. 903; and Icenhilde weg near Wenbeargan (Wanborough) in a charter of the eleventh century. The name under various forms designates roads from the borders of Norfolk through Cambridgeshire, Bucks, Berks, Hants, and Wilts into Dorset.

Higden, however, gives the name of the fourth road as Rikenild Strete, which, he says, tends from the south-west to the north, and begins at St. David's and continues to the mouth of the Tyne, passing Worcester, Droitwich, Birmingham, Lichfield, Derby, and Chesterfield. Dr. Guest suggests that the monk of Chester in passing along Watling Street would cross Riknild Street, and was led to adopt it as Icknild Street; however that may be, Riknild Street, as Higden describes it, can now be followed from Worcester to near Chesterfield, and can be traced as far north as Aldborough, and it has borne that name, or Rigning, Recnald, or Rignall, from early times to the present.[1]

Confusion has arisen from an attempt to ignore Riknild Street as a road distinct from Iknild Street. Dr. Plot is a good deal responsible for this; he not only extended Icknild Street into Staffordshire, but he established the Iceni there as a ground for so doing.

These names are all applied to roads which seem to have little or no connexion with those to which they properly belong. Thus Watling Street is the name of a road running north from Kenchester in Herefordshire, of a road between Chester and Manchester, and of a road between Manchester and Blackburn. Leland [2] calls the road crossing the river Wharfe at St. Helen's Ford, the road at Aldborough on Erming Street, and the road by Greta Bridge on the

---

[1] In three of the four MSS. of Higden, collated and printed under the authority of the Master of the Rolls, the name is given Rikenilde, Rikenyldes, and in the fourth, which is said to be one of the earliest, Hikenil Street. Trevisa's English translation (1387) calls it Rykeneldes Strete.

[2] Itinerary, 1535–43.

way to Carlisle, Watling Street, and says that "Ancaster standeth on Wateling." Watling Street is the name borne by the road which runs through Northumberland into Scotland, where it seems to be the usual designation of a Roman road. The names Foss and Erming Street are also applied to roads having no connexion with the roads properly so called, and the wide distribution of Icknild Street under various forms has been noticed.

Akeman Street, Portway, Peddars Way, Maiden Way, Sarn Helen, are old names of Roman roads, but Latin names, such as Julia Strata or Via Julia, Via Devana, Via Badonica, are not Roman and are generally modern.

The straightness of Roman roads is the characteristic which strikes ordinary observers, and has been, perhaps, too much insisted upon, while the skill and the comprehensive grasp of the features of the country displayed in laying them out has received too little notice. In an open country like much of the south of England, the general course of the Roman roads is often wonderfully direct, perhaps not deviating more than a quarter or half-a-mile from an absolutely straight line in 20 or 30 miles. But even here between the extreme points there are many pieces of straight road not quite in the same line, and where a difficulty, such as an unnecessary crossing of a river, or a steep hill which need not be passed over, could be avoided by leaving the straight line, it was generally done. Where steep-sided valleys had to be crossed the road winds down and up, and resumes the straight line on the other side. In a broken country, or along valleys, a winding course to suit the ground was usually followed, and in a hilly country straightness is sometimes not a characteristic at all. Considerations of a military nature sometimes caused difficulties to be faced which might have been avoided, and it is plain that high ground was generally preferred.

The directness and straightness of Roman roads seems to be largely a matter of convenience in setting them out. In many cases the general course may have been laid out from one end, perhaps with the help of a smoke signal, as the road from Lincoln to the Humber, the road from Notting Hill to Staines, and the 19 miles of Watling Street south-east of Chatham Hill. But there can be no doubt that the Roman engineers made use of a method well known

to surveyors for laying out a straight line between extreme
points not visible from each other, from two or more intermediate points from which the extreme points are visible.
By shifting the intermediate points alternately all are
brought to lie in a straight line. The general course of
many roads must have been thus laid out.

Between the extreme points there are often many straight
pieces not quite in the same line, generally pointing to some
landmark which can often be identified, either on the
ground, or with the help of the Ordnance map with levels
and contours.

Changes of direction from one straight line to another,
when the change is not at a station or some other point
through which the road had to pass, almost always occur
at points on high ground. There are several instances
where a barrow or tumulus was the landmark, the road
passing round it on nearing it. Silbury affords one example,
and Brinklow, on the Foss, another.

It is curious to find that the same method has been
employed in setting out a railway in a new country. On
the "Cape to Cairo" railway in the high bush-covered
country of Northern Rhodesia, long straight pieces of line
are to be seen pointing to a kopje, or to a large anthill,
from or towards which it has been set out. Sometimes an
anthill, perhaps more than 15 feet high, has been cut through
leaving part of it standing on one or both sides, but often,
on approaching the kopje or anthill, the line avoids it by
curving round it to another straight line, either following
the same course as before, or taking a new direction. As with
the Roman engineers in England, the exact location of the
line did not matter so long as the general direction was kept.

The straightness is often less apparent in travelling along
a Roman road than on a map. When the roads were
enclosed, of course long after they were made, the usual
width between the fences appears to have been about
20 yards, or even more, and where that width has been
preserved the present road, perhaps not more than 12 or
15 feet wide, often winds from fence to fence. Hedges and
trees overgrowing the sides, and other encroachments on
the width are frequent. Parts have been taken in to
adjacent fields, or long strips have been fenced off as separate
enclosures on which houses have often been built. The

original width between the fences has thus been often reduced to one-half or even one-third, sometimes on one side of the road and sometimes on the other; and especially where trees and hedgerows hinder the view of any length of road the straightness is far from being obvious. A way in which the original straightness has been lost is shown on heaths and commons where the ridge remains, and a cart-track runs sometimes on the ridge, and sometimes alongside it on one side or the other, as the best way along the neglected road has been followed.

Some Roman roads are noticeable for their isolation from villages and existing traffic. The cause is that while the roads, whether they followed older tracks or not, kept to high and dry ground, the villages afterwards arose where springs and streams afforded water, and without any relation to the Roman road. If the road did not suit the local traffic it was abandoned, and if not destroyed, it remains deserted on the high ground on the flank of which the villages lie, where springs and streams break out.

Certain place-names constantly recur on or near Roman roads. The more numerous are those connected with Street, such as Old Street, High Street, Green Street, Stretton, Stratton, Stretford, Stratford, etc. Others refer to the elevation above the surface, as the Ridge, Roman Ridge, Ridgeway, Long Causeway, Devil's Causeway, High Dyke, Atchling Dyke. Others to the paving or solid construction, as Stone Street, Stane Street, Stanegate, Stangate, Staney Street, Stoney Stratford, Stanford. "Street," however, must not always be taken as evidence of a Roman road, places so called having originated in modern times where houses have sprung up along roads. In Wales such names as Sarn, Sarn Helen, Sarn Swsog, Fforddfawr, Henffordd, Heol fawr, Heol-las, Hen heol, mark the course of Roman roads.

Chester, Cester, Caster, Castor, Caistor, alone or in composition, refer of course to camps and forts often on or near Roman roads. In the north, Birrens, Burwens, Burrens, Borrans, Borrowens are names given to the sites of Roman camps.

"Cold Harbour" is a name which in the south of England is found constantly accompanying Roman roads, the meaning of which has been a moot point. In the north, "Windy

Arbour" takes its place, which seems fatal to more than
one suggested derivation, and to favour the more natural
explanation that a place of shelter is meant, of Roman or
later times.   Caldecot, a name of similar meaning, is nearly
always found near the course of a Roman road.

"Toot" is claimed as a name connected with Roman
roads, and it is so, but it is not confined to them.   The
word is said on good authority to signify a place of look-
out, and though some Toots, like that of Tothill Fields,
Westminster, the Toot of Toot Baldon, or Toat Hill in
Sussex, may have looked out along Roman roads, there are
many others with no such connexion.

In studying the courses of the Roman roads of England,
and the manner in which they were laid out, observation
on the ground is greatly aided by a careful study of the
Ordnance maps both of the old and the new survey.   In
these days of cheap and accurate maps, the imperfection
of those at the disposal of earlier writers is apt to be for-
gotten.   To go no further back than the eighteenth century,
Stukeley appears to have had no map, and to have guessed
his distances as he travelled, and he falls into mistakes in
consequence.   Thus in passing over the Foss Way from
Lincoln to Leicester, by wrongly estimating his distances,
he brings *Margidunum* to Willoughby, some ten miles too
far south, and he says he " must with the Itinerary make
an excursion to take in *Vernometum*," which he does by
going to Burrow, an earthwork seven miles away from the
Foss road, with no sign of a Roman road to it.   In making
Burrow *Verometum* he, however, followed Camden.   He
goes entirely astray between Silchester and Salisbury in
his 7th Iter.

Horsley (1732) was evidently without a map from which
he could ascertain distances.   He relied on Ogilby's survey
of the principal roads,[1] and when that did not serve he

[1] Ogilby's *Britannia* was published in folio in 1675.   It consists
of 100 double-page plates on which the roads are mapped on scrolls
to a scale of an inch to a mile from a survey made by a measuring
wheel and compass bearings; with 200 pages of letter-press.   It
shows how the principal roads of that date, sometimes following the
course of Roman roads, have been superseded by modern roads,
and are now byeways, or are closed altogether.   Ogilby's work is the
origin of many road books.   It was soon issued in a more portable
form as " improved," and one of these was probably used by Horsley.

sometimes trusted to the landlords of inns or others he met with. It is not surprising that his distances are often wrong, and his conclusions from them sometimes erroneous. He measures by a " computed " English mile, and finds that wherever he is sure of his distances the proportion of Itinerary miles to English computed miles is generally as four to three; and he gives a table of distances between Lincoln and Corbridge, and between Catterick and Carlisle in proof. But his computed miles are far longer than a statute mile. Thus the distance from Lincoln to Littleborough, which is 14 statute miles, he makes 10½ computed miles, and from Littleborough to Doncaster, which is 21½ statute miles, he makes 16 computed miles, and so on throughout, and if statute miles as measured on the map be substituted for the computed miles in his table, it will be found that Itinerary miles and English statute miles are about the same. According to the usual authorities, the Roman M. P. would be about eleven-twelfths of an English statute mile, but absolute accuracy is not to be expected in Itinerary distances, which were probably measured by pacing. There is sometimes a difference of a mile or two in the distance between the same stations in one Iter and another.

Modern maps not only give correct distances, but throw valuable light on other things. It is well known that the ridges of Roman roads were often made the boundary between parishes and townships; and boundaries follow roads which are certainly Roman for many miles together. On Watling Street, south of London, from Kidbrook over Shooter's Hill, and through Dartford, parish boundaries run along seven and a half out of 12 miles, and on the north of London parish boundaries follow Watling Street along the Edgware Road continuously for five miles, from Oxford Street to the river Brent, and again for two miles after an interval of one and a half miles, or for seven out of eight and a half miles. Watling Street marks the north-east boundary of Warwickshire for 22 miles continuously, and between Bath and Cirencester parish boundaries follow the Foss road almost continuously for another 22 miles. Parish boundaries run along the Roman road from the north of Lincoln to the Humber for 14½ miles without a break, and almost continuously along Erming Street, south of

c

Lincoln, for 18 miles, and many other examples might be given of undoubted Roman roads which are followed by parish boundaries. A boundary running straight along a road, track, or hedgerow, or across country, often indicates the course of a Roman road when all other trace has disappeared.

The form of the ground as shown by contour lines and levels on the modern maps often gives suggestive information as to the probable way in which the roads were laid out where, as is often the case, modern enclosures, planting, or building prevent access to or a look-out from prominent points to which the course of roads appears to be directed.

The older Ordnance maps dating from early in the last century afford a record of ridges of Roman roads which have since disappeared, and generally seem to be more trustworthy in such matters than the new survey, the maps of which mark Roman roads for which there is little or no evidence or authority.

In describing the courses of the Roman roads it will be best to follow as far as possible those which have generally recognised names, grouping with them such other roads as may be convenient. Thus with Watling Street will be described the three roads which meet at Canterbury, and the Sussex Stane Street; and the road will be followed from Wroxeter into Herefordshire, to Chester and Carnarvon, and to Manchester, Lancashire, etc. In the same way Erming Street will be followed into Scotland, though bearing the name of Watling Street in Northumberland, and the roads connected with it in Lincolnshire, Yorkshire, Durham, and Northumberland will be grouped with it. One very important group of roads, from London to Silchester and the west, has no authentic name of a road by which to distinguish it.

It will also be convenient to follow, in the first place, a road about the course of which there is no doubt, and which is in all respects characteristic. Watling Street, by which Britain was entered, fulfils these conditions, and it does not appear that confusion will arise from beginning with it, a road passing through the middle of England. Erming Street will be taken next, then the roads to the east of it and Icknild Street, then the Foss and Ryknild Street, and then the roads from London to Silchester, branching to the south, and to Salisbury, Dorchester, and Exeter, and to Speen, Bath, Gloucester, and South Wales. The Roman roads in connexion with these main lines will be followed up, but it will be impossible to notice all that are known, and the continual discovery by chance of remains of Roman roads shows how much remains unknown, which a judicious use of the spade might reveal.

CHAPTER II

WATLING STREET AND BRANCHES

(1) *General course.*—If the course of Watling Street from Dover to Wroxeter be followed on a map, it will be seen that it consists of 11 lengths of nearly straight road, which change in direction, sometimes through considerable angles, where they join. It would appear that Canterbury was made for because it was the highest point on the Stour to which Roman ships could ascend from *Portus Ritupis*, the usual port of arrival in England. At Canterbury the direction of the road changes 40°, while between Canterbury and Dover, 15 miles, and between Canterbury and Lambeth, $52\frac{1}{2}$ miles, no part of the road is one and a half miles away from an absolutely straight line, although on the latter length is the crossing of the Medway. The Thames must have been crossed at a point determined probably by a ford, and then a new direction was taken to Brockley Hill, Elstree, so nearly straight that no part of the road deviates one-eighth of a mile from it. North of Elstree the next length of straight road continues to *Verolamium*, and the stations *Durocobrivæ* at Dunstable and *Magiovintum* at

Fenny Stratford are passed through without any change
of course, alterations in direction occurring on high points
between them.   The bend west to Towcester was probably
made to avoid the low ground of the valley of the Tove,
and then there is a turn through 25°, and the road for 28
miles to High Cross (*Venonæ*) is nowhere three-quarters
of a mile away from an absolutely straight line.   The
situation of High Cross on the summit of high ground
is in itself a sufficient reason for its having been a point
to be made for, and there is there a turn of 29°, and the
road goes on to Wall (*Etocetum*), 25 miles, passing through
the station *Manduesedum* near Atherstone, nowhere a mile
out of a straight line.   At *Etocetum* Watling Street is crossed
by Riknild Street, and the four roads converge on different
lines.   From Wall to *Pennocrucium*, near Gailey, a length
of 13 miles is nowhere a mile out of a straight line, and
thence to Wellington for 16 miles no part of the road is
100 yard out of a straight line.   From Wellington a
length of six miles with a slight turn ends at Wroxeter,
on the Severn, the lowest point according to Camden at
which that river was fordable.

Between London and Wroxeter Watling Street keeps
on high ground, from which rivers flow away on either
hand.   It is crossed nearly at right angles by Iknild Street,
the Foss Way, and Riknild Street, that part of the Foss
between Watling Street and Lincoln becoming the Itinerary
route to York and the north.   An important branch is
that which turns off towards Chester, from which, four
miles south of Chester, another road turns off at right
angles to Carnarvon.   These branchings-off may be
supposed to mark the advance of Roman dominion first
to the Severn, then to Chester, and then to Carnarvon.
The continuation of Watling Street beyond the Severn
and southwards along the Welsh border may mark the
campaign against the Silures.

If, as it has been supposed, a British trackway previously
existed along the course of Watling Street, it is evident
that the road was laid out and reconstructed by the Romans
in their own manner.

There appear to have been two lines of road through
Cheshire and Lancashire to the north, one by Northwich,
Warrington and Wigan to Lancaster, and the other by

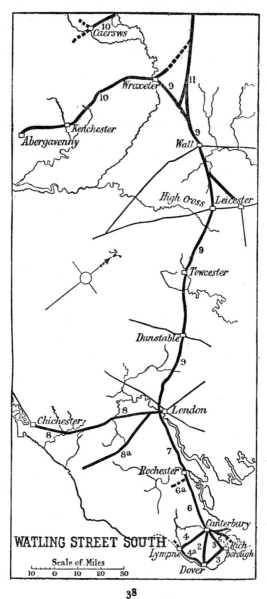

10
Caersws

Wroxeter 9 11

10
Kenchester
Abergavenny
Wall 9

High Cross Leicester

9

Towcester

Dunstable

9

London

Chichester 8

8

8a

7

Rochester

6a

8a

6

Canterbury

4
2 3 Rich-
WATLING STREET SOUTH borough
4a
Lympne 3
Dover

Manchester, Ribchester, over the fells to the Lune valley,
and then over the Westmoreland fells to Kirkby Thore
and the Maiden Way.   From Manchester and from
Ribchester roads crossed the moors into Yorkshire.

(2) *Dover to Canterbury.*—From Dover (*Dubris*) Watling
Street ascended the valley by River very much on a line
with the present road.   In 1719 Harris,[1] apparently on the
authority of Dr. Plot, wrote that between Buckland and
Ewell the old road " lay fair and high where it joins the
common road," but modern improvements have demolished
it.   To the south of Lydden, a piece apparently of the old
road may be seen on the west side of the modern road at
a higher level, and Harris describes it as plain enough to
be seen at several places on the north of Lydden, where
the modern road up the hill has since been constructed
on a different line.   At the top of the hill (455'),[2] a parish
boundary runs along the modern road for one-eighth of a
mile, and then on in the same straight line, rejoining the
road beyond the small Roman Camp on Barham Down,
the modern road diverging to the west for about four
miles.   Harris describes the remains of Watling Street,
apparently from Dr. Plot's observations, along this line,
and it is one of the many instances which prove the depend-
ence that can be placed on parish boundaries to show
the lines of Roman roads of which no other trace remains.

From the top of Lydden Hill to Canterbury, Watling
Street was laid out in almost a straight line for nine miles.
On Barham Down, Harris, and later Stukeley,[3] describe
it as entire with a high ridge composed of chalk and flint
blended together, and in use as the common road.   The
modern road, which has since superseded it, is followed by
two short lengths of parish boundary, but near Higham
a straight parish boundary on the north-east of the modern
road may perhaps represent Watling Street.   At the end
of the 18th century it was to be seen entire and high on the
west side of Bridge.[4]   Beyond, from Stone Farm to where
the new Dover road branches from the old road, a parish

---

[1] Hasted's *History of Kent.*
[2] The height above Ordnance datum, or mean sea-level, is thus
indicated.
[3] *Itinerarium Curiosum*, 1776, p. 127.
[4] Hasted, iii. 725.

boundary runs along the existing road for three-eighths
of a mile. There are two lengths of parish boundary of
a quarter of a mile and one-eighth of a mile along the middle
of the old Dover road, which is doubtless on the line of
Watling Street. It leads to Watling Street in Canterbury,
a name by which it has been known from an early date
down to the present time. When Canterbury was sewered
the hard crust of the Roman road was found near the
north and south gates of the Roman *Durovernum*.

(3) *Dover to Richborough and Canterbury.*—From Dover
to within a short distance of Richborough traces of a
Roman road are plain. It creeps up a coombe by the
cemetery on to the chalk down as a narrow sunk road, a
parish boundary following it all the way up, and on nearly
to Whitfield. On gaining the high ground (200′) a straight
road begins pointing to Woodnesborough (100′), and after
winding slightly, it continues straight for six miles, except
where interrupted for a quarter of a mile at Betteshanger
Park, parish boundaries following it for more than half
the distance. Woodnesborough is on the nearest high
ground to Richborough, most of the intervening two miles
being marsh still below level of high water. *Portus Ritupis*
must have been on an island in the channel between Thanet
and the mainland in Roman times, as it is now cut off by
marsh-land below high-water level. This road is shown
on the *Tabula Peutingeriana*, and also one turning off
from it to Canterbury which represents the road from
Portus Ritupis. It would seem from this that one causeway across the tidal land between that station and the
mainland served for both roads. The walls of Richborough enclose an area 160 yards from north to south,
and 100 to 160 yards from the west wall to the cliff
on the east. It is curious that there are very few traces
of the Roman road from *Portus Ritupis*, the usual port
of entry into Britain, to Canterbury. Those recorded by
Harris,[1] as observed by Dr. Plot and himself in 1719,
are but vague, and between Shatterling and Richborough
they could find no further traces. Stukeley, a little later,
found no trace, and existing roads and parish boundaries
give very little indication of the line of it. Between
Shatterling and Ash a parish boundary runs along the

[1] Hasted's *History of Kent.*

road for half-a-mile, and another bit follows the road east of Ash, and thereabouts the road may have joined the road from Dover. The line of the road between Ash and Shatterling produced is taken up after an interval of three miles by the road on to Canterbury.

(4) *Stone Street.*—A Roman road from Canterbury to *Portus Lemanis*, called Stone Street, is plainly traceable. Camden describes it as paved with stones.[1] Its course in rising up out of the Stour Valley from the west of Canterbury is no doubt that of the present road, along which the city boundary runs for one and a half miles. It then makes straight for a point (600′) on the high ground north of Horton, 10 miles off, and for that length the deviations from an absolutely straight line are very slight, and are in hollows where the intermediate points from which the road must have been set out are not visible. Leland says of the road, " It is the straightest that ever I saw, and toward Canterbury ward the pavement continually appereth a iiii or v myles." [2] The centre of the road is a parish boundary for more than three-quarters of the 10 miles to Horton. If the straight line had been continued further it would have led down a steep hill, falling 200 feet in a quarter of a mile, where it would have been commanded by the high ground it had quitted. The road therefore bends to the eastward, and keeping on high ground (550′ to 600′) for a mile, makes almost a semi-circle before descending to the 400 feet contour, a parish boundary following it for most of the way. A straight course is then resumed, pointing to West Hythe, the present road following it, with parish boundaries along it for more than half the way, through Stanford, and by Westenhanger railway-station to near New Inn Green. The present road bends to the east, but a hedge-row continues the line of the road for one-eighth of a mile. No trace of the road then appears for three-quarters of a mile, and then at Shepway Cross the same line is taken up by a road, with a parish boundary along it, which descends to the old sea-shore at West Hythe. About half-a-mile to the west, below Lympne, are the Roman remains of Stutfall Castle extending down to the sea-level. The walls, of which portions remain, are said by Stukeley to have enclosed about twelve acres,

[1] *Britannia,* i. 321.   [2] *Itinerary,* Part viii. p. 141.

" in form somewhat squarish." A good deal of the walls would seem to have been standing in Stukeley's time,[1] and also old foundations at West Hythe, where Stukeley with good reason placed the port. The construction of the military canal has since altered the ground.

The distance from *Durovernum* to *Portus Lemanis* in Iter IV., 16 M. P., agrees with the mileage from Canterbury to West Hythe.

Boundaries along roads suggest a Roman road from Watling Street at about three-quarters of a mile south of Canterbury, by Nackington and Street End, to Stone Street near Hermansole Farm.

Stone Street affords a good example of straightness of direction abandoned for a winding course when the form of the ground required it.

(*a*) In the *Tabula Peutingeriana* no road is shown from Canterbury to *Portus Lemanis*, but one is shown from Dover, of which perhaps there are traces from Shorncliff to Shepway Cross. Further on are Court at Street and Stonestreet Green, so that this, the ancient place of assembly of the Cinque Ports, appears to have been at the crossing of Roman roads.

A Roman road is considered probable [2] onwards by Smeeth, Ashford, and Charing, to Maidstone, but parish boundaries afford no evidence of it.

(5) *Canterbury to Reculver and Thanet.*—A Roman road from Canterbury towards the north-east appears to have crossed the Stour at Fordwich. A parish boundary follows the present road from the river at Fordwich through Sturry and for two miles on through Westbere. At about three-quarters of a mile from Sturry the road to Reculver branched off, represented by the present road through Up Street, which a parish boundary follows for two miles near Hoath. The present road through Westbere, Up Street and Sarre is supposed to be in the course of a Roman road across tidal land to the Isle of Thanet.

(6) *Canterbury to Rochester.*—From Canterbury northwards, the course of Watling Street through Harbledown is uncertain, the road having been re-made, but from Harbledown Church the centre of the present road is the

---

[1] *Itinerarium Curiosum*, p. 132.
[2] G. Payne, F.S.A., *Archæological Survey of Kent,* 1888.

WATLING STREET AND BRANCHES 43

parish boundary, which seems to show that the modern
road winding down the hill is on the site of Watling Street.
At Harbledown Lodge a piece of straight road two and
a half miles long, with a parish boundary along it for
three-quarters of a mile, begins and leads to the high
ground (317′) at Dunkirk. Between this point and the
high ground (255′) on Chatham Hill a length of 19 miles
of straight road was laid out. From Dunkirk to Norton,
six miles, and from Key Street to Chatham Hill, seven
miles, the road lies in one straight line, and the intervening
six miles in the lower ground deviates less than a quarter
of a mile from the same line. Parish boundaries follow
the road at intervals for nearly seven miles out of the 19,
and are now the chief vestiges of Watling Street. Harris
in 1719, and Hasted in 1790, however, described the old road
as being still visible between Harbledown and Boughton
Street, and between Sittingbourne and Chatham.

Half-way between Canterbury and Rochester was the
station *Durolevum* in Iter II. of Antonine, and from
Sittingbourne a Roman road is supposed to have gone to
Maidstone,[1] where many foundations of buildings and
interments testify to Roman occupation, but no evidences
of a road are afforded by parish boundaries.

(a) From the Star Inn on the top of Chatham Hill a parish
boundary runs for two and a half miles across country to
near Lidsing, and appears to represent a Roman road to
Maidstone by Boxley and Penenden Heath, where there
is a parish boundary, and again for half-a-mile, and a
quarter of a mile along the road beyond. A Roman road
from Chatham to Maidstone is marked in the *Archæological
Survey of Kent*, continued on to Ightham, and as probably
going on to Westerham and Limpsfield, and from Westerham to Keston and Lewisham. Parish boundaries afford
no evidence of these roads west of Maidstone.

The course of Watling Street through Chatham was
described in 1897 by Mr. G. Payne, F.S.A.[2] From near
the foot of Chatham Hill, to which parish boundaries
follow the main road, the latter now continues on through
the High Street of Chatham, on land reclaimed from the
estuary of the Medway. Watling Street, however, kept

[1] *Archæological Survey of Kent.*
[2] *Archæologia Canitana,* vol. xxiii. p. 1.

on higher ground to the south, nearly in the line of New Road, and on by Old Street Road, and at the back of St. Bartholomew's Hospital, and by Nag's Head Lane, to the south-east gate of the Roman station *Durobrivæ* at Rochester. A section of the road where it was exposed in Chatham exhibited one foot of small flints on the subsoil of brick earth, then a layer of mortar or grout, above which was a bed of gravel two feet thick grouted with mortar, and then flints to the present surface. It is probable that the gravel grouted with mortar is the uppermost layer of the Roman road remaining, from which a paving of some sort has been removed.

The south-east gate of *Durobrivæ* has been proved to have been on the High Street of Rochester, which follows the line of Watling Street to the site of the north-west gate, opposite the modern bridge, and the site of the Roman bridge across the Medway. The Roman walls, as traced by Mr. Payne, enclosed an area measuring 450 yards from the south-east to the north-west, and in width from 150 yards at the south-east to 350 yards towards the north-west. In digging the foundations of the Technical School near the Guildhall in 1892, the Roman road was found : it consisted of a roughly-prepared bed of sand, earth, and flint, one foot three inches thick on the natural clay, on which was six inches of chalk rammed, then one foot of round and angular gravel, on which was six inches of flints laid in, and then another one foot two inches of round and angular gravel, making a thickness of four feet five inches, over which there was seven feet of earth and *débris*. No paving was found.[1]

Piles of the Roman bridge over the Medway are said to have been met with in the foundation of the modern bridge in 1847.

(7) *Rochester to London.*—On the Strood side of the river a causeway on piles has been traced almost from the bridge nearly to the foot of Strood Hill. It was cut through opposite Station Road in laying a drain in 1897. In the river mud, met with at about eight feet six inches below the present surface of the road, were remains of oak piles about four feet long with timber cills laid across them ; upon these was a layer of flints and rag with fragments

[1] *Archæologia Cantiana*, vol. xxi. p. 10.

of Roman tiles, three feet six inches thick, then five inches of rammed chalk, then seven inches of flint broken fine, covered with nine inches of small pebble gravel mixed with black earth; and upon this was found a paved surface, six to eight inches thick, of Kentish rag of polygonal shape fitted together, and jointed with fine gravel. The width of the causeway was about 14 feet, and there were four ruts in the paving, three on the south side about three inches apart, and one on the north side, six feet three inches from the outer track on the south side. The paved surface was again met with where High Street is joined by North Street.[1] A causeway branching off opposite Station Road, and inclining downwards past Aveling and Porter's Works to the water's edge, was also exposed in pipe-laying. It perhaps led to a ford or ferry which was superseded by a bridge. A boundary follows the line of the causeway from the river to the north end of High Street, Strood, and turns along Strood Hill.

The London road turns off at the north end of High Street after having followed the Roman road for 43 miles from Dover, and the course of Watling Street continues straight on up Strood Hill, where there is a bit of parish boundary, and then along the north of Cobham Park, followed by parish boundaries for three and a half miles. There are traces of the ridge in Cobham Park close to the present road, and for a quarter of a mile from the cross-roads at Scales Hill. At the cross-roads there is a change in the general direction on to Springhead, but the road is not straight, and it is generally narrow, and sunk below the adjoining land. Harris, in 1719,[2] says that the old road was visible between Cobham Park and Springhead with hedges standing on it, sometimes on the one side and sometimes on the other of the existing road. Parish boundaries follow it for nearly half the distance, and it may be noticed that where the ridge is visible the boundaries follow the road and not the ridge.

At Springhead, half-a-mile west of where the Gravesend railway crosses the road, there is a decided bend, and here considerable remains of a Roman town have been found.

[1] G. Payne, F.S.A., *Archæologia Cantiana*, vol. xxiii., and information from Mr. Banks, City Engineer.

[2] Hasted, i. 501.

It may possibly be *Vagniacæ*, the distance from *Durobrivæ*
corresponding. The road, followed by a parish boundary,
ascends to Swanscombe Wood, and from this point (200′)
to Shooter's Hill (400′) there is a straight road for 10½
miles, with very slight turns on high ground, only interrupted where the road drops down to cross the river at
Dartford and at Crayford. Parish boundaries follow it
almost continuously to Dartford, and through Crayford,
and from Welling to Shooter's Hill. About half-a-mile
east of Dartford the modern road from Rochester through
Gravesend rejoins Watling Street, and on the common
close by, the bank or ridge of the latter is evident, eight
yards wide and two or three feet high. At the foot of
East Hill, Dartford, the paved surface of the Roman road
was discovered in 1897 at two feet six inches below the
surface of the present road. It consisted of stones set in
gravel, like the pavement at Strood. In 1790, according
to Hasted,[1] it was plainly visible on Bexley Heath and
through Welling.

From Shooter's Hill the straight line is continued with
a very slight change in direction for one and a half miles
further. Harris (1719) says that the road half-a-mile
from Shooter's Hill was very plain and high with ditches
on each side of it, and Stukeley observed that some of the
agger was left in his time, and that from the top of Shooter's
Hill it butted upon Westminster Abbey. This is so, and
a straight line of road from Swanscombe, ten and a half
miles east of Shooter's Hill, points direct to the passage
over the Thames to Westminster, at Stangate, eight and
a half miles further on.

Near Kidbrooke End the straight line ends, and the
road bends to the south, and parish boundaries which
have followed the straight road continuously for four
and a half miles from Welling follow the road on over
Blackheath, where in 1719 Watling Street was pretty
plain.[2] Further on the course is less certain. After crossing the valley of the Ravensbourne at Deptford bridge
it possibly followed the line of the old road now cut in two
by the railway at New Cross, and represented by Batavia
Park Road and Hatcham Park Road. It no doubt crossed
the Thames from Stangate to Thorney, now Westminster;

---

[1] *History of Kent*, i. 211.   [2] Harris.

but before the river was enclosed by an embankment
from Vauxhall to Deptford, there lay between the higher
ground of New Cross and Stangate more than three miles
of ground, nearly all below the level of high water, and
most of it covered by four or five feet of water at every
tide.   It was not, however, such a swamp as it has been
described to have been, but a wide passage through which
the tides flowed between Limehouse Reach and Vauxhall
for some hours before and after high water.   Excavations
show that to the west of the Old Kent Road, there was
generally a bottom of gravel or sand at about half tide
level.   Eyots, now represented by St. George's Fields,
Stangate, the old part of Lambeth, Bermondsey, and
others, stood above high-water level, with tidal channels
between them.   On the north side of the river, opposite
Stangate, two streams, the Westbourne, and the Tyburn
discharged through tidal marshes extending from Millbank
to Whitehall by several channels, forming a sort of delta
with Thorney Island in the midst.

The wide area open to the tides no doubt gave rise to
a shallow fordable place in the main stream between
Stangate and Thorney, presenting a convenient crossing
place for the pre-Roman Watling Street, accessible without
much difficulty for some hours before and after low tide
by avoiding swampy places, and fording low water
channels.[1]   But it is difficult to suppose that the Romans
constructed a permanent road between New Cross and
Stangate across a wide channel through which the tides
swept as much as 8 or 10 feet deep.   They may have
improved an existing track, but no permanent road was
possible until the tides were shut out.

[1] It is probable that this, the ford of the pre-Roman Watling
Street, was where Aulus Plautius crossed the Thames in the
Claudian invasion.   It is described by Dion Cassius as being near
where the Thames empties itself into the ocean, overflowing at high
tide and forming a lake,* where the Britons knowing the place
well easily crossed, but the Romans following them got into difficulties.   When the Romans did get across the river by the help of
their Celtic Allies, we learn also that they fell into almost impassable
marshes, as they would do after landing on Thorney, surrounded
by the marshes at the mouths of the Westbourne and Tyburn
streams, covered by every high tide, and as difficult to cross without
guides as the river itself.

* πλημύροντος τε αὐτοῦ λιμνάζει, Dion Cassius, lx. 20.

There was not the skill and organization for such a
work as a tidal embankment before the Roman Conquest,
and Roman interments 10 feet below high-water level,
and broken pottery, and other Roman refuse on the old
surface of the ground at from 9 to 15 or 16 feet below high-
water level, covered by a considerable thickness of soil
containing objects of Roman and later date, are evidences
that the tides were banked out in Roman times, and
probably at an early period.   Gibson, in his edition of
Camden's *Britannia* in 1695, said that a Roman highway
was still visible in St. George's Fields, and Stukeley, in
1722,[1] says that it went from Stangate across St. George's
Fields and south of the Lock Hospital, and that a small
part of the ancient way pointing to Westminster Abbey
was then the common road " on this side the nearest
turnpike," by which he must mean the turnpike which
stood at the south end of Newington Causeway.   St.
George's Fields were, however, above high-water level, and
these remains may have been those of a road made before
or after the river was embanked.

The Roman Watling Street probably kept on the higher
ground as far as New Cross Road, and then turned and
made for St. George's Fields, following the course of New
Cross Road and Old Kent Road, and falling at once below
the level of high water.   New Cross Road and Old Kent
Road lie in a straight line as far as Commercial Road,
and are several feet above the level of the ground on
each side, as if they were on a causeway.   Then Old Kent
Road turns to the north, and beyond is but little above
the ground adjoining, while the straight course of it
prolonged would pass in a mile near the site of St. Thomas
Watering.   This, the " Waterynge of Seint Thomas " of
the Prologue to the *Canterbury Tales*, is now marked by
a parish boundary where the stream formerly ran across
Old Kent Road at St. Thomas Street, a little to the north
of Albany Road.   In a garden near the road here, in ground
at least four feet below high-water level, it is recorded [2]
that a head of Janus in marble, said by Dr. Woodward to
be unquestionably Roman, was dug up about 1690, together
with large flat bricks and other Roman remains.   Accord-

---

[1] *Itinerarium Curiosum*, p. 119.
[2] Preface to Leland's *Collectanea*, p. 19.

ing to Defoe [1] it was found with remains of a building,
and a second head was found and left in quicksand.   The
straight course of the road onward would pass to the south
of the Lock Hospital, which stood at the south end of
Great Dover Street, and cross Newington Causeway a little
to the north of the turnpike shown on Rocques map in
1746, and reach St. George's Fields, which were above the
level of the marshes.   There was then a change of direction
to Stangate, and the ancient way, mentioned by Stukeley,
pointing to Westminster, would bring the road to near the
front of Bethlehem Hospital, opposite to which a great
quantity of Roman remains, tesseræ, and pottery were
discovered at different times.   Between St. George's Fields
and Stangate low ground had to be crossed, but before
the tides were shut out the ford could have been reached,
and the river crossed at and near low water.   After the
river was embanked, it could have been reached at any
time, but the ford could only have been crossed as before
for a few hours before and after low water.   It must have
been an inconvenient way of reaching *Londinium* from
the south, and the effect of confining the river by an embankment would have been to deepen the ford and add to the
inconvenience, and a bridge with a road to it, must soon
have followed the embankment of the river.

The course of the road from Watling Street to the bridge
certainly passed through Tabard Street, and the line of
the latter prolonged southwards follows Old Kent Road
to within a quarter of a mile of St. Thomas Watering, where
it would cut the course, as above suggested, of Watling
Street.   From this point the site of Tabard Street would
have appeared about half a mile off, as a promontory
above high-water level jutting out into the marsh which
then extended to the river, and to it the road was laid
out.   Roman burials have been found on both sides of
Old Kent Road near the Deaf and Dumb Asylum, in ground
four feet below Trinity high-water level, and the surface
of the road is not much higher until Tabard Street is
reached, when there is a sudden rise to one foot six inches
above that level, and the street maintains that level for
its whole length of half-a-mile in a straight line.

In a shaft sunk by the side of Tabard Street " mould "

[1] *Tour Through Britain*, vol. i. p. 234.

D

was met with five feet below the road level, corresponding to the level of the ground adjoining, and being no doubt the original surface upon which the causeway was raised. The boundary between St. George's Southwark and Bermondsey runs along the middle of the street, and Roman remains, cinerary urns, *ampullæ*, etc., have been found all along, particularly on the western side.[1] In 1882, in clearing the site of Nos. 6 and 8 for a new street, many fragments of so-called Samian and other Roman ware were met with to a considerable depth.

Tabard Street, or Kent Street, as it was before its name was altered towards the latter part of the last century, was from early times the chief approach to London from the south. By it state entries were made, the Lord Mayor attending at the boundary of the city liberty at St. Thomas Watering. It was described by Strype in 1720 as ill built, and narrow, with alleys and courts on both sides very meanly built and dirty, with narrow and dark entries, and chiefly inhabited by broom-men and mumpers. It retained its reputation as one of the dirtiest and meanest streets in London, and it was little improved by a change of name. It may be supposed that for such inhabitants a street having one side in Southwark and the other outside it had its advantages, which they owed to the boundary following the middle of the causeway of a Roman road. Early in the last century it was superseded as a main thoroughfare by Great Dover Street, made alongside it, but it still remains a curious survival, lying in a straight line with Old Kent Road, and a great contrast to it in width and general appearance.

At the north end of Tabard Street, near St. George's Church, the branch road from Watling Street joins the Sussex Stane Street, which from Clapham Rise to Newington Butts is straight, and points to the south end of old London Bridge. Towards London its course is not known, but from the junction near St. George's Church onward to the bridge Roman remains are continuous.

(8) *The Sussex Stane Street* seems to have continued in the same straight line from Clapham Road for about 11 miles, and then by a more uncertain course through the gap in the Surrey downs at Dorking. On the south of

----

[1] Strype, *App.* p. 23. Bagford's letter to Hearne.

that lay the forest of Anderida, with nothing to determine the course of the road through it except perhaps a crossing of the river Arun at a point which would afford communication with the sea. A crossing place at Pulborough just below the confluence of the Rother having been fixed upon, a straight line to it from the flank of Leith Hill on the south of the Dorking gap was laid out. Leith Hill is visible from near Pulborough, and from the flank of Leith Hill (400' contour) the high downs beyond Pulborough can be seen. From the ground between, on the south of Slinfold (200'+) there is a good view along the course of the road in both directions, over Pulborough to the downs 13 miles to the south-south-west, and to Leith Hill and Anstiebury 10 miles to the north-north-east, Boxhill (600') 15 miles distant appearing beyond. It seems probable that from this high ground the direction of the 18 miles of almost straight road from Hardham to Minnick Wood near Anstiebury was laid out by the method of ranging a straight line between two extreme points from two intermediate points, by shifting them alternately until they lie in a straight line with the extreme points. The general line having been thus got, intermediate landmarks were made use of as points of direction; but so close is the road to an absolutely straight line that no part of the 15 miles from Todhurst Farm to Minnick Wood is one-eighth of a mile away from it Between Pulborough and Chichester another straight line was set out, no doubt in the same manner. From Bignor Hill (686') both Pulborough and Chichester can be seen, and Stane Street for nine miles from Chichester lies in a straight line pointing directly to Pulborough Bridge. The length of Stane Street is 57 miles, passing for nearly half its course through what was a wild forest. The sites of neither stations nor camps upon it are known except perhaps the doubtful camp at Hardham near Pulborough.

Chichester, the *Regnum* of the Itinerary of Antonine, is still surrounded by walls, which in position, and partly in construction, are Roman. They enclose an irregular area 752 yards from the east to the west gate, and 757 yards from the north to the south gate; as if a considerable town already existed when the walls were built. The Stane Street left Chichester by the east gate along the

line of the street now called St. Pancras.   It makes straight
for nine miles to high ground (686') on Bignor Hill, the
modern road following its course to beyond Halnaker,
and then a lane taking the line on to Halnaker Down.
There the ridge is plainly visible, about 13 feet wide,
although on the south-east side it is interfered with by a
later earthwork.   At Seabeach the modern road again
follows the course of Stane Street for a quarter of a mile,
and then the ridge is traceable in the woods to the north
of Eartham, where it is known as Stane Street.   Towards
Bignor Hill the ridge is covered by a hedgerow, and on the
open down beyond it is conspicuous, five to six feet high,
and two to two and a half yards wide, now of a rounded
profile.   On each side of the ridge, about 13 yards apart,
are the remains of trenches.   A profile of the road here
was given by Mr. Martin,[1] who described two stoned roads
inside the trenches, separated by a *vallum* two yards wide,
rising 10 feet above the adjacent surfaces to a rounded top
only wide enough for two or three men to march abreast.
In 1913 a section was cut through Stane Street, 383 yards
south-west of the lane leading down to Coldharbour Farm, by
Dr. Eliot Curwen.[2]   The section, carefully measured, shows
a ridge or *vallum* with a narrow rounded top rising five
feet above the original surface, with spaces on each side
supposed to be roads, and ditches outside about two feet
deep from the present surface, and 28 yards apart.   On the
original surface, which slopes to the southward at an
inclination of about one in ten, lies what is described as
rammed chalk, 27 inches thick near the middle of the section,
and thicker as the old surface falls, with flints in horizontal
layers about a foot apart.   The highest horizontal layer
of flints, which is not much more than a foot above the old
surface on the north-west of the section, in 14 feet is nearly
2½ feet above it as the ground falls, and there are three
horizontal flint layers below, which abut against the
sloping old surface.   There can be little doubt that the
" rammed chalk " with these horizontal layers of flint
are remains of the carefully constructed Roman road.
The structure of the bank above is quite different.   The
layers of which it is composed thin out towards the
sides of the bank, and bend downwards, overlapping the

    [1] *Sussex Archæological Collections*, xi. 127.   [2] *Ibid*., lvii. 136.

horizontal beds of flint in the chalk below and conforming with the profile of the bank. It is evident from the section that a bank has been thrown up over the ridge of the Roman road. On Halnaker Down Stane Street has been altered for defence, and the conversion of 13 miles of Roman road into Wansdyke will be mentioned further on.

On Bignor Hill (683') the nine miles of straight road ends. Looking towards Chichester the spire appears almost in line with the Roman road, and to the north-north-east Leith Hill and Box Hill, on the sides of the Dorking gap in the chalk through which the course of Stane Street lies, can be seen. On leaving the high ground of Bignor Hill the road slants down the steep northern side of the hill as a terrace in the slope. It can be traced in Bignortail Wood, but in the ploughed land below the course is now lost. According to Mr. Martin it was traceable on to Grevatt Copse, about a mile east of Bignor, where it appeared as a slightly raised causeway, and could be traced on Waters-field Hill and for about a quarter of a mile on the north of Coldwaltham. The new Ordnance map shows it by a dotted line in this direction passing through Hardham camp, and across half-a-mile of land subject to floods to Pulborough Bridge. There is an ancient bridge over the Arun to the west of Pulborough Bridge, but there is no trace of a causeway in that direction. The present road is carried across the meadows between Hardham and Pulborough Bridge for 600 yards on a causeway which is very nearly in a line with Stane Street on the north of Pulborough, and may very possibly be of Roman origin. A continuation of that line southwards would however lead again into the low ground bordering on the river Arun, and there must have been a turn near Hardham if the present road to Pulborough Bridge represents Stane Street. Portions of the road between Hardham and Watersfield are in a straight line in the direction of Grevatt Wood.

From Pulborough to Rowhook, 15 miles, the modern road follows the line of the Roman road, passing through Billinghurst and Five Oaks. Near Todhurst Farm there is a slight change of direction. At Rowhook a Roman road is indicated on the new Ordnance map, on what evidence does not appear, branching in the direction of

Guildford. From Rowhook the line of the old road is
followed for two and a half miles by hedgerows and lanes
to a public road called Stone Street Causeway, which passes
through Stone Street, Ockley, to Bucking Hill Farm.
Dr. Burton, who passed over it about 1750, describes it
as being here excellently paved in a stoneless country,
and remaining firm and hard for four miles.[1] Manning
states that the causeway in Ockley parish had, in 1814,
lately been dug through, and found to be four and a half
feet thick of flints and other stones laid alternately and
bedded in fine sand or gravel.[2] About a mile north of
Bucking Hill Farm, in the same line, the old road has
been since found beneath the surface. Opposite Minnick-
wood the crown of the causeway four feet wide was found
at less than two feet from the surface; the sides were
broken up, but the width did not appear to exceed 15 feet.
There was a thickness of one foot of flints set in mortar
on sand beneath.[3] So lately as September 1898 it was
again exposed near the same place in a trench for laying
a water main.

Hereabouts, about half-way between Anstiebury and
Holmwood station, the direction appears to change rather
more towards the west, and the course is uncertain. Not
many years ago the old road could be seen a little to the
west of Folly Farm, a mile and a quarter further on, beyond
which the line lies a little to the west of the modern road
to near the south end of Dorking. Aubrey says [4] that the
road went " through Darking churchyard, which they find
by digging graves"; it has of late years been exposed in
drainage works in East Street. The same line appears
to be taken up on the north side of Dorking by the modern
road, the east side of the Dorking gap having apparently
been taken as a point to make for from the high ground
near Minnick Farm. In 1861 a length of 200 yards of the
ridge was to be seen in a meadow near Burford Bridge
close to and parallel to the turnpike road.[5] From Juniper
Hall the old road seems to have wound up in about the

[1] *Sussex Archæological Collections*, xxix. 45.
[2] *History of Surrey*, vol. iii. p. xlv.
[3] *Surrey Archæological Collections*, x. 105.
[4] *Survey*, vol. iv. p. 187.
[5] C. Warne, *Proc. Soc. Antiq.*, 2nd Series, vol. i. p. 311.

line of Downs Road to the east of Mickleham, skirting the
heads of the chalk coombes to Mickleham Down, on which
the ridge is traceable. Further on, on Leatherhead Down,
it is still very much as described by Aubrey, and fortunately
it is fenced in and likely to be preserved. He describes
it as in some places 10 yards broad and one and a half yards
deep. The mound is now in places upwards of four feet
high, measuring from the surface of the Down on the
lower side, and six yards wide across the top. The upper
part appears to be made of flints, and tertiary pebbles
are visible in places. The old road here appears to have
for a long time borne the name of Ermyn Street. Beyond
Leatherhead Down a lane and hedgerow occupy the site
of the road, the lane sometimes being upon and sometimes
at the side of the mound. The old coating is visible in
places, consisting of flints and tertiary pebbles; the latter,
which must have been brought to the road, appear to have
given the name " Pebble Lane " to the lane, which continues on in the same straight line to high ground (410')
near Thirty Acres barn. Towards Epsom and Ewell the
line is lost, but in 1876 it was conspicuous for 200 yards
in a field adjoining the Reigate road at Ewell.[1] On the
north of Ewell by North Cheam and Pilford Bridge, the
modern road in a straight line seems to follow it to Morden,
and it seems to be continued after a break by the present
road through Tooting, which a parish boundary follows.
After an interval of two miles the road from Clapham
Rise to Newington Butts takes up the same straight line
as that between Ewell and Morden, pointing to the south
end of Old London Bridge for two miles. High-water
level is reached at Kennington Park, and the straight
road continues below that level for more than half-a-mile.
Onwards in the low ground bordering on what was formerly
the Lock stream there is no trace of the Roman road.[2]

[1] Roach Smith, *Journ. Archæol. Assoc.*, vol. xxxii. p. 481.

[2] It is to be observed that the Roman roads on the south of the
Thames, which perhaps crossed the embanked marsh on raised
causeways, have disappeared on ground below high-water level,
while traces remain above that level. It is probable that after the
Roman evacuation the river embankments fell to ruin, and the
roads were washed away by the action of the tide. There are
records of many breaches in the banks in more settled times.
Dugdale notices 28 between 1294 and 1475 in that part of the bank

Newington Causeway and Stone End are suggestive names, but the former seems to have originated in a causeway leading to a bridge over the Lock brook, and Stone End is called by Ogilby [1] " the end of the pavement " of Southwark, of which there was a "stone end" in Kent Street, and another in Bermondsey Street.

(a) Stane Street appears to have been joined by another road on approaching London, the course of which through Sussex was described in 1780,[2] when it was being dug up for the construction of the Brighton turnpike road. From Clayton, one mile south of Hassocks station, and seven miles from Shoreham, it was traced to St. John's Common, where it was 18 to 20 feet wide, of flints eight inches thick. It passed to the east of Butler's Green to Ardingly Church, by Wakehurst Place, and along the London road to Selsfield Common in a line pointing to New Chapel. A parish boundary along or near the road for a mile and three-quarters to the south of St. John's Common, and along the London road for half-a-mile, are the only evidences now left. After an interval of four miles on the north of Selsfield Common, the line seems to be taken up by the road to Godstone, passing Stansted House, Cold Harbour, and Stratton, and it is said to have gone by Caterham and Coulsdon. From the Brighton road near Purley railway-station a parish boundary follows a rough bank along the east of Russell Hill, and runs along Merebank to Waddon Court, with Cold Harbour close by, and seems to mark the course. The boundary continues on in the same line to the Wandle between Waddon and Beddington, and on in the same direction to the railway. The road was formerly visible on the west side of Broad Green,[3] from which the course appears to be by Streatham to Stane Street. At Woodcot, on this

---

of the river on the Surrey side between Vauxhall and Deptford, and many others are recorded. When Canute passed his ships to the river above London Bridge in 1016 the marshes were most likely open to the tides. The ground levels in 1850 show that ships drawing five feet of water could then have passed at high water of an ordinary spring tide from Limehouse Reach to Lambeth Reach over all ground not now covered by docks, wharves, and raised roads.

[1] *Britannia*, 1675.   [2] Vine, *Gent. Mag.*, vol. li.
[3] Manning and Bray, vol. iii. p. 381.

line of road, Camden and others have placed *Noviomagus*,
a station ten M. P. from London on Iter II., which rejoins
Watling Street by a course which is not known.

Southwards from Clayton this road may have led to the
mouth of the river Adur, where Camden and others have
placed the *Portus Adurni* of the *Notitia*. It may possibly
also have communicated with *Anderida* by a road along
the downs, through Lewes, and following a very old road
through Glynde and Alciston. The Roman walls of
Anderida at Pevensey, enclosing an area of 220 yards by
115 yards, remain, but there are no traces of a Roman road
to it. It is almost surrounded by land but little, if at all,
above the sea level, and the natural access is from the west,
and it was from near Eastbourne, in that direction, that
the squared blocks of calcareous sandstone came with
which the Roman walls are faced.

Part of a supposed Roman road from Newhaven to
London has been described, from Isfield, five miles north
of Lewes, passing east of East Grinstead, and through
Lingfield Camp, on what evidence is not apparent; the
maps afford none.

At the time of the Itinerary of Antonine the road to
Londinium was no doubt by the bridge, and the Itinerary
distance from Rochester agrees fairly well with the
mileage. The earlier Roman London appears to have
extended eastward from Lambeth Hill and Old Change
(a little to the east of St. Paul's) to Miles Lane, Clement's
Lane, and Birchin Lane (a little to the west of King
William Street); and from Cheapside and Poultry to
Thames Street.[1] The area thus enclosed was a rectangle
about 800 yards by 400 yards, or perhaps rather less.
The present Watling Street runs through the western
half of it, and if, as Sir Christopher Wren supposed, it
represents the Prætorian Way of the camp, it is suggestive
of a still earlier camp through the middle of which it would
have run, extending southwards only as far as the brow
of the slope to the river, marked by the line of Knightrider
Street, Great St. Thomas Apostle, and Cloak Lane; and
eastwards perhaps to Walbrook. This would enclose an
area about 240 yards by 530 yards. From the west gate

[1] The evidence for these boundaries is given in a paper by A. J.
Kempe, in the *Gentleman's Magazine*, 1842, part i. p. 267.

the Roman road must have turned towards the north
to cross the Fleet.   On the south side of Cheapside, Wren
sunk 18 feet through made ground and then came upon
a Roman causeway of rough stone firmly cemented, with
brick and rubbish at the bottom, and four feet thick, on
which he founded Bow Church steeple.[1] For various
reasons he thought that the causeway ran along the north
boundary of the older London, and his conclusion has
been confirmed by its discovery, in 1765, at the middle of
Birchin Lane.   Outside the eastern wall, where it crossed
Eastcheap (where the statue of William IV. now stands),
a raised causeway of gravel seven feet six inches in depth,
and 16 feet wide, supported by walls of ragstone with
layers of Roman tiles was displayed in 1831.[2] It pointed
to the north-east in the direction of Aldgate, and many
cinerary urns on either side showed it to have been outside
the station.   The Roman bridge over the Thames, on the
site of Old London Bridge, was also outside the earlier
boundary.

The enlarged *Londinium* extended east and west for
about a mile and a quarter, from the Tower to the Old
Bailey, and northwards from Thames Street for about
half-a-mile to London Wall.   From the Tower, by Aldgate,
Bishopsgate and London Wall streets run inside the course
of the Roman Wall, and Minories and Houndsditch follow
the ditch outside it as far as Bishopsgate.   From the
west end of London Wall the Roman wall turned south,
and then west, and then south again by Newgate to Thames
Street, the latter marking the line of the southern wall.
The irregular shape seems to show that the walls enclosed
an area already occupied by buildings.   Both Newgate
and Aldgate stand on the courses of the roads from the
gates of the older city, to the crossing of the Fleet and to
Old Ford respectively.

(9) *Westminster to Wroxeter.*—A Roman sarcophagus,
tessellated pavement, fragments of Roman buildings, and
Roman bricks, are evidences of the Roman occupation of
the island, which afterwards became the site of Westminster.
This, until the river was shut out, was bounded on the
north by the lower course of the Tyburn stream, flowing
through a tidal marsh, now St. James Park, to the Thames.

[1] *Parentalia*, p. 265.   [2] *Gentleman's Magazine*, 1833, p. 421.

The course of Watling Street onwards is probably that of
Tothill Street,[1] continuing on in the same line as far as
Buckingham Gate, so as to keep above high-water level,
and then turning to the north-west across ground which
is even now below the level of high tide.   When the brow
of the rising ground in the Green Park was reached the
straight line of Edgware Road may have been entered
upon.   If so, the course of Watling Street is now covered
by the houses of Mayfair from Piccadilly near Down Street
nearly to the top of Park Lane.   An attempt to find the
road on this line was made in 1912 inside the Park about
40 yards south of Green Street.   A trench 97 feet long
and 7 feet to 9 feet 6 inches deep was cut across it, but
only made ground over yellow clay and undisturbed gravel
was met with.[2]

At the south end of Edgware Road Watling Street was
crossed by the Roman road from London to the west,
which after crossing the Fleet, followed the line of Holborn
and Oxford Street, and was continued on to Staines and
Silchester by Bayswater Road.   The remains of the Roman
road, pointing to Newgate, were discovered in digging the
foundations for Holborn Bridge,[3] and the road onwards
to Tyburn is referred to in a charter of Edgar as the wide
Here Street, *i. e.* military way.   High Holborn lies in a
straight line with the older part of Oxford Street, and with
the Bayswater Road to Notting Hill.   It is followed by a
parish boundary, and from Tottenham Court Road parish
boundaries follow the straight road to Notting Hill.

The course of Watling Street onwards is plain, Edgware
Road and the continuation of it occupying the line for
10½ miles to Brockley Hill.   From Kilburn to Brockley Hill,
eight miles, the road is in a line between Brockley Hill (416')
and Sydenham Hill (350'), 17 miles distant to the south-
east.   It may have been set out from Brockley Hill in a line
with Sydenham Hill, on which the Crystal Palace is now
visible from Brockley, or it may have been set out from intermediate points, which may very well have been Shootup Hill,

[1] Tothill Street and Tothill Fields, suggests a Toot-hill, or look-
out.   Hollar's view of London shows a hill, and Stow (Book vi.
p. 56) mentions St. Hermit's Hill near Tothill Street.

[2] *Proc. Soc. Antiq.*, 1912, p. 138.

[3] *Gentleman's Magazine*, 1750.

and near Hendon. At Kilburn there is a slight turn to the east, but only enough to throw the Oxford Street end of the road 100 yards away from the straight line. There are slight deviations all along the modern road, which appear the greater from the encroachments which have been made, but from the Marble Arch to Brockley Hill the road is nowhere one-eighth of a mile out of a straight line. Parish boundaries run along the road from Oxford Street to the Brent, five miles, and from the Hyde to Edgware, a mile and a half.

The Roman paving has recently been cut through in a trench for laying a telephone tube along the Edgware Road. Beneath the wood paving and its concrete foundation, on about a foot of brick rubbish, there was generally found four inches to a foot of ordinary soil, but sometimes the brick rubbish rested immediately on the Roman paving. The latter was found to consist of large black nodular flints, weighing from four to seven pounds each, on a bed of rammed reddish-brown gravel of thickness varying according to the inequalities of the clay surface below. A large opening opposite Market Street showed that the gravel was supported by dwarf walls of gravel concrete a foot high, at the sides of a trench cut in the clay. On the levelled surface of the gravel, lime grouting appears to have been laid, in which the flints were set, every advantage having been taken of the protuberances of the nodules to dovetail and interlock them. The workmen found that it gave them much more trouble to break up than the modern concrete floor above. The trench extended for half-a-mile from the south end of Edgware Road, and the paving was cut through all along except where the trench was too near the footway. The width of the paved road appeared to be 24 feet. The flints are from the chalk of Hertfordshire, and the gravel is such as is found at Radlett. A block of Totternhoe stone from near Dunstable, a boulder of granite, and a sandstone block, possibly from the boulder clay, occurred in the paving.[1]

Many Roman remains have been found on Brockley Hill, the site of a Roman station, *Sulloniacæ*. From it

[1] James G. Wood, M.A., F.S.A., in *Home Counties Magazine*, vol. iv. p. 238 and p. 259.

a road is supposed to have branched off in the direction of Watford, King's Langley, Berkhampstead, and Tring,[1] but parish boundaries afford no evidence of it.

From the station on Brockley Hill onwards Watling Street has a remarkable double bend, curving first to the north-east through Elstree and then back again, making a reversed curve one mile and a quarter long. From the north end of the curve a straight line runs to Verulam in a line with a point on high ground on the top of Elstree Hill (470′), which is half-a-mile to the east of the point on Brockley Hill, to which the road from the south is directed. The effect is to ease considerably the ascent of the hill coming from Verulam. That the course of the Roman road was along the double bend is shown by parish boundaries following it all through and along the straight road beyond, and it is another instance of that straightness which has been so much insisted upon, having been abandoned when there was cause for it. From Aldenham onwards Watling Street is now a narrow road, with signs that it has been encroached upon. The Midland Railway runs alongside it for two miles near Radlett station. At Park Street the straight line is again broken by a slight bend to avoid more than one crossing of the river; the road resuming the same line when the difficulty has been passed. At St. Stephen's Church the road from Watford to St. Albans is crossed, and there are some traces of Watling Street on in the same line for three-eighths of a mile to the walls of *Verolamium*.

The area enclosed by the remains of these walls is a rough oval about 1500 yards from south to north and 850 yards from east to west. Watling Street, which passes through it lengthways, was dug up and robbed of its materials as far as St. Michael's Church in 1800.[2] Near the south side of the church it is crossed by Camlet Way, visible in 1795,[3] but of which nothing is now known in either direction.

On the north side of the Roman city Watling Street

[1] Sir J. Evans, *Archæological Survey of Hertfordshire*, 1892.

[2] J. W. Grover, *Journal of Archæological Association*, 1870. Mr. Grover points out that Verulam and Pompeii are very much of the same shape and size, the former being rather the larger.

[3] Newcome, *History of St. Albans*.

can be traced through the fields in line with the modern London and Holyhead road, which joins it about two miles north of St. Albans and thence follows the course of it nearly all the way to Weedon. The direction is at first between the higher part of Verulam (336') and a point on high ground (416') beyond Bylands Farm, four miles distant. There is then a curve to the west, with a parish boundary continuing along the middle of the road, to another straight line two miles long, for the greater part of which Watling Street, as a narrow lane, lies to the north-east of the modern road, passing over a hill which the latter avoids. At Markyate Street the modern road rejoins Watling Street, and winds in a shallow valley with county and parish boundaries along the middle of it to Dunstable.

About midway, at Hensworth Lynch, the Roman road was lately exposed in the side ditch of the present road, nine inches thick of flints and other stone for a width of four or five feet. A similar road surface was found in the town of Dunstable in 1900. Horsley placed *Durocobrivæ* at Dunstable, and it would seem correctly, judging from the distances apart of the stations as given in the Itinerary, although there is no river or water. Here Icknild Way crosses Watling Street, which runs straight through Dunstable for five and a half miles to a knoll (445') beyond Hockliffe, having parish boundaries along the middle or side of it for the last three and a half miles. It then goes on straight in nearly the same line for four miles to high ground (508') half-a-mile south of Little Brickhill, parish boundaries following it all the way. The course thence down the hill is rather uncertain, modern road improvements here as in other places having interfered with the old road, but from one mile south of Fenny Stratford (*Magiovintum*) parish boundaries run along the middle of the road, which goes straight for seven miles, crossed by the North-Western Railway one mile north of Bletchley station, and then, with a slight turn on high ground, on for nine miles in almost the same straight line through Stony Stratford to Towcester, with parish boundaries following it for most of the way.

In Camden's time [1] the ridge of the old road was very conspicuous between Stony Stratford and Towcester,

[1] *Britannia*, ii. 265.

and, according to Ogilby, beyond Potterspury there were " visible remains of the old Roman way " in 1675.

From Fenny Stratford strips of waste begin to be frequent at the sides of the road. Nearly all the way from London the width is 20 yards or more between the fences where the road has not been encroached upon, but encroachments are frequent, sometimes on one side and sometimes on the other, and the modern road in some degree loses the appearance of straightness to a traveller passing along it.

At Towcester (*Lactodorum*) Watling Street passes through a Roman camp, three sides of which can be traced in the town, the east side being now bounded by a branch of the river Tove. It is about 480 yards long in the direction of Watling Street, and 200 to 400 yards wide. On leaving the Roman station there is a decided change in direction, and the road for 28 miles is in straight lengths, making up approximately an arc of a circle of which no part is as much as three-quarters of a mile away from the chord. It is not difficult to trace how the line was laid out from intermediate points on high ground. The first point is near Pattishall (480'), four miles from Towcester, to which the road is straight, with a parish boundary along a mile of it ; beyond, the present road is not straight, and a parish boundary which does not follow it in places may be the line of Watling Street. At Weedon, called in Leland's Itinerary Weedon on the Street, the Holyhead road, after having followed the course of the Roman road for 45 miles, turns off to Daventry ; and Watling Street, about 20 yards wide between the fences with a road 12 to 15 feet wide, continues on in the same general direction. It bends to avoid the Nene river, parish boundaries following it for half-a-mile. After the North-Western Railway has been crossed, a straight line begins which is in line between high ground over Weedon Tunnel (400') and Watford Gap (500'), and for three miles out of six parish boundaries run along the middle of the road. On the west of Norton Park the road, followed by the parish boundary, turns out of the straight line to the east and back again to it in half-a-mile. In the field through which the straight line thus quitted passes, a shallow pit, in the summer of 1900, afforded fragments of Roman pottery, mortaria, etc., and about 18 inches below the surface there were traces of a pavement of flat stones too thin to be part of a road.   Somewhere here, according to the distances in the Itinerary, should be the site of *Bannaventa*, which Camden and Stukeley place at Weedon, three miles to the south, and Horsley at Borough Hill near Daventry, two miles away from Watling Street.

The same straight line is resumed, parallel to and less than half-a-mile west of the North-Western Railway, after crossing which the present road, 12 to 15 feet wide, winds between fences 20 yards or more apart.   Near Watford in 1712 Watling Street is said [1] to have run very high, and to have been seven yards wide.   The ridge is still to be seen between Weedon and Norton Park, especially where a fence runs along the east side of it for some distance.

From near Watford Gap, with a slight turn, there is a straight line to Gibbet Hill (429') seven miles distant. For half-a-mile the modern road follows the line of the old road, but from the cross-roads from Ashby St. Leger to Crick, Watling Street is now grassed over for two and a half miles.   For one and a half miles there are hedges on both sides, 23 to 25 yards apart, and there is little or no trace of a ridge.   Beyond, the old road is in a grass field with a hedge on one side ; a brown track in the turf marks the line all along, and as the ground falls the ridge is more evident.   On the north of the road from Rugby to Crick it is as much as five feet high and eight yards wide.   Stukeley found the ridge hereabouts very high for miles together,[2] but it has since evidently been dug into for the sake of the gravel.   A little further on there is not much ridge, but a stream that runs alongside has cut into it in places, exposing gravel a yard deep, with a layer of large cobble stones at the base on the clayey subsoil.   A little further on the present road from Kilsby joins, and the hedges are 25 yards apart, with a hard road 12 or 15 feet wide between them. A parish boundary has followed the road all along, and here it becomes a county boundary, and for the next 21 miles Watling Street is the boundary between the counties of Warwick on the south and Northampton and Leicester on the north-east.

At Gibbet Hill (429') there is a slight turn to Cross-in-Hand (429'), and then another length of straight road three

[1] Morton, *Natural History of Northamptonshire*, p. 501.
[2] *Itinerarium Curiosum*, p. 113.

and a half miles long reaches High Cross (440'), the station *Venonæ* at the intersection of Watling Street and the Foss.

Where Watling Street crosses the river Avon, about two miles east of Rugby, *Tripontium*, which appears in Iter VI. as eight M. P. from *Venonæ*, has been placed; the position agrees with this distance from High Cross, but it is to be noticed that from *Venonæ* to stations further south the distance is three M. P. longer than it is by Iter II., or by measurement. It is possible that *Tripontium* was not on the direct line of Watling Street.

This part of Watling Street is now an unimportant thoroughfare where it is not grassed over and disused. It is generally enclosed by hedges 20 yards or more apart where there are no encroachments, and the modern road is not more than 12 or 15 feet wide. Towards High Cross the hedges are as much as 30 yards apart, a cart-way winding from side to side between them. Though the general direction of the road is straight from point to point, the straight line appears to have been slightly departed from in crossing streams and in hollows. Encroachments, sometimes on one side, sometimes on the other, and the devious course of the present road, detract from the appearance of straightness as one passes along the road. Though little used for road traffic, this part of Watling Street still serves as a main line of communication for one of the principal telegraph routes.

At High Cross there is a considerable change of direction to the westward, and the road makes for Wall (*Etocetum*) 25 miles off, by straight lengths between intermediate points on high ground, none of which is as much as a mile out of a straight line from High Cross to Wall. For nearly eight miles from High Cross the road runs straight in the direction of high ground (300') south of Higham-on-the-Hill, keeping to the north of the river Anker, and then there is a very slight turn more towards the west, and another straight line seven miles long to Hall End (343') begins. Near Mancetter a straight road joins, pointing for five miles to Leicester, and continued on in the same line by other roads, which represents a Roman road from Leicester.[1] At Mancetter, the station *Manduesedum*, a rectangle 233

[1] On this road Henry VII., coming by Watling Street from Wales, and Richard III., coming from Leicester, met at Bosworth Field.

E

yards by 166 yards, is passed through longitudinally, half the camp being in one county and half in the other.   Beyond Atherstone, at Hall End, there is a bend more to the west, and a straight road runs by Wilnecote railway-station, and through Fazeley, for six miles to high ground near Hints (400'), from which there is an extensive view in both directions.   A change of direction occurs a quarter of a mile further on, on the north side of a large tumulus (380'), and thence the road went straight to Wall (*Etocetum*) (369').

From High Cross to within two and a half miles of Wall a turnpike road was constructed along the line of Watling Street, and for $10\frac{1}{2}$ miles a county boundary follows it to near Atherstone.   A highway continues the line on from Weeford Gate to within three-quarters of a mile of Wall, and then a footpath preserves the line.   The gravelled Watling Street was here found 4 feet below the surface in draining, seemingly about 15 feet wide.

About half-a-mile east of Wall Watling Street is crossed by Riknild Street, and towards Wall Roman masonry and the remains of a villa mark the site of station *Etocetum*. Here there is an extensive prospect, particularly to the south and west, and a decided change of direction, and Watling Street runs straight due west for four and a half miles to high ground (500') on the west of Brownhills, with a parish boundary following it nearly all the way. Camden describes a fair, bold and uninterrupted ridge running from Wall till it comes to the river Penk,[1] and in Stukeley's time the ridge was perfect for a great length, but it has since been destroyed in making the modern road.

On the high ground (500') west of Brownhills the direction changes to west-north-west, and with a very slight turn on high ground (389') south of Cannock, continues in the same line for eight miles, with parish boundaries along it in places, to the river Penk.   Hereabouts, 12 M. P. from Wall, and two miles to the south of Penkridge, must have been the station *Pennocrucium*.   The road then turns due west, and for 13 miles to Oakengates is nowhere more than 200 yards out of a straight line, which was probably laid out to pass on the north side of the Wrekin (1335').   It is made up of several straight lengths between points on high ground, and for nine miles parish boundaries run along the

[1] *Britannia*, ii. 496.

middle of the road, and continuously for five and a half miles to Oakengates. Stukeley says that the old road was " laid very broad and deep with gravel not yet worn out, where it goes over commons and moors," and was raised a good height above the soil.[1]

On this straight length of road, 12 M. P. from *Penno-crucium* and 11 M. P. from *Uriconium*, according to the Itinerary was the station *Uxacona*.

Through Oakengates and by Wellington the course is rather uncertain, but on the south-west of Wellington the London and Holyhead road joins Watling Street, and for two miles follows the course of it in a straight line pointing to the top of Overly Hill (462'), with a parish boundary along the middle. The modern road skirts round the north of the hill, but the old road straight on over the hill was used by coaches at the beginning of the last century. Now only about 250 yards remain on the top of the hill, where it is narrowed from 20 yards to about four yards by a long strip of garden with a house on it; and beyond that a hedgerow and footway indicate the line of the old road. From where the modern road diverges to where it again joins Watling Street parish boundaries follow the old line of Watling Street almost continuously, and run along the modern road, after it rejoins Watling Street. From the top of Overly Hill the site of *Viroconium* or *Uriconium* at Wroxeter three miles distant is plainly visible, and Watling Street with a slight turn goes straight to it, the main road turning off to Shrewsbury. Recent excavations show that the earlier houses of *Uriconium* were of wood and wattle and daub, in date about A.D. 75 to 81. There must have been an early fortress, traces of which may be revealed in further excavations, to the north gate of which perhaps Watling Street led. The later walls appear to have enclosed about 170 acres in a rough oval about 1400 yards from north to south and 1000 yards from east to west. Watling Street enters the later walls on the north-east, and the ford across the Severn is opposite the village of Wroxeter at the south-west of the Roman city.

Parts of Itinera III. and II. of Antonine's Itinerary make up the whole length of Watling Street from Dover to Wroxeter. They are here arranged in order, with the names

---

[1] *Itinerarium Curiosum*, p. 60.

of the Roman stations, and their distances in M.P., and the
modern names with the distances in miles.

	M. P.		STATUTE MILES
ITER III.			
Portus Dubris ad Duro-vernum	xiv	Dover to Canterbury .	15
ITER II.			
Durolevo	xii	Rochester	26
Durobrivis	xiii		
ITER III.			
Londinio	xxvii	London	29
ITER II.			
Sulloniacis	xii	Brockley Hill . . .	$13\frac{1}{2}$
Verolamio	ix	Verulam	$8\frac{1}{2}$
Durocobrivis	xii	Dunstable	12
Magiovinto	xii	Fenny Stratford . .	$11\frac{1}{4}$
Lactodoro	xvii	Towcester	$15\frac{1}{2}$
Bannaventa	xii	near Norton Park . .	11
Venonis	xvii	High Cross	18
Manduesedo	xii	Mancetter	11
Etoceto	xvi	Wall	15
Pennocrucio	xii	Gailey	$12\frac{1}{4}$
Uxacona	xii	Redhill	$11\frac{1}{2}$
Urioconio	xi	Wroxeter	$10\frac{1}{2}$
	M. P. 220		Miles 220

It will be seen that the Itinerary distances make up a
total the same as the total in English miles, and that the
intermediate distances agree fairly well. Beyond Uriconium
Iter II. leads to Chester by an unknown route of 53 M.P.,
the direct distance being less than forty miles.

(10) *Wroxeter to Abergavenny.*—The name Watling Street
is borne by a road from Wroxeter in a south-westerly
direction. It crossed the Severn opposite the south end
of the village of Wroxeter on the south-west of the Roman
city. Camden [1] mentions the foundations of a bridge, which
Bishop Gibson says were still to be seen in his time, about
1700. The foundations of the piers were said in 1879 still

[1] *Britannia,* iii. 5.

to remain.[1]   After leaving the Severn valley and crossing
Cound Brook the course is followed by a lane passing to the
east of Pitchford, through Frodesley and Longnor Green,
and then a parish boundary follows it for two miles, and
the ridge is traceable, having a fence upon it for a considerable distance.   A lane continues the line along the east
side of the railway past All Stretton, and Church Stretton
railway-station, and at Little Stretton the ridge appears with
a cart-track on one side.   The general section of the road
hereabouts seems to be eight inches of gravel on a layer of
stone one foot deep and raised two or three feet above the
surface.[2]   For a mile the main road follows the course with
a parish boundary along it.   At Marshbrook Station Watling
Street is crossed by the railway, and is followed by the old
road by Wistanstow to Stretford Bridge.   Beyond, another
lane with a parish boundary along it for three-quarters of a
mile takes up the line past Craven Arms station, half-a-
mile west of which the railway to Knighton crosses over it,
and it can be seen ascending the hill in the direction of
Clungunford, which it leaves half-a-mile to the west.   At
Leintwardine it passes through the remains of a rectagular
camp about 310 × 220 yards, the High Street of the town
dividing the camp longitudinally in halves.   Here was
probably *Bravonium* of Iter XII., 27 M.P. from *Viroconium.*
Turning east of south by Stanway to near Wigmore the
road passes through Aymestrey to Mortimer's Cross.   From
Wroxeter thus far, about 33 miles, the character of the road
is different from that of Watling Street proper, due perhaps
partly to the more broken nature of the country.   There
are no long pieces of straight road, but parish boundaries
follow it and indicate the line where no traces remain.
From Mortimer's Cross a lane with a parish boundary along
it runs straight pointing to high ground (400') near Bush
Bank, eight miles distant, immediately to the east of which
Bayley Hill rises to 775 feet.   The straightness of the road,
which here bears the name of Watling Street, is deviated from
at the crossing of the river Arrow near Stretford, where it is
joined by the modern road.   To the south of Bush Bank
the present road occupies the course for two miles, the
direction changing slightly to avoid the high ground (700')

[1] *Trans. Shropshire Arch. and Nat. Hist. Soc.*, vol. ii. p. 358.
[2] *Shropshire Arch. and Nat. Hist. Soc.*, N.S. x. p. 173.

of Nupton Hill. Then the present road turns towards
the east, while the Roman road seems to have bent in the
opposite direction, its course in about a mile being indicated
by a lane which, near Tillington, joins a road bearing the
name of Watling Street, leading straight to *Magnæ*, the camp
near Kenchester, passing through Credenhill, and by Credenhill railway-station, from which a parish boundary runs
to the east side of the camp. The station *Magnæ*, about
half-a-mile east of Kenchester, on the north of the river
Wye, is now represented by irregular earthworks about
500 yards from east to west by 300 yards, of which Stukeley
gives a complete plan.[1] A footpath and a lane mark the
course southwards, and near Old Weir the road was found in
1893 a foot beneath the surface, of gravel 12 inches thick and
15 feet wide.[2] On the south of the Wye a parish boundary
continues the same line for more than half-a-mile, and then
a hedgerow, and a road called Stone Street, carry on the
same line for three miles farther. Near Woodyatts Cross
some of the pavement of the road remained lately. The
road went on by Brampton and Carey's Gate to Abbey
Dore, where at the railway-station it was found in 1901
at a depth of 18 inches beneath the surface. The pavement,
13 feet wide, of rough stone pitching, is said to have had ruts
4 feet 8 inches apart, 8 inches deep and 9 inches wide.[3] In
1908 it was uncovered for a length of 10 yards for the full
width of 13 feet. The paving, 18 inches to 2 feet beneath
the surface, of unworked local limestone, without a kerb,
averaged 9 inches in thickness and was laid on a hard red
marl. A wheel track towards one side of the road of a
gauge of about 4 feet 6 inches is mentioned.[4] Farther south
the course is obscure. Iter XII. of Antonine passes over
this road coming from Caerleon by *Burrium* (Usk) and
Gobannium (Abergavenny) to *Magnæ* and on to *Viroconium*.
The Itinerary distances agree with the mileage between these
places.

Through *Magnæ* a Roman road ran east and west, which
will be reverted to (p. 292).

(*a*) From Wroxeter it is probable that a Roman road

[1] *Itinerarium Curiosum*, pl. 85.
[2] *Trans. Woolhope Field Club*, 1893, p. 60.
[3] *Ibid.*, 1901–2, p. 190.
[4] *Archæologia Cambrensis*, Jan. 1909, p. 154.

went to Caersws, an undoubted Roman station three miles west of Newton, Montgomeryshire, and 34 miles in a straight line from Wroxeter. The natural access to it would have been from Wroxeter, and a road to it would be in the direction, of Higden's continuation of Watling Street to Cardigan, but there is no trace of it.

Westward from Caersws the Ordnance map shows a Roman road for four miles to Rhyd-y-Carw on the river Taranon. A Roman road in continuation of the Brecknockshire Sarn Helen is supposed to have reached Caersws from the south, and to the north of it the course of Sarn Swsog was described in 1806 by the Rev. Walter Davies [1] in great detail as far as the river Vyrnwy near Dolanog, about 14 miles. The Ordnance maps show it for three miles, beyond which the local names in the description do not help in an attempt to follow the course. The road was visible on the hills, where large side stones appeared, and the hard surface of the road could be felt by thrusting a stick down through the grass and moss. The width was five yards, and the space between the sides of large stones was filled in with stones and gravel, the middle being somewhat raised.

A paved road called Devil's Causeway, generally referred to as being near Pitchford, but really three miles south of it, is described by Hartshorne [2] as branching from Watling Street on the west of the Severn, and passing through Acton Burnell, to the east of Cardington, and to Rushbury, where it turns to the south-east over Wenlock Edge to Tugford and Nordybank camp on the Brown Clee Hills. The paving of a local gritstone is very distinct for half-a-mile in the road near Causeway Wood Farm, but the road generally has nothing of the character of a Roman road. It points towards Worcester, from which a Roman road is said to have formerly been traced in a north-westerly direction.

[1] Hoare's *Giraldus Cambrensis*, p. clviii.
[2] *Salopia Antiqua*, p. 133.

CHAPTER III

WATLING STREET AND BRANCHES (*continued*)

(11) *Watling Street to Chester.*—Higden, the monk of Chester, though he describes the course of Watling Street with considerable fulness, does not say that it led to Chester. Horsley [1] had been informed that Watling Street, or a branch of it, went by Newport and Whitchurch from Wall to Chester, and that it appeared in several places. It is probably represented by a line of highways branching from Watling Street on the west of Gailey near the site of *Pennocrucium*, 22 miles east of Wroxeter. From Stretton, half-a-mile north of Watling Street, a highway lies in very nearly one straight line for two miles and a third to near Longnor brook, where the present road turns north to cross the brook by Stonyford Bridge. A lane for an eighth of a

---

[1] *Britannia Romana*, p. 417.

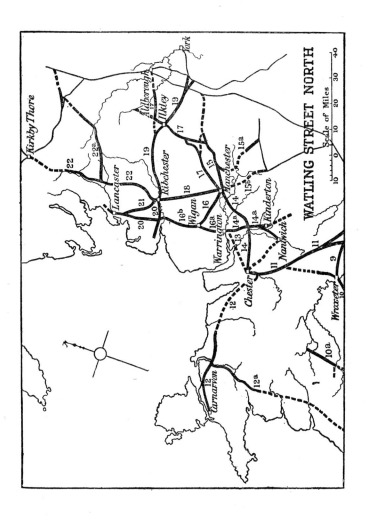

WATLING STREET NORTH

Scale of Miles
10 0 10 20 30 40

mile on the south-east of Little Onn Hall, and three-
quarters of a mile of a track and a highway in the same
direction on the north-east of High Onn, are the only indications for five miles; and then highways follow the same
direction for nearly two miles on the north-east of Aqualate,
past what is marked as a Roman Well on the Ordnance
map. After an interval of a mile Gorsey Lane, with a
parish boundary, and a highway with a county boundary
along it, lie in a straight line in very nearly the same direction for nearly two miles to The Camp, where there is a
slight turn and then a lane, followed by the county boundary
for three-quarters of a mile to Ellerton Hall, and a track
and a highway onwards for another half-mile, continue
the line to within a mile of the road called Long Ford
near Hinstock. No part of the line indicated by the
highways is more than half-a-mile out of a straight line
in the sixteen miles, and the three slight changes of
direction take place at high points, giving a Roman
character of setting out. The Long Ford is the continuation of a line of highways crossing Watling Street
a mile west of Weston-under-Lizard, which may be a
Roman road from the direction of Worcester, of which
there are some indications. This road on the north of
Watling Street is followed by a parish boundary for three-
quarters of a mile, and three-quarters of a mile further on
in the same line the road bears the name of Pave Lane.
It is marked on the new Ordnance map as a Roman road,
leading through Chetwynd Aston to Newport, three miles
north of which the present road, pointing straight to Newport, is followed for a mile by parish boundaries. At
Stanford Bridge, over the river Meese, a road called the
Long Ford is entered upon, which continues for eight miles
by Hinstock to Bletchley, parish boundaries following it
for most of the way. This road was called the Long Ford,
and the crossing of the river Tarn, Streatford, in the time of
Henry III; and in a writ relating to the repair of the road
in 1319 it is described as the Royal road called Longeford.[1]
Near Hinstock the road from Watling Street near Stretton
must have joined. At Bletchley the straight line of Long
Ford ends, and the course is lost, but it seems to have
gone through Whitchurch to Malpas, whence the present

[1] Eyton, *Antiquities of Shropshire*, vol. ix. p. 339.

road, followed for two miles by parish boundaries, runs on straight to Tilston. A mile further on is Stretton, where Horsley placed *Bovium*, and then there is no trace for five miles. The line is picked up at Aldford, where a paved causeway is said to be visible in the river Dee at low water.[1] Between the Dee and Chester, Stukeley observed the remains of the Roman road. It runs straight for four miles to Chester through Eaton Park, where it is still to be traced, and along the Eccleston Road, where the pavement was broken through in 1884 for about 600 yards. On boulder stones set in hard clay a layer of coarse gravel was found on which a pavement of flags had formerly rested. Nearer Chester the flags were found, of red sandstone 18 inches by 12 inches and 8 inches thick. On approaching the Dee the modern street is in a line with Bridge Street, Chester, to within 300 yards of the river, and further on the Roman road was found on the brow of the slope, and it was visible in Edgar's Field in Pennant's time. The Dee was crossed between the Castle and Dee Bridge, and the ferry and ford were in use until the building of Dee Bridge.

The south wall of the Roman *Deva* is supposed to have extended westward from Newgate, from which northwards the present city wall follows the line of the Roman wall. If Bridge Street is on the course of the middle road dividing the camp into two equal halves, the breadth of the early station was about 400 yards, compared with 450 and 440 yards at Caerleon and Caerwent; and with 435 yards at the similar station at Gloucester. Following the proportion of those stations, the length of *Deva* would be about 470 yards, which would bring the north wall to near the Deanery, and the principal cross street, represented by East gate and West gate, would be in the same relative position as in the above-named stations. There is no doubt that the city was enlarged in Roman times, and how far the present walls of Chester are on the lines of the Roman walls has been a subject of controversy.

A Roman road northwards from Wroxeter probably joined the latter road to Chester on the south of Whitchurch. The straight road from the north gate through Norton seems to follow it, and traces of the ridge appear between the forking roads beyond. A footway continues it to the river

[1] Ormerod's *Hist. of Cheshire*, p. 584.

Tern, and onwards a parish boundary marks the course for a mile and three-quarters to a line of highways in the same direction for a mile and a half. After an interval of the same length, straight roads from Poynton Grange to Shawbury, and on to Moreton Corbet lie in the same direction. There is then no trace for six and a half miles, but fragments of two Roman milliaries were found in 1812 when Moston Pool, two miles north of Moreton Corbet, was drained.[1] On the north of Prees the Whitchurch road resumes the line of the road for two and a half miles to within two miles of Whitchurch.

(12) *Chester to Carnarvon.*—From *Deva* Iter XI. of Antonine goes by *Varae* and *Conovium* to *Segontium.* The road appears to have branched from the road leading to Chester from the south after it had crossed the river Dee near Aldford, thus avoiding the Saltney Marshes on the south and west of Chester. The course according to Mr. Shrubsole [2] is along the present road by Poulton Hall, Pulford, and Dodleston to Hawarden. He thought that the course could be traced for several hundred yards, passing near the castle, by the church and through the vicarage grounds; and he continued it by Kesterton to Flint, and thence by a doubtful course to Caerwys, where he placed *Varae*, 32 M. P. from *Deva*, and 29½ miles from Chester by the course followed. Camden, probably led by sound, placed *Varae* at Bodfari, where there are no traces of Roman occupation; and Gale altered the Itinerary distance to 22 M. P. to suit a direct course from Chester.

It was suggested many years ago that the road from Chester to *Varae* and *Conovium* may have branched at Eaton in the direction of Hawarden, some fields on the north of Belgrave Avenue being named Stratton, or Streatons.

A course for the road onwards has been suggested by the Rev. George Herbert, which is worthy of consideration. From Hawarden it follows the road by Ewloe to Dublin, called Stamford Way, and then the old road on to Northop, a mile and a half to the west of which place Croes-y-Stryt may indicate the line. On the road onwards near Pen-y-park there is paving along one side of the road, and partly under the turf bordering it. From Pentre Halkin, on the

1 *Eph. Ep. Add.*, vol. vii. No. 692.
2 *Archæol. Cambrensis*, 5th Series, vol. ix. p. 257.

east side of Halkin mountain, a line of highway continues
for eight miles, past Babell and Wernfawr, joining the main
road at Rhiewallt, two miles and a half from St. Asaph.
On the west of St. Asaph a road runs due west for three
miles and a half, with a county boundary along it for two
miles and a half; the boundary going straight on where,
at Glascoed, the present road diverges from the straight
line. The line of highways continues on by Sarn-rug,
Bettws-yn-Rhos, and Gofer to the Conwy river, a mile
north of Caerhun. If this line of roads represents with some
deviations the course of the Roman road, by distance along
it from Caerhun, *Varae* would be placed at or near St.
Asaph, which is not inconsistent with the itinerary distances
from Deva, M. P. xxxii., and from *Conovium*, M. P. xviii.

Conovium is placed at Caerhun on the river Conway,
where the site of a Roman camp is still traceable about
144 yards square, and from it in 1846 [1] a raised turf road
was traced, by Bwlch-y-Ddeufaen, and along the hillside
above Llydiart-y-Mynydd towards Aber. This road is
shown on the Ordnance map for four miles to Maes-y-gaer
near Aber, a large camp apparently not Roman. Near
it, at Rhiwiau Uchaf, a Roman milestone was found in
1883 with an inscription to Hadrian marking the eighth
mile *a Kanovio*.[2] Traces of the road are lost in the
lower ground, and the only indication of its course seems
to be a Roman milestone found near Tycoch Bangor,[3]
and another near Llanddeniniolen, 4 miles north-east of Carnarvon, described as a stone 4 feet long, one foot wide at
top, and one foot six inches at bottom, with an inscription
to Trajan.[4] The site of *Segontium*, near the mouth of the
river Seiont, on the south-east of Carnarvon, is marked
by the remains of a walled fort about 183 yards by 153 yards,
including the Church of Llanbladig.

(*a*) *Sarn Helen.*—From *Conovium* a Roman road known
as Sarn Helen ran due south. The course is described in
1864 [5] to be along the foot of the cliffs on the west side of
the vale of Llanrwst as far as Trefriew, where, however, it
was then obliterated, and over the moor behind Gwydir,

[1] *Archæol. Cambrensis*, vol. i. p. 72.
[2] *Ibid.* iv., xiv., p. 170.   [3] *Ibid.* i., ii. 1847.
[4] *Gent. Mag.*, 1795, part 2, p. 559.
[5] *Archæol Cambrensis*, 3rd Series, vol. xi. p. 215.

crossing the valley of the Llugwy between Bettws-y-coed and Swallow Falls, and then over the moors, where there are remains of the paving, to Pont-y-pant on the Lugwy. South of this the railway to Festiniog seems to have effaced it for a mile and a half to the village of Dolwyddelan, and then Sarn Helen is plainly traceable over the moors, passing on the east of Manad Mawr, and by Bwlch-y-fran (or Bwlch-carrig-y-fran) to Rhyd-y-Halen, leaving Festiniog about a mile to the west. Camden [1] mentions this part as being paved with stones, and Pennant [2] noticed it near Festiniog " quite bare, exhibiting the rude stones of which it was made." In his time it appears to have been visible on to Tomen-y-mûr, a walled Roman fort measuring about 300 yards by 200 yards, from which Sarn Helen is traceable south to Trawsfynydd. It ascends the mountain to Pen-y-street, where it is visible, and also along the ridge between the Afon Eden and the Gair. Its further course is by Dolmelynllen, and on to Dolgelly. It is supposed to have passed the mountains to the east of Cader Idris, and to have gone on south to join the other Sarn Helen, which, after an interval of 30 miles, can be followed through Llanio to Carmarthen, and towards Llandovery.

(13) *Chester to Wilderspool.*—A Roman road is supposed [3] to have left Chester by the north gate, now represented by " The Street " or " Back Street," through Hoole, in the direction of Helsby Hill; and to be traceable towards the ford at Bridge Trafford. It is continued on by Dunham, Frodsham, and Preston-on-the-Hill, beyond which the present road carries on the line for three miles towards Wilderspool. It would there have crossed the Mersey with Kind Street to Wigan and the north.

(14) *Chester to Manchester.*—The Roman road from Chester to Northwich and Manchester, called Watling Street, was on the line of the present road for four miles to Stamford Bridge, and then along a highway with a parish boundary for another mile, pointing straight to Edisbury Hill (460'—550') in Delamere Forest, visible from Chester. After an interval of a mile, a road with a parish boundary along it for three-quarters of a mile east of Salter's Brook

[1] *Britannia*, iii. 169.
[2] *Tour in Wales* (edited by Prof. Rhys), vol. ii. p. 286.
[3] Watkin, *Roman Cheshire*, p. 55.

takes up the line. Mr. Robson traced the road through Delamere Forest before it was effaced by disafforesting operations.[1] At the west of the forest he describes the ridge as being more or less distinctly marked for half-a-mile, nine or ten yards across, with a well-marked crown, and shallow ditches and traces of mounds beyond them on each side. There was a thickness of 18 inches of solid gravel. Traces appeared after a mile and a half in the same course, and the ridge is still conspicuous on the west of Stony Lane, 3 feet 4 inches high, with gravel a few inches beneath the turf. At Edisbury Hill there is a slight turn, and the line is taken by a lane, and where that joins the road to Delamere railway-station the Roman road was cut through two feet beneath the surface in laying the Vyrnwy water-main.[2] It is visible on the east of the road, and in about a mile and a half the Northwich road rejoins it for a short distance, and the ridge is traceable onwards on the north of the road to Sandiway, from which onwards the present road seems to follow very nearly the course of the Roman road on to Northwich, where remains have been found in several places.

Mr. W. T. Watkin[3] supposes that a road branched at Nettlefold to Kinderton, near Middlewich. The supposed junction consists of two sunk roads, not ridges, and the evidences of a Roman road to Middlewich appear to be but slight. He also gives the course of a Roman road from Chester, by Waverton and Beeston Castle to Wardle and Nantwich, and on to Chesterton. The line of the road was plainly to be distinguished in 1810 for two and a half miles on the west of Beeston Castle,[4] on the north of which there were lately some remains of a paved road, but the evidence of a Roman road in this direction is inconclusive.

(a) The connexion of the Roman roads of Cheshire and Lancashire with the south is not very plain. It would seem to have been by the road leading to Chester

---

[1] *Trans. Hist. Soc. Lanc. and Chesh.*, 1851, p. 71.

[2] Watkin, p. 38.

[3] *Roman Cheshire*, p. 32.

[4] Bishop Bennet in *Lysons*, vol. ii. 432. Bennet, Bishop of Cloyne, is said to have walked over most of the Roman roads of England at the beginning of the last century, when many traces remained which have now disappeared. Unfortunately nearly all that is known of his observations is contained in **Lysons'** *Magna Britannia*, which includes only nine English counties.

by Hinstock and Whitchurch, which has already been mentioned, but there is no trace of any connexion between this road and Nantwich, nine miles distant. Between Nantwich and Middlewich there are evident traces of a Roman road. About a mile north-north-east of Worleston Station, near Red Hall, the road was found in laying a water-main thirty years since two feet below the surface, consisting of a hard concrete two feet thick, and it was cut through at another place near Minshall Vernon, 18 inches thick of gravel almost as hard as concrete, and 15 feet wide. There was no sign of the road at either place on the surface. The course is indicated by roads and lanes with parish boundaries along them by Park Hall—near which the ridge was quite plain in 1810 [1]—by Occleston Green, and Sutton, and on to Middlewich, where it seems to have joined another Roman road from the south. There are some remains of the ridge of the latter on the south of Middlewich, and a quarter of a mile of it is shown in the same line on the new Ordnance map near the railway junction at Sandbach. The Roman road near Sandbach was unearthed in forming a bowling-green at Elworth a few years ago. From information afforded by Mr. F. J. Poole, it appears that it was found about a foot beneath the surface, and consisted of a solid bed of gravel about 15 inches thick, and four to five yards wide. It can be traced by the stones showing on the surface up to and beyond the railway for some distance in the direction of Kinderton. It may have continued on by a road which was thought by Ormerod to have gone to Chesterton, where the remains of a walled fort 370 yards by 300 yards were, it is said, visible until the beginning of the last century, and of which portions can still be traced,[2] and on perhaps by Meir and Rocester to Derby, but there are no evidences of it remaining, except perhaps parish boundaries here and there, and a Windy Arbour near Red Street.

At Kinderton, half-a-mile north of Middlewich, on the south bank of the river Dane, Whitaker [3] and others place *Condate* of the Itinerary. That there was a station there is shown by the remains of a Roman camp, now destroyed,

1 Bishop Bennet, *Lysons*, vol. ii. p. 433.
2 Watkin, *Roman Cheshire*, p. 20.
3 *Hist. of Manchester*, vol. i. p. 145.

and by the meeting of at least three Roman roads, but that it was *Condate* is unlikely; the distance from Manchester would be, going by Kind Street, 23 miles, instead of 18 M. P., as both Iter II. and Iter X. give it.

Kind Street.—From the river Dane north of Middlewich, Kind Street, or King Street, runs straight for four miles to Broken Cross near Northwich, parish boundaries following it for two and a half miles. It is 20 yards between the fences where not encroached upon, and towards Kinderton it is raised above the adjoining land. Camden says [1] that the road between Middlewich and Northwich was raised with gravel to such a height as easily to be known for a Roman work, and gravel being very scarce all over those parts it was being carried away from the road. That process appears to have been continued, and there is now little of the ridge remaining. It is visible in the fields to the north of Broken Cross, and a parish boundary follows the line for a quarter of a mile on from Wade Brook to Over Street, on the road from Chester to Manchester, one and a quarter miles east of Northwich.

Kind Street continued on to Wilderspool on the south of the Mersey opposite Warrington. On the north of the Chester and Manchester road it has been traced near Wincham brook, and a footway follows the line, and near Great Budworth falls into the road to Stretton. The Roman road was cut through in widening the highway on the south of Lower Stretton, and in Stretton, and farther on it was laid bare between the road and Appleton Hall. It was of gravel, and 18 to 20 feet wide.[2] Parish boundaries run along the present road for three-eighths of a mile and three-quarters of a mile.

There are remains of a Roman camp at Wilderspool, measuring 141 yards by 140 yards, and Wilderspool causeway leads to the ford at Latchford across the Mersey to Warrington.

On the east of Northwich the present Altrincham road bears the name of Watling Street, but there is reason to think that the Roman road followed a line of highways straight on from Northwich to near the south-east of Pickmere, where it was laid bare in draining at about two

[1] *Britannia,* iii. 43.
[2] Watkin's *Roman Cheshire,* pp. 66, 67.

F

feet below the surface, composed of gravel paved with boulders.   Leland seems to have followed this line on a causeway for 5 miles after leaving Northwich.[1]   The present road is partly upon it for several miles, and it seems to have fallen into the Altrincham road near Over Tabley.

Where Kind Street crosses Watling Street on the east of Northwich, Horsley with reason places *Condate*.   According to Iter II. it is 20 M. P. from *Deva* and 18 M. P. from *Mamucium*, which are doubtless Chester and Manchester, 36 miles apart, compared with 38 M. P.   The intersection of King Street is exactly midway, and if *Condate* were to the west of that the distances would agree fairly well.

From Over Tabley the Roman road from Northwich to Manchester seems to have followed the course of the present road to Bucklow Hill, where a parish boundary begins to follow the road.   At three-eighths of a mile further on there is a slight turn, and the general course of the Roman road is straight to near Old Trafford.   It may have been directed towards some point (1300' to 1500') on the moor to the south-east of Todmorden, some 27 miles distant.   Parish boundaries follow the present road, which is straight except where the river Bollin is crossed.   Where the present road turns towards the east to Altrincham, the Roman road continues straight on up Bowden Hill into Dunham Park, where there seems to be a very slight change in direction, and from which the road can be seen for some miles in both directions.   In 1751 the road was very plain in Dunham Park and to the west of it.[2]   From the railway on the north of Dunham Park to the Mersey at Crossford the present road is straight in the same direction for three miles, with a parish boundary along it, and the same line is taken up for a mile by the road through Stretford.   Between the Mersey and Stretford remains of the road were visible in the meadows about the middle of the eighteenth century.[3]

From Stretford to Manchester, and on as far as Ancoats Lane, an interval of three and a half miles, there were no traces of the road in Whitaker's day.   In 1885 a section of the Roman road was exposed for three-quarters of a mile in the Chester Road, which showed that after passing through Stretford it turned to the north-east, and subse-

---

[1] *Itin.*, part vii. fol. 82.
[2] Percival, *Phil. Trans.*, xlvii. p. 216.   [3] *Ibid.*

quent discoveries of the road in Manchester prove that
the course of it was in the same straight line as Chester
Road and the known course from Ancoats Lane to Oldham.
The road was laid out from the turn at Stretford towards
high ground (1000') on Austerlands, more than 12 miles
distant, and it probably marks a Roman advance from the
west against the Brigantes inhabiting the highlands of the
middle of England. The section in the Chester Road
showed a foundation consisting of a thick bed of gorse, ling,
and brushwood, upon which was a layer of boulders, of a
total thickness of three to four feet.[1] A section seen to
the south of the Central railway-station in the same line
consisted of three inches of stiff clay on the pre-Roman
surface, covered by five inches of burnt brick, small stones,
charcoal, fragments of pottery and nails, on which boulders
$8'' \times 6'' \times 4''$ were bedded, about eight inches in thickness,
and then eight inches of gravel with two inches of rubble
stone and clay over it, making a total thickness of 26
inches. The road passed about 100 yards south of the walled
castrum near the confluence of the Medlock and the Irwell,
the *Mamucium* or *Mancunium* of the Itinerary. It was a
rectangle with rounded corners, 175 yards by 140 yards,
the walls of which were still to be seen in Whitaker's time.
They were pulled down about sixty years ago, but a fragment remains under an arch of the viaduct of the Cheshire
Lines Railway in Castle Fields, and the course of them
can still be traced. A short branch road on the north of
the Medlock led to the east gate. Whitaker tells us [2] that
it was cut down to the base in 1765, and was found to
be 14 yards wide, and one and a half yards deep of strong
gravel mingled with boulders.

(15) *Manchester to Oldham and the North-east.*—Beyond
Ancoats Lane the ridge was 16 to 17 yards wide, and three-
quarters of a yard high in gravel, with a quarter of a yard
of marl laid upon it, and it was visible to Butler's Lane,
where the width was five or six yards.[3] Ridgeway Street

---

[1] C. Roeder, *Lanc. and Ches. Antiq. Soc. Proc.*, 1899, p. 119.

[2] *History of Manchester*, by J. Whitaker, 1771, part i. p. 120.
It may here be said that in referring to him it is necessary to distinguish between his statements of fact, and what he so often says must
have been.

[3] Whitaker, *loc. cit.*, p. 120.

now marks the course for half-a-mile onward, and it continued by what was formerly called Roman Road to Newton Heath Church, which stands on the site of the old road. Beyond, the construction of the canal has destroyed all traces of the road, but near Failsworth it appears with houses on one side, and is called Roman Road, and Street Lane, and it is still to be seen as a lane across grass fields, the ridge remaining 10 yards wide and three or four feet high. Further on, across swampy ground, the ridge is narrower and higher for several hundred yards, and here Whitaker tells us [1] that he found that the moss had been trenched on each side of the road, and that the larger and more solid plates of turf had been laid on the original surface over a base 12 or 14 yards wide, from which the road was carried up to a crest three or four yards wide finished by about a yard of gravel. The ridge beyond has disappeared, and further on the lane is below the surface, but near the Hollinwood Cemetery the ridge is very evident, seven yards wide and two to four feet high. All trace of the road is then lost, after being plainly visible for a mile. The same line is taken up a mile further on, near Alexandra Park, Oldham, by a street called Honeywell Lane on the old Ordnance map, and then Oldham intervenes.

In Whitaker's time it was visible on to Glodwick to the south of Oldham, and also at Wellihole a mile further on.

After an interval of two miles the road is again to be seen in the same straight line on High Moor Austerlands (1000') for half-a-mile. From this spot the view to Manchester is unimpeded except by smoke, but in the opposite direction there is no prospect, and the road no longer keeps a straight course. It curves round by Doctor Head to Delph, and on to Castleshaw, where there are remains of a Roman camp. Excavation in 1908 showed that there were two camps, one about 130 yards by 110 yards, and within it, against the south-east side, another about 60 yards by 50 yards square. The ramparts proved to be of piled sods, and four gateways were found, with paved roads from those on the south-west, north-west, and north-east,[2] According to Percival,[3] the road proceeded direct to

[1] *Manchester*, vol. i. p. 125.
[2] *Yorkshire Archæol. Jour.*, xx. 100.
[3] *Phil. Trans.*, vol. xlvii. p. 216.

Clowes Moor, where it can still be traced over Stanedge tunnel (1300'), and then turning to the north-east, it passed to the north of Marsden to Slack, where numerous Roman remains have been found, and traces of a walled fort about 133 yards square. About three miles beyond Marsden a parish boundary follows bits of an old road along the north of the present road to Brighouse for a mile and a half, past Slack to Outlane. The present road continues on in the same line, followed for a mile by the parish boundary, and on Lindley Moor [1] the ridge was formerly visible for a mile, raised considerably above the adjoining ground, and about 12 yards wide. It has been supposed that a Roman road went onwards through Rastick, Brighouse, and Cleckheaton in the direction of Leeds and York. There seems to be little or no evidence of a road in that direction, and it may have gone to Woodlesford as Warburton shows it on his map.

At Rastrick a Roman road joins which branches from the road from Manchester over Blackstone Edge near Ripponden (p. 92). From Rastrick westward the course of it is followed by the present road by Elland Lower Edge, through Elland to Greetland, and Greetland Wall Nook to Ripponden Bank. The old road descends by a direct course to Ripponden, and continues on by Old Lane to the Manchester and Ilkley road at Westgate Head. Traces of the paving are to be seen in various parts, and it was taken up in Old Lane about the middle of the last century. [2]

From Slack a Roman road has been traced due north [3] by Sowood Green and Stainland, over Greetland Moor from near Turbury, across the river Calder at Sterne Mill, over Skircoat Moor, passing on the west of Halifax to Illingworth, and by St. John's to Causeway Foot and Cockhill. Near the last-named place the straight line of road from Illingworth northward to beyond Denholm is joined at an angle of about 45° by the road from Manchester by Blackstone Edge. At Hill Top near St. John's a portion of the Roman way a quarter of a mile long remained *in situ* not many years ago, paved with boulders, 20 feet wide, and with

[1] Watson, *Hist. of Halifax*, 1775, p. 39.
[2] Leyland, *Jour. Brit. Archæol. Ass.*, vol. xx. (1864), p. 208.
[3] F. A. Leyland in Watson's *Hist. of Halifax*, 2nd edition, 1854, p. 141.

ditches at the sides.   By some the road from Blackstone
Edge has been supposed to follow the straight line northward from Illingworth, instead of the course which will
presently be described (p. 92).

Slack has been supposed to be the site of *Cambodunum*
in Iter II. of Antonine, 18 M. P. from *Mancunium*.   It is
more than 20 miles from Manchester, and as the Itinerary
distance from *Calcaria* to *Mancunium* is 10 miles less than
the actual distance in a direct line, the intermediate station
cannot be fixed by measuring from either place, if we
knew which road Iter II. follows.   It may be by Slack, or
by Elland, or by Adel and Sowerby.

Warburton's map of Yorkshire, made from actual
survey in 1720,[1] bears the following note where this road
enters Yorkshire near Oldham :—" This Roman way goes
from York to Manchester, but disappears in places," and it
is shown by a broken line, as not being visible, by Almond-
bury and on by Thornhill and Ossett to Woodlesford, where
Riknild Street crosses the river Aire.   There is no further
evidence of a road in that direction.   Castle Hill, Almond-
bury, has no claim to be a Roman station, as it was
supposed to be by Camden.

(*a*) *Doctor Gate*.—At Doctor Lane Head, on the east of

---

[1] The map of Yorkshire, by John Warburton, Somserset Herald,
F.R.S., F.S.A., was made to a scale of two and a half miles to an
inch from a survey by compass bearings and measured distances, the
field books of which remain among the Lansdowne MSS. in the
British Museum.   Several volumes (Lansdowne MSS. 909–914) of
Warburton's notes and memoranda contain references to Roman
roads, and show that his map was produced after observation in all
parts of the county.   He had previously surveyed the Roman wall,
and had published a map of Northumberland from actual survey,
upon which Roman roads are laid down.   The map of Yorkshire
was published by subscription in 1720.   A note on it says that
" The Roman military ways are shown by two unequal black lines,
and when discontinued or broken off are not visible."   The map
shows that the meaning is that a pair of lines, a thick and a thin line,
indicate a Roman road visible, and where the lines are broken, the
road is not visible.   Warburton's map is now very scarce, but there
are copies in the Bodleian Library, and in the Bradford Free Library.
A map of Yorkshire by Overton and Bowles, 1728, and other maps
of the Ridings published about 1750 by E. Bowen, are evidently
copied from it, the curiously expressed notes relating to Roman
roads being repeated verbatim, except that a reference by Warburton in one of them to his map of Northumberland is omitted.

Austerlands, a Roman road from the south joins this road, coming from Melandra Castle, a walled Roman fort seven and a half miles distant, on the south bank of the river Etherow and about three-quarters of a mile west of Dinting railway station. The road is marked as Roman on the old Ordnance Map from Lidgate southwards along Qulck Edge and on for a mile to the south of Mossley, and again after an interval of a mile, between Millbrook and Roe Cross, and then the present road seems to follow the course of it to near Mottram, a mile from Melandra. The fort here was excavated by the Manchester Classical Association in 1906–7. It is a rectangle with rounded corners, 133 yards by 112 yards to the outside face of the walls, which are backed inside with earth. Doctor Gate continues on to Brough on Batham Gate. It seems to have passed to the north of Glossop, where several fragments of a Roman road are said to have been met with. In 1772 Doctor Gate between Melandra and Brough was described [1] as still used for a good part of the way, " being set with large stones in the middle, and where it runs over mossy ground, has proper drains cut on each side of it." A modern road has superseded it, but a good deal of the track remains. It passes up the valley of the Shelf brook at first on the north bank, and thus on the south, and ascends to Cold Harbour Moor (1621') by Crooked Clough.

A section of Doctor Gate as it now appears on Cold Harbour Moor has been published by Mr. W. Smithard [2] which is of considerable interest. The track lies on a sandy clay 5 feet below the general surface of the moor, in a cutting through the peat moss, 50 feet wide at top. The roadway is 4 feet 9 inches wide between kerbs which rise 6 inches above a paved surface between them. In the middle, stones 9 inches wide are laid lengthways, and the sides between them and the kerbs are paved with stones 2 feet long, 6 inches wide, and 2 to 6 inches thick. Side ditches on each side are 2 feet wide at the road level and about 18 inches deep. The ditches are now choked, and the paving is overgrown with vegetation. The section is on ground nearly level, with a slight fall towards the south. It may be what

---

[1] *Archæologia*, vol. iii. p. 237.

[2] *Jour. Derbyshire Archæol. and Nat. Hist. Soc.*, vol. xxxiii. (911).

was described in 1772, but it is difficult to suppose that it is a Roman road in an unaltered state.

From Cold Harbour Moor the road descends by Lady Clough and joins the modern road at Doctor Gate Culvert. It then appears between the road and the river, and crossing the former on the south of Birchen Clough, winds round Osyter Clough more than a quarter of a mile above the modern road, and continues on the slope above it to Alport Bridge. Between Doctor Gate Culvert and Alport Bridge it is a narrow sunken track often hidden in heather and whin bushes, and is now quite disused. At Alport Bridge Doctor Gate crosses the river Ashop, and mounts the southern slope of Woodland Dale to the height of 1250 feet, and then soon falls into a road marked as Roman on the Ordnance map. Further on it appears to be represented by a cart track on the east of the river Noe, and by a lane for half a mile to Fulwood Stile. It probably passed through Hope to Brough on Batham Gate.

(*b*) *Manchester to Buxton.*—The Roman road from Manchester through Stockport is said to have crossed the river Medlock at Old Ford, and to have fallen into the present Stockport road at Longsight. The road through Levenshulme to Stockport has long been called High Street, and onwards the present road is followed by a parish boundary from Stockport Great Moor to Hazelgrove, beyond which the course is uncertain. The road on to Buxton perhaps followed the course of the old Manchester and Buxton road, nearly straight from High Lane to Disley, over the hill to Whalley Bridge, and on by Wythe Lache, beyond which a parish boundary follows the lane for a mile and a quarter. Whitaker and others seem to refer to a road by Adlington, but there appears to be no evidence of it.

Whitaker [1] says that a road appears to have branched off from the road from Manchester to the north-east near Ancoats Lane, by Streetfold near Harpurhey, and Street Bridge and Street Gate, near Royton, in the direction of Littleborough, but nothing now seems to be known of this road.

(16) *Manchester to Wigan.*—According to Whitaker, a road to Blackrod branched from the road from Northwich, crossing the Irwell near Old Trafford, beyond which

[1] *Hist. of Manchester*, vol. i. p. 191.

he admits that the road was wholly invisible as far as Hope Hall.[1] His account of this road has been questioned. Sibson[2] makes the road, of which the ridge was still to be traced for nearly a mile between Hope Hall and Chorlton Fold, leave *Mancunium* by the west gate, and cross the Irwell in the line of Regent Street, Salford, at Wodensford (now Hulme Bridge), described in an old writing as a paved causeway. It cannot now be traced for the two and three-quarter miles to Hope Hall, nor to beyond Chorlton Fold, but it was found in constructing the railway from Eccles to Wigan near Worsley at about a foot below the surface, about seven yards wide.[3] A small piece, said to have been very perfect, near Brick House on Mawdesley (? Mosley) Common is not now traceable. Further on it was found near Cleworth Hall, half-a-mile east of Tyldesley, and in the lane between Chowbent and Hindley, and on the south side of Hindley Vicarage, where it was two feet below the surface, formed of stone and gravel. The course is crossed by the Lancashire and Yorkshire Railway on Amber Common, two miles from Wigan, where Sibson describes it as being 14 yards broad and one yard thick of earth and gravel. Wigan agrees with the Itinerary distance of *Coccium* from *Mancunium*, 17 M. P.

(a) *Wigan to Warrington.*—From Wigan Sibson traced a Roman road south to Warrington, and north to Walton-le-Dale on the south of the Ribble near Preston. The former road is described as crossing the river Douglas at Haddon Bridge and going nearly straight to Nearer Nagwood, and then, with a turn to the east, straight to the top of Whitehill (242'), where there is a change of direction to Old Heywood. The ridge is described as being very perfect in several places; it was discovered in Ashton-in-Makerfield, and it is still visible in Nagwood and in the plantation on the east side of the road at Haydock Lodge, where Sibson saw a complete line of road for 200 yards, of earth covered with a layer of red freestone with a coat of gravel over. The road was traceable on to Warrington, crossing the Orford Brook at Longford Bridge. It probably crossed the Mersey at Latchford, a ford which was in use until

---

[1] *Hist of Manchester*, vol. i. p. 154.
[2] Baine's *Hist. of Lancashire*, 1836, vol. iii. p. 573.
[3] *Gent. Mag.*, 1862, part i. p. 419.

Warrington Bridge was built, to Wilderspool and Kind Street (p. 81).

(b) *Wigan to Walton.*—The road from Wigan to the north, according to the same authority, was found one and a half miles from Wigan, and was traced back towards the town. Standish Wood Lane seems to occupy the course of it, which was easily traced up the hill to Standish, beyond which it continued through Welsh Whithill, Euxton Burgh, Rose Whithill, and Bamber Green, to Walton, probably the site of a camp at the passage of the Ribble.

(17) *Manchester to Ilkley and Aldborough.*—From the north gate of *Mancunium* this road ran in the direction of the Cathedral. In Whitaker's time the ridge was visible, five yards wide, bordered with large stones. It followed the course of Byrom Street as far as Quay Street, and then turned in the direction of the Cathedral; traces were found in Wood Street, and it was discovered in 1898 beneath the foundations of the old deanery in Dean's Gate, where it consisted of a layer of sandstone flags on five inches of clay and rubble, overlying six inches of gravel, below which were four inches of blackish soil, bricks, charcoal, and scoria resting on the original soil.[1] The road continued in the same line to the east side of Victoria Station, and then, with a slight turn, crossed the river Irk at Scotland Bridge. Stukeley[2] found that the Roman road went across the churchyard to Scotland Bridge, and then ascended the hill and proceeded with its original direction, north-east, to Rochdale. According to a MS. of the Rev. J. Watson,[3] it went through Blackley (beyond which the present straight road probably occupies the course for one and a half miles) to the east of Alkrington Hall, and by Middleton Hall and Trub Smithy to the east of Rochdale, where Whitaker tells us a Roman road had lately (in 1771) been dug up, and to the south of Littleborough. The Roman road appears to have passed by Lydgate, about a mile east of Littleborough, and on to the remarkable paved causeway over Blackstone Edge, about two miles east-north-east of Littleborough. The track now appears a little to the south of the Halifax road near the fourth

---

[1] C. Roeder, *Proc. Lanc. and Ches. Antiq. Soc.*, 1899, p. 119.

[2] *Iter Boreale*, p. 29, 1776.

[3] Quoted by Mr. Earwaker in *Manchester Guardian*, Dec. 5, 1883. The MS. (*circa* 1760–70) is in the Bodleian Library.

milestone from Rochdale, and the paving of the causeway soon becomes plain, ascending in a straight line for more than half-a-mile to the top of Blackstone Edge. The paving is in regular courses across the road, and seems to be bedded on rubble upon the rock; it is now several feet below the level of the surface of the moor, the peat which covered it having apparently been removed. It is about 18 feet wide, and is bordered with stones set on edge, and in the middle there is a line of large blocks hollowed out so as to form a longitudinal trough 14 inches wide and eight or nine inches deep, the bottom of which is rather higher in the middle than at the sides. Higher up the hill the trough ceases, and a paved causeway twelve feet wide branches off on the north, at an angle of 20°, and continues for a short distance in a westerly direction at a flatter gradient. The trough stones reappear above the branch, and a rut in the paving two-feet four inches from the centre of the trough is soon very plain on the north side, in places three or four inches deep. Higher up a rut appears on the south side, well marked, with traces of the rut on the north side, both at the same distance (two feet four inches) from the middle of the trough. Appearances suggest two wheel-tracks of about two-feet gauge, with one wheel in the trough, rather than one track of four feet eight inches gauge, as has been suggested. Above the catchwater drain which crosses the causeway, the latter is as high or higher than the surface of the moor, and there are traces of side trenches, but higher up the pavement is again several feet lower than the surface. Towards the summit the pavement is a good deal broken up, and the bare rock appears. There is no middle trough, but the large flat stones forming the pavement are slightly grooved by wear in the line of it. The causeway bends towards the north at the summit (1300′), where the pavement is partly covered by peat. On the descent on the Yorkshire side the trough stones again appear, and the causeway runs in a straight line for half-a-mile, and then winds down Blackcastle Clough. Towards the Halifax road the paving has been removed, but the course of the road can be easily followed. On the Yorkshire side it is known as the Devil's Pavement.[1]

---

[1] The various opinions about the trough, and the Roman or other origin of the causeway, are summarized by Dr. H. C. Marsh in the *Journal of the Archæological Association*, vol. i., N. S., p. 259.

The road is plainly traceable for two miles; it ascends from the west with an average gradient of one in seven, and at one part is as steep as one in five. The trough in the middle has given occasion for much speculation, and for doubts whether the causeway is Roman.[1] Of its Roman origin there can be not much doubt, but it has probably been altered to serve as an incline for bringing stone down from a large quarry at the top. The quarry remains; the growth of peat in the bottom and over the sides testifying to its antiquity, and there is no record of its having been worked.

Warburton's map bears the note at the Yorkshire boundary on Blackstone Edge: "This Roman way extends from Manchester in Lancashire unto Aldborough near Borrow bridge, is all paved with stone and near eight yards wide." He marks it as visible from the Yorkshire boundary to the river Nidd, and his notes in the Lansdowne MSS. describe the course from Ilkley southwards, and both map and description prove to be fairly accurate. The course of the road through Yorkshire was investigated by Mr. Leyland in 1864,[2] and the information collected by him and others has been summarized by Mr. Norton Dickon.[3] Further investigation of that part of the road between Cock Hill and Ilkley has lately been made by Mr. J. J. Brigg and Dr. F. Villy of Keighley.

At Baitingsgate, about three-quarters of a mile to the east of Blackcastle Clough, the course of the Roman road leaves the present Halifax road and follows the old road on the north of it for two and a half miles by Westgate Head, where a road already described (p. 85) branched to Rastrick, and thence to Lane Head and Fosson Lane, where some remains of the paving lately existed. It then turns northwards, by Mill Bank and through Sowerby, and on to the river Calder by Finkle Street, where some of the pavement not long ago remained. The ford across the Calder was still paved with large blocks of stone, to the width of about 20 feet, within the memory of men living

---

[1] It is remarkable that Horsley, who passed over Blackstone Edge, only mentions the causeway to express his surprise to find how much it was below the surface.—*Brit. Rom.*, p. 291.

[2] *Jour. Brit. Archæol. Ass.*, vol. xx. p. 208.

[3] *Bradford Antiquary*, vol. iii. p. 239 (1898–9).

in 1834, and the road ascended in a north-easterly direction by Hollin Hall, where part of the causeway was visible not long before, to Newland. Then the road turned more to the north, and the course is along the high ground by Clough Head, Sentry Edge,[1] Balklam Edge, and Hamilton Hill to Hunter's Hill (1300'). From this point traces of the road are marked on the six-inch Ordnance map of 1847 in a north-easterly direction for two miles to Cock Hill on the Halifax and Keighley road. The pavement was entire at the junction of the Ogden and Skirden brook until it was removed about sixty years ago to make fences, and more of the road was destroyed when the Ogden reservoir was made. When the road was destroyed, near Hunter's Hill, it was found to consist of layers of gravel and clay mixed with rubble, upon which was a pavement of stones admirably jointed, and showing signs of having been long used.[2]

At Cock Hill the road now followed falls into the Roman road from Slack northward, which has already been noticed (p. 85), and which is here represented by the Halifax and Keighley road. For half a mile a parish boundary follows the present road, which then turns to avoid the hill, while the Roman road went straight on. Traces are marked for three-quarters of a mile on the six-inch Ordnance map of 1847 until it crosses the modern road. It was then a raised way plainly visible, and remains have been dug up within living memory. Warburton says that it crossed Denholme Edge, where it was met with probably not far from the present road, in digging the foundation of a barn,[3] and a mile further on, about 400 yards to the west of the road, at Manywells Height, about 20 yards of a rough paving of boulders was found by Dr. Villy in 1909, some of the stones protruding and others eight inches deep in moor soil and peat.[4] In about half a mile traces are marked on the six-inch Ordnance map for a quarter of a mile at Coldspring House, and they were faintly discernible in

---

[1] A low mound, called " Intrenchment," marked on the six-inch Ordnance map, running straight for one-third of a mile on the west of the present road on Sentry Edge may mark the course of the road.

[2] Watson, *Hist. of Halifax by Leyland,* p. 136.

[3] Notes in Lansdowne MSS. 911.

[4] *Yorkshire Notes and Queries,* vol. v. p. 62.

1885.[1] The course onwards seems to be straight on to Eller Car, and the road seems to have been visible in 1712 between Cullingworth and Hainworth, as a paved way about 12 feet broad, neatly set with such stones as the place afforded, traceable where the ground was pretty hard, as a ridge in some places only covered with grass; and said to have been met with at a depth of several feet on the moors in digging for peats.[2] Warburton says [3] that the road appeared near the mere stones, a little to the west of the road to Halifax, and went by Eller Car, taking its course inside the boundary stones to Hainworth Shaw; that is, on the line of the old, straight, Beuty Lane, up the gill from Eller Car, along which stones mark the boundary between Harden and Hainworth. At the south end of Cradle Edge allotments on Harden Moor, Dr. Villy, in 1906, uncovered a paved road 15 feet wide, of large flagstones, lying a few inches beneath the turf. Across the two adjoining allotments the paved road was dug up in the middle of the last century. Beyond, quarries encroach on the line, and then it is taken up by a levelled terrace, 15 feet wide, on the south of the lane by Moorside Farm to Back Shaw Lane. In the same line a paving of large flat stones was found by Dr. Villy for about 30 yards, crossing the north-west corner of the enclosure called the playground, with a width of about 16 feet.

A detached piece of road, apparently Roman, on Harden Moor must be noticed here. The ridge is marked on the six-inch Ordnance map of 1847 for 130 yards to the south of Cradle Edge quarry, 230 yards east of the road which has now been followed, and pointing a little west of north. About 80 yards now remains, a ridge about one foot six inches high, much overgrown with ling and rough grass, which was found to cover stones about three inches in diameter set on a pavement of larger stones, about 16 feet wide, with a kerbing of stones about 12 inches by 6 inches on each side.[4] The continuation southwards from the moor is unknown, but it has been supposed that the road from Bank Top, one and a half mile distant, in a south-

[1] Leyland, *Watson's Halifax*, p. 135.
[2] Hearne's *Leland's Itinerary*, vol. 1. p. 143.
[3] Notes in Lansdowne MSS.
[4] Mr. J. J. Brigg, *Yorkshire Notes and Queries*, March 1907.

easterly direction to Nook Nick, represents it. It is in straight lengths for nearly two miles, and then points to Nook Nick, where some remains, considered by Dr. Villy to be of a Roman road, were found.[1]

If continued northwards this piece of road on Harden Moor would join the road to Ilkley a little beyond Black Shaw Farm, but Dr. Villy connects it with Spring Gardens Lane, which runs from the north of Keighley in a north-westerly direction. After a mile he finds traces more or less definite, for most of the way to Steeton. Opposite The Hollins the ridge is plain, and a clearing showed the stonework of the road in a dilapidated state, 19 feet wide, with a kerb remaining on one side. On nearing the crest above Steeton the low ridge appears on the south of the present road, and faint traces seem to wind down into Steeton. After a break of a mile and a half the course seems to be taken up by a road, and then signs of the Roman road appear on the north of it near Ling Haw, and becomes plainer under Well Head Lathe as a terrace. Transverse sections there seemed to show the remains of a substantial but much destroyed road, as much as 15 inches thick on a cambered bed, and 18 feet wide. This, six and a half miles from Harden Moor, is as far as the road has been definitely traced. It points to the " col " (805') between Gib Hill and Gallows Hill.[2]

There are no traces of the road onwards from Harden Moor towards Ilkley; it most likely went by Thwaites Brow, and crossed the Aire near East Riddesden. According to Warburton it crossed Rumbold Moor (coming from Ilkley), by Black Knowl, and appeared near to Morton High Gate, which is identified with High Ash near West Morton. It is also stated [3] that a paved road was destroyed near Upwood about 50 years ago. High Ash and Upwood are about a quarter of a mile apart, and two and a half miles from the last traces of the road. The course for a mile and three-quarters over Rumbold Moor to Black Knowl and Keighley Gate has been explored by Dr. F. Villy.[4] He traced a ridge northwards from the road between High

[1] *Bradford Antiquary*, 1913.
[2] Dr. Villy, *Bradford Antiquary*, 1914, p. 121.
[3] Norton Dickon, *Bradford Antiquary*, vol. iii. p. 220.
[4] *Yorkshire Notes and Queries*, June 1908.

Ash and Upton cross roads, and considers that the line is taken up by an old road, now allotment road, a raised way beneath which there seem to be fragmentary bits of the Roman road. Bradup beck appears to have been crossed near the present bridge, between the deep gorge on the east and the bogs higher up the course of the stream. Traces appear onwards in a course bending eastward round the boggy ground, and in a short distance the paving of the road was found beneath the soil for 300 yards, and in places was plainly to be seen; a layer of boulder stones, 15 to 19 feet wide, kerbed with large rough stones at the edges with a camber of about eight inches. Close under Black Knowl there is a turn to the west of north, and the road runs straight for about half a mile to Keighley Gate (Whetstone Gate on the new Ordnance map), the gap (1217′) in the ridge of the moor. The paving is to be seen here and there all along, where not grown over with rough grass. From Keighley Gate the line of the Roman road appears to have been generally followed by the present road to Ilkley.

The result of Mr. Leyland's inquiries was to show that up to the middle of the eighteenth century the road was fairly passable for foot-passengers along the whole distance from Littleborough to Ilkley, but was then in a ruinous condition; in some places it had been enclosed, or incorporated with the highway, and in others the paving had been taken up and used for building. In 1864 the road within the parish of Halifax (about ten miles) had ceased to exist as a highway, though it was traceable, by the help of information from old inhabitants, very much on the line along which Warburton marks it as visible on his map of 1720.

From about five miles to the west of this road, on the north of the Calder valley, an ancient road known as The Long Causeway can be followed for more than six miles in the direction of Burnley. There does not seem to be any evidence that it is a Roman road.

A Roman road is marked by broken lines, as not being visible, on Warburton's map, leaving the road at right angles on Ilkley Moor—probably the " ancient road " marked on the Ordnance map. The old Ordnance map shows a straight ridge for more than a quarter of a mile on

Lanshaw Delves, a mile and a half from the Ilkley road in the direction of the Chevin, to which the road may have crossed to join York Gate, a Roman road which can still be traced in the direction of York (p. 103).

The Roman station at Ilkley, supposed to be *Olicana* of Ptolemy, was on a steep brow overlooking the river Wharfe, between two tributary brooks.   Whitaker describes it as an area about 160 yards by 100 yards round the church, the enclosing walls being traceable all round.[1] The site, viewed from the riverside, is still well defined, although the rivulet on the west side has been filled in.

The Roman road is supposed to have crossed the Wharfe on the east of Ilkley Bridge.   The paved way is to be found under the sod from near Middleton Hall, and it can be traced along the course marked on the old Ordnance map on the east of Ing Gill to Raw Shaw, where a Roman road is shown on the same map branching in the direction of Addingham, of which, however, there seems to be no trace on the ground.   About a mile further on, on the south-east of Round Hill (1341′) the road, here bearing the name of Watling Street, turns through 50° to the east over Blubberhouse Moor.   Dr. Villy supposes that a road continued straight on, pointing to Thruscross Hill (909′), four miles distant, and after an interval of two miles is represented for three-quarters of a mile by a road past Burnt House, and by a terrace on the slope down to the river Washburne, on the north of which the line is taken up by Street Lane and a track beyond.   He traces the road on towards Hayshaw, where two pigs of lead of the time of Domitian were found in 1735.

The road that turns sharply to the east near Round Hill is still faintly traceable on Blubberhouse Moor.   In the middle of the eighteenth century it is described [2] as being paved with stones uncommonly large, and edged with stones still larger.   The road can be traced in the same straight line from near Round Hill across the Washburne valley to near Crag Hall, where the line is taken up by a road, also called Watling Street, for two miles, and then by a footway on a ridge in the fields.   The paving of the road, of native boulders, was here taken up about 1848.   At Whitehall Nook (600′), where seven miles of straight road ends, a

[1] Whitaker, *Hist. of Manchester*, vol. i. p. 195.   [2] *Ibid.*, p. 193.

G

small portion of the road nine feet wide, fenced on both
sides, remained in 1882.[1]   The course of the road, bending
more towards the north, crosses the river Nidd near
Hampsthwaite Church, and a little further on, in Holly
Bank Wood, remains of paving were noticed in 1894.
Dr. Villy, who saw this road in 1911, describes it as paved
between kerbs with cobbles, six feet wide, and in one place
nine feet, sunk and winding.   It is known locally as the
Roman road, but it is doubtful.

Warburton's map shows the road as visible as far as the
river Nidd, and continues it by broken lines, as not being
visible, on by the south of Ripley to Aldborough.

(18) *Manchester to Ribchester.*—The Roman road from
Manchester to Ribchester branched off from the last road
near where the Cathedral now stands, at an angle of 65°.
It crossed the river Irk at its confluence with the Irwell,
and passed through Strangeways very much on the line
of the Bury road.   At Broughton a fragment was visible
in 1851.   The course appears to have been straight from
Hunts Bank to Bowstock Hill (890'), ten miles distant,
the road over which has for centuries borne the name of
Watling Street.   A description of the road by Mr. Just
in 1839 and 1842 [2] notices slight traces at the corner of
Kersall Moor, and one mile south of Prestwich the Bury
road joins the line and follows it through Prestwich.   A
mile further on Higher Lane, on the Ordnance map, is on
the line of the old road, but building seems to have altered
this, and destroyed other traces existing 50 years ago.
North of Radcliffe the line is preserved by a parish boundary
for seven-eighths of a mile from Spenmoor to Blackburn
Street.   There are traces beyond, and then the line is taken
up by Watling Street over Bowstock Hill, with a parish
boundary along it for one and a half miles.   From the
highest point (890') the course of the road is seen through
Radcliffe, five miles to the south, and to the high ground
beyond, and looking northward the road is seen five miles
off mounting Rushton Height (1062'), to which, with a very
slight turn, the course is now directed.   There were lately
remains of the ridge of the Roman road between the Bolton
road and the Wanves Reservoir, which is on the line of

---

[1] Grainge, *Hist. of Harrogate*, p. 33.
[2] *Trans. Lit. and Phil. Soc. Lanc. and Cheshire*, vols. vi. and vii.

the road, and there are traces here and there by Edgeworth
and on to Pike House; the same straight line is then taken
up by the present road, on the west of which, just beyond,
a trace of the ridge is to be seen. From Grimehills Moor,
over Rushton Height, and through Blacksnape, the present
road follows the course of the Roman road, which seems
to have been once wide between the enclosing fences, and
to have been encroached upon by houses and enclosures,
so that, seen in detail, the straightness is somewhat lost.
Before enclosures at the beginning of the nineteenth
century the ridge was everywhere conspicuous.[1] On Rushton Height, from which the whole length of Longridge
Fell, 12¾ miles off, is plainly visible to the north, there is
a very slight turn, and the general course of the road lies
in a straight line to Jeffrey Hill (900′) on the east end of
Longridge Fell, three miles north of Ribchester. Beyond
Blacksnape a parish boundary follows the present road
for a quarter of a mile, and then the latter turns off to
the west to join the line again in rather more than a mile.
Mr. Just there noticed a stony line across the fields, marking
the course of the old road. From Ranter's Row to the
outskirts of Blackburn the present road follows the course
of the Roman road, which was opened in 1890 at Lower
Darwen. It was traced on further by Mr. Just over ground
now covered with building. On the north of Blackburn,
in 1839, there was a bold ridge on approaching Revidge,
and it was visible beyond Revidge Lane. A footway
appears to indicate the line towards Higher Waves, where
remains lately existed. The line is taken up by a lane on
Top-of-Ramsgrave (730′), from which Rushton Height to
the south, and Longridge Fell to the north beyond the vale
of the Ribble, are plainly visible. Traces of the ridge
remain near Midge Hole Farm, and a lane to Stubby Head,
and another lane, and a line of hedges, seem to mark the
course to the river Ribble about a quarter of a mile to the
east of Ribchester.

For the whole distance from Manchester to the Ribble,
25 miles, no part of the road is three-quarters of a mile out
of a perfectly straight line, the greatest deviation being
at the top of Rushton Height (1062′), and on the top of
Bowstock Hill (890′), where slight changes of direction occur.

[1] Dr. T. D. Whitaker, *History of Whalley*, vol. i. p. 28.

After crossing the Ribble, the road from the south
probably joined the road from the east, and by it crossed
the Boyce brook to Ribchester, but it may also have continued straight on in the direction of Jeffrey Hill. The
site of the Roman station is on the west side of Boyce Brook,
which flowed round the east and north side of it. It appears
to have extended from the churchyard to the Ribble, and
to have been a walled rectangle about 200 yards by 143
yards.

(19) *Ribchester to Skipton, Ilkley and Tadcaster.*—The
Roman road from Ribchester eastward crossed the Ribble at
the ford at Little Town. There is a piece of the ridge south
of Salusbury Hall, and three-quarters of a mile to the east of
it another piece, which bends to the north-east and points
towards Backing Hall (200′). The ridge appears again at
Dole Farm, and then Kenyon Lane takes up the line.
East of Dinckley Brook the ridge is again visible, and there
are traces of it to the south of Backing Hall. It then
turns due north-east in a line straight towards high ground
(410′) a quarter of a mile north of Worston on the east
of the river Ribble. It crosses the river Calder, and in
about two miles, where the railway crosses it, the ridge
is plain for more than half a mile on to Standen Hey,
where a road takes up the line. In old deeds the road
hereabouts is called Brede Street.[1] A bit of the ridge
remains on the west of the Clitheroe Road at the cross-
roads, and half-a-mile further on it is very plain on both
sides of the Pendleton Brook. In 1850 Mr. Just saw a
section there, 21 feet wide, of flags on gravel, the flags not
of any definite shape or size, but nicely fitted.[2] A plantation of trees now covers it. The ridge, with a fence and
lane along it, is followed by the municipal boundary of
Clitheroe for two miles to the east of Chatburn, with a very
slight change of direction after Worston has been passed.
Then there is a turn through 45° to the east, and the ridge
is visible on the south of the road to Downham, and with
a slight wind it keeps on the crest of the hill to Hey
House. The ridge follows a straight line across Smithies
Brook and continues in about the same line on to Ings
beck, and is shown on the old Ordnance map to the south

---

[1] Dr. Whitaker's *History of Hallamshire*, vol. ii. p. 100.
[2] *Trans. Hist. Soc. Lancs. and Cheshire*, vol. iii. p. 7.

of Newby nearly on to Howgill, when a lane takes the line of the Roman road. In about a mile some remains appear on the east of Coverdale beck, and further on the ridge is plain. It can be followed across another beck until it is joined by a farm road which follows it to Brogden Lane. The ridge is 16 feet wide, raised 12 to 18 inches above the ground.[1] From Brogden Hall, Brogden Lane, and Old Lane carry on the line, the ridge appearing in places on the north of the lane, to Greenlees, where traces of the ridge are shown on the Ordnance map on the east of the canal and beyond. The road appears to run straight on to the high point at Thornton Rectory. To the east of Thornton, beyond some rubbish-tips, the Roman road can be traced up a hill, along the top of which the paving can be seen beneath the turf. At about three-quarters of a mile east of Thornton railway-station the railway cuts into the old road and occupies its course for a quarter of a mile, and then passes a rectangular earth-work called Burwen Castle, situated on the west side of a stream about 150 yards west of Elslack Station. It was systematically excavated in 1909, when two forts were revealed, the foundations of an earlier one with earthen ramparts measuring 126 yards by 127 yards to the outside of the ramparts, enclosed by a later walled fort, 201 yards by 136 yards. The road, running between the south wall of the later fort and the ditch outside, was found to consist of gravel between squared stone kerbs, 18 to 19 feet wide.[2] The road can be traced on the south side of the railway further on for more than a mile, and the pavement was found there in some draining operations in the spring of 1899. It seems to have followed much the same course as the railway now does to Skipton Station, and then perhaps that of the road, and Newmarket Street in the same line, to Short Bank Lane at the south-east of Skipton. There it would seem that a Roman road crossed at an angle of about 45°. Straight onwards a track, and other traces mark the course of a supposed Roman road, which Dr. Villy, after investigation by digging, considers to have gone on by Droughton to join the road over Blubberhouse Moor towards Aldborough.

[1] P. Ross, *Bradford Antiquary*, vol. vi. p. 44.
[2] *Yorks. Archæol. Jour.*, vol. xxi. pp. 113–167.

The straight line of Shortbank Lane, running north-west and south-east, is continued to the north-west of Skipton by a road pointing to Whitehill (575') a mile distant, and is considered by Dr. Villy to be the course of a Roman road up Airedale into Ribblesdale. He traces it [1] by Stirton to the Gargrave road, following that for about a quarter of a mile, and then striking across the Aire to the south of Gargrave church, passing Kirk Sink, regarded by Whitaker as the site of a Roman villa, of which there are now no definite remains. Thence he traces it along the south of the Aire to Coniston, where an old road, which leaves the present road near the entrance to Coniston House, takes up the line. The old road, now disused, can be plainly traced, crossing the present road near The Switchers, and again near Hellifield. There are traces of it on towards Long Preston, and beyond that Green Bank Lane takes up the line over the moor to Settle and the Ribble, which was crossed to the south of Giggleswick. Dr. Villy made many excavations, and certainly found traces of an old road. From Skipton to the Gargrave road beyond Stirton, and from Coniston nearly to Hellifield, and on to Long Preston, and over the moor to Settle, the course is that of the road followed by Ogilby in 1677, but the evidence that it was the course of a Roman road is hardly conclusive.

Between Skipton and the railway bridge Dr. Villy notices traces of the Roman road along Short Bank Lane, and on for about 100 yards close to the east side of the lane towards the ascent to the moor. There is no evidence that a road continued up to Skipton Moor, but the lane, which was formerly the road from Skipton to Ilkley, turns sharply to the east, and passes along the steep slope of the moor on a terrace, mostly natural, but in places artificial. The track of the Roman road is fairly easy to follow over most of the way, and it can be seen that the present road is a few yards to the south of the Roman line for about three-quarters of a mile. Where the Roman road crossed a gully a partial section is to be seen. A width of about 12 feet remains, some of the southern edge having been destroyed. On the northern side a thickness of one foot eight inches or more of stone is supported by a kerb of two

[1] *The Antiquary*, vol. xi. pp. 16, 61.

courses of large stones.[1] The road was, no doubt, raised
and carried across the stream by a small bridge or culvert.
On a spur (1000') at the east end of Draughton Moor, the
road turns to the south-east and runs in a straight line
over Addingham Low Moor, where Whitaker [2] described
the road in 1771 as being very conspicuous for a mile, and
where it is still visible. After an interval of half a mile it
is continued in very nearly the same straight line by The
Street, Addingham, along which traces were lately visible
in several places, the stones showing through the turf
covering them. The continuation of the " Street " joins
the modern road one and a half miles from Ilkley, and
further on remains of the Roman road were exposed close
to the north side of the railway. Whitaker says in 1771
that the road was traceable for three miles on the west of
Ilkley, and that the present main road is on the line of the
Roman road through Ilkley. Traces of the Roman road
are shown on the Ordnance map just to the west of Ben
Rhydding, and onwards by The Mount towards Scalebor
Park. It appears to have crossed the lower ground near
Burley Junction, and to have ascended by Chevin End,
but no traces are visible. The old Ordnance map marks
the Roman road on Guiseley Moor, which is now enclosed,
and it has lately been traced for nearly a mile by Mr.
Percival Ross. Excavation showed it to consist of broken
stones 12 inches thick on the millstone grit rock, bordered
by kerb stones, and 13½ feet wide. The middle of the
road was 6 inches beneath the surface.[3] Further on the
road can be seen on Carlton Moor, where it is known as
York Gate, and it is shown on the Ordnance map from
near the Black Horse Inn, by Green Gates to the Cook-
ridge and Bramhope road on the north of Crag Hill, and
then, with a turn southward, straight by the north of the
Roman fort at Adel to a hill (531') half a mile beyond it.
From that the course of the road is marked continuously
on the old Ordnance map for four miles, by Alwoodly
Gates to the north of Brandon Lodge. From hereabouts
there seem to have been two Roman roads to York, one
through Bramham to Tadcaster, and another by Scarcroft,

[1] Dr. Villy, *loc. cit.*   [2] *Hist. of Manchester*, vol. i. 193.
[3] *Bradford Antiquary*, vol. vi. p. 56. Mr. Ross has lately described
this Roman road in detail from Ribchester to Bramham.

through Bramham Park to the road from Aberford near Hazelwood.   The former is shown on the map by a dotted line for three-quarters of a mile, from the north of Mount Pleasant to half a mile south of Bardsey, marked as the site of a Roman station, *Pompocali*.   Onwards " Roman road " is marked in two places to the north of Wother-some House, where a high raised road had been recently broken up in 1862.[1]   It is marked again " Roman road " between Wothersome and Bramham, and is called Stany-gate.   On the other road bits of Roman road are marked on the south of Scarcroft, on the north of Nova Scotia farm, in Bramham Park, and on both sides of the Bramham road on the north of Bramham Moor.   It would seem from the way that this latter road turns off from the more direct course of the former, that the former is the original road between York and the west.

Warburton's map of 1720 bears the note where this road enters Yorkshire from the west—" This Roman Way goes to York, and for the most part is visible, being paved with stone throughout."

(20) *Ribchester to Fulwood and to Lancaster.*—A road went westward from Ribchester along the north of the river Ribble.   A raised *agger* was noticed by Just[2] near the parsonage, where it is still visible, but nothing beyond for two miles, and it is possible that this road turned off from the road to Lancaster.   At Stubbins Nook the road is visible, and a lane is in the line, and there are traces east of Marsh House, and between Tun Hook and the Clitheroe road, all in one straight line.   There is then a change of direction, and on the west of the railway the road bearing the name of Watling Street runs to Fulwood Barracks and on to Withy Tree and the North-Western Railway, beyond which there are traces of a road called Dane's Pad to Kirkham.

A Roman road from near Preston to Lancaster is men-tioned by E. Gibson[3] as going over Fulwood Moor, by Cadley Causeway, through Broughton, Barton, and Bils-borough, and along Fleet Street in Claughton, and through Burrow.   From a quarter of a mile north of Barton and

[1] *Gent. Mag.*
[2] *Trans. Hist. Soc. Lancs. and Cheshire*, vol. iii. p. 3.
[3] Baines, *History of Lancashire*, vol. iii. 1836.

Broughton railway station a parish boundary follows the present road for three miles. The only other sign of a Roman road appears to be "Windy Arbour," near Forton, four miles north of Garstang.

(21) *Ribchester to Lancaster.*—A Roman road left Ribchester in the direction of Lancaster by Dale Hey to the cross-roads, two miles from Ribchester. About three-quarters of a mile further on the course of an ancient causeway is shown on the Ordnance map, running across country for a mile and a half to Derby Arms, continued by a highway to the south of the river Loud. The course is uncertain onwards, but passing Windy Arbour it seems to have crossed the river Brock to Snape Rake Lane, where a paved road was well preserved in 1897.[1]

About a mile further on a parish boundary joins the road at Stanygate, and follows it for one and a half miles across the river Calder at Oaken Clough, and on to Grizedale Brook, to the south of which there are remains of the Roman road. From Grizedale Brook the road was traced on by Mr. Jackson past Gregory's Barn and Fell End Farm to Burns Farm, and from that to Street he found it in good preservation for a considerable distance. At Street there are remains of a bridge over the river Wyre, about 80 yards below the present Street Bridge, which, if not Roman, appears to mark where the Roman road crossed. An "ancient causeway" is marked on the Ordnance map along the road beyond, which leads to Methurst, about half-a-mile east of the railway at a mile south of Galgate station. It probably fell into the road from the direction of Preston to Lancaster, which on the north of Galgate is followed by a parish boundary. At Scotforth, one and a half miles south of Lancaster, it is thought that a Roman road branched to the north-east by Caton and Hornby. A milliary dedicated to Hadrian, and marked M. P. III found near Caton in the bed of Caton beck, seems to be the chief evidence of a road in that direction.

Little is known of Roman roads to the north of Lancaster. A paving of cobbles, grouted with lime, four to four and a half yards wide, was dug up in 1882 for a length of 130 to 140 yards, which pointed to Scaleford, on the river Lune, and on the north of the river a supposed Roman road was

[1] S. Jackson, *Lanc. and Ches. Antiq. Soc. Trans.*, 1897, p. 221.

uncovered in 1892 on the road from Lancaster to Kirkby Lonsdale, at about four and a half miles from Lancaster.[1] A little further on a parish boundary follows the road for a mile, but there is no further trace beyond. There appears to be no indication of a Roman road in the direction of Kendal, a mile and a half south of which, near Natland, there are remains of a Roman camp, measuring about 176 yards by 132 yards.

According to Rauthmell and R. S. Ferguson,[2] a Roman road from Lancaster crossed the sands of Morecambe Bay for about seven miles to Wyke, in Cartmel, and across Cartmel Sands (three miles) and Duddon Sands (two miles) to the west coast of Cumberland. A Roman road is said to be visible in Cartmel, and in Furness between Conishead and Duddon Sands, but the crossing of the wide treacherous sands by a road appears to be impossible.

(22) *Ribchester to Lowborow and Kirkby Thore.*—The course of the Roman road from Ribchester to the north is a little east of north for half-a-mile to near Stidd brook. It then turns to the N.N.W. and takes the straight line of the road from Manchester pointing to Jeffrey Hill. There are traces of the ridge alongside the present road, which is called Stony Gate Lane. At Cock House the present road turns to the north-west and back again with a sharp angle to the line of the road on the south of the Ribble, between Rushton Height and Jeffrey Hill. The ridge at once appears, and the road, with traces of the ridge, continues on to Jeffrey Hill (900′), at the west end of the Longridge Fell. There is then a turn of nearly 60° to the north-east, and the course is in a line with a point (825′) on the west flank of Marl Hill in Bowland Forest, and also, as Mr. Just remarked, with the top of Penyghent (2273′), 25 miles distant. There are traces of the ridge in this line as far as the river Hodder, which is crossed a quarter of a mile east of Doeford Bridge. Gough says[3] that over Longridge Fell the Roman road, appearing green when the fell on both sides is heathy or morassy, was called Green Lane. North of the river Hodder the line of the old road

---

[1] *Lanc. and Ches. Antiq. Soc.*, vol. xi. p. 184.
[2] *Archæological Survey of Lancashire, and Trans. Cumberland and Westmoreland Antiq. Soc.*, vol. iii. p. 64.
[3] Camden, iii. 393.

is taken up by a lane for two miles from Doeburn, with pieces of the ridge remaining. The lane then turns off, but the ridge is marked on the Ordnance map (1847) as continuing on in the same line for a quarter of a mile. After entering Bowland Forest there is no trace for three miles, and then at Gamble Hole the ridge appears in a new direction, pointing southward to Brownsholme Heights (950′), a little to the east of the last trace of the ridge, and northwards to the top of Croasdale Fell (1433′). The ridge is visible in this line on to Low Fell, to the east of which it passes, and then turns to the north-west up Croasdale. A road without traces of a ridge continues on over Whitendale Fell and round Bottonhead Fell (1784′), where the ridge was formerly conspicuous.[1] Further on, a quarter of a mile of ridge is shown on the Ordnance map pointing a little west of north, and there is another bit in the same line near the source of Hindburn Beck. In 1824 the ridge was visible seven yards wide on to Ivah, where the present road appears to take up the line; the original pavement was laid bare at Low Gill, half-a-mile further on, early in that century,[2] and remains were visible to the west of Tatham Fell Church. The present road appears to be on the line for half-a-mile beyond Tatham Fell Church, and there are several traces of the ridge beyond in the direction of Old Wennington, and between that and the river Greta, the line passing about a mile west of Lower Bentham. On the north of the river Wenning, Rauthmell[3] in 1746 saw the causeway ploughed up. It was a deep bed of large pebbly gravel seven yards wide, and was paved with large, broad, flat stones. The Greta was crossed by a bridge, the abutments of which are said still to remain.[4]

North of the Greta the course is straight between a hill (250′) one and a quarter miles east of Greta Bridge on the north of Cantsfield Beck, and high ground (412′) at Casterton, four miles to the north, which is plainly visible from the hill near Cantsfield. A piece of ridge several feet high remains, and a lane with a parish boundary along it for three-quarters of a mile is in the line to Overtown, a mile to the west of which, at Overborow,

---

[1] Just, *Lanc. and Ches. Antiq. Soc.*, vol. i. p. 68.   [2] *Ibid.*

[3] *Antiquitates Bremetonacenses*, 1824 ed., p. 21.

[4] W. T. Watkin's *Roman Lancashire*, p. 81.

the station *Bremetonacæ* has been placed by Camden and others.

From Overborow a road is supposed to have run through Kirkby Lonsdale to the Roman camp at Natland, a mile and a quarter south of Kendal, and thence on to Windermere, but there are no evidences of it from parish boundaries, nor are any traces of it known.

Northwards from Overtown a road called High Gate takes up the line of the Roman road, and Wandles Lane continues it by Kirkby Lonsdale railway-station to Gate House, Casterton (412'), looking south from which the course of the road from Botton Head Fell is in sight.

Beyond Barbon the course of the Roman road is perhaps along the lane between the railway and the modern road, through Borrowens and Applegarth, rejoining the latter road near Middleton Hall. Near Middleton a cylindrical Roman milliary has been re-erected not far from where it is said to have been found bearing the letters M. P. LIII.[1] In a mile the present road crosses under the railway, and a lane continues straight on for one and a quarter miles to Fordholme on the river Rawthey, and the same line is taken up by a track on the high ground on the east side of the Lune valley, passing Howgill, Low Carlingill and High Carlingill. The Roman road seems to have crossed the river Lune at Salterwath, a quarter of a mile from which, on the south of the Borrow Beck, at its confluence with the river Lune at Lowborow, is the Roman walled fort, a rectangle (133 by 103 yards) close to the railway and between it and the Lune, which, it has been suggested, is the station *Alona*. In 1853 there were the remains of walls, and of the abutment of a Roman bridge across the Borrow;[2] the walls still remain.

The present road seems to follow the course of the old road for a mile north of the camp, and it can be traced in the Tebay gorge and in Crosby Ravensworth parish.[3] A parish boundary for one and a quarter miles is continued by a track in a straight line for two miles over Crosby

[1] *Bradford Antiquary*, vol. v. p. 260; which contains further details of the course of this road from Mr. P. Ross's observation.

[2] Just, *Brit. Archæological Journal*, vol. viii. p. 35.

[3] R. S. Ferguson, *Trans. Cumb. and West Antiq. and Archæol. Soc.*, vol. iii. p. 64.

Ravensworth Fell. At Ewe Close on the moor a mile south of Crosby Ravensworth the line is well marked. Sections of the causeway revealed a cobble pavement 25 to 33 feet wide, edged with large stones, having upon it a slightly raised metalled road 20 feet wide.[1] The road probably went on to the camp at Crackenthorp, or to Kirkby Thore, joining the Roman road from Catterick to Carlisle, and continuing northwards by the Maiden Way.

A Roman road has been traced [2] from Lowborow westward, pointing to Whinfell Beacon, and bending southwards by Whinfell Tarn, where the suggestive name of Borrans occurs. No traces seem to have been seen further on.

(a) Warburton's map of Yorkshire shows a Roman road branching near Overborow, which he calls " The Devil's Causeway," crossing the moors to Askrigg. It now bears the names of Cam High Road and Priest Bank, and can be followed from Gayle Beck, near Ribble Head, over Cam Pastures (1900') and Wether Fell, where parish boundaries follow it for two miles and a half, and thence in a straight line for three miles to the Roman fort at Brough, on the south of the river Ure, near Askrigg. Warburton continues it on by broken lines from Askrigg to Feetham, and thence by hard lines over Hope Moor, and to the Roman road to Carlisle, beyond which it is shown on to Barnard Castle, where it falls into the straight road from Bowes to Streatlam Castle, pointing in the direction of Bishop Auckland. The latter road crossed the Tees at Streatford, as noticed by Warburton, and was visible in his time from Barnard Castle to Streatlam Castle, which is as far as he follows it.[3] At the beginning of the last century it was distinctly to be seen on the pasture called The Flats, opposite Streatford, and below Paddockmire, and also where it joined the Northumberland Watling Street on the south of the river Gauntlees.

(23) *Iter X. of Antonine.*—It has been supposed that Iter X. of Antonine passed over the road that has now been followed. It is not known where either *Clanoventa*, where

[1] *Trans. Cumb. and West. Antiq. and Archæol. Soc.*, vol. viii. N.S. p. 355.
[2] *Ibid.*, vol. iii. O.S. p. 90.
[3] Lansdowne MSS., 911.

it begins, or *Mediolanum*, where it ends, are, nor is there certainty as to the position of any other stations except *Mancunium* and *Condate*. Camden suggested that *Coccium* was at Ribchester, and supposed Overborough to be *Bremetonacæ*, from its distance from Ribchester, and Horsley and others followed him. Horsley, who had first placed *Clanoventa* at South Shields, afterwards fixed it at Lancaster, and the way in which he dealt with the Itinerary distances is remarkable.

In Gale's copy, in Wesseling's edition, and in that of Parthey and Pinder, there are only two differences, each of one M. P., in the distances between stations in Iter X.; but Horsley, to suit his localities for the stations, alters five Roman numerals out of the eight in the Iter. The Itinerary distance of *Coccium*, 17 M. P. from Manchester, which agrees with the distance either to Blackrod or to Wigan, he makes 27 M. P. to suit Ribchester; he alters the distance between *Coccium* and *Bremetonacæ* from 20 to 25 M. P., and the distance between *Bremetonacæ* and *Calacum* from 27 to 32 M. P., and in two other places changes the distance from 18 to 28 M. P. to suit his positions of the stations. He thus increases the length of the Iter from 150 M. P., which is the length stated in the heading, and is the sum of the intermediate distances, to 189 M. P. Taking the Itinerary distances as we find them, and putting *Coccium* at Wigan, it will be found that, following the road from Wigan to Walton-le-Dale, and thence to Ribchester, it is 23 miles compared with 20 M. P. to *Bremetonacæ*, a considerable difference; but from Ribchester to Overborow on the river Leck it is 29 miles compared with 27 M. P. from *Bremetonacæ* to *Calacum*; and from Overborow to Lowborow at the confluence of Borrow Beck with the river Lune, 17 miles compared with 19 M. P. from *Calacum* to *Alona*, the river names and the names of the stations in both cases bearing some affinity. This arrangement of the stations was suggested by Mr. W. T. Watkin in 1883.

CHAPTER IV

ERMING STREET AND BRANCHES

(1) *General Course.*—Erming Street, according to some, extended to the south coast, and part of the road from London to Chichester, which has already been described, bears the name. Others have denied that the Roman Erming Street came as far south as London. Dr. Guest [1] was of opinion that Erming Street from London to Huntingdon was not Roman, because there are no Roman remains on it, and because if there had been a paved road there would have been an Iter on it, whereas of the three from London to Lincoln, two go by Watling Street and one by Colchester. He, however, says that there is evidence that it existed in the time of Edgar, and he shows it in his map of the " Four Roman Ways." Dr. Guest's view was adopted and more widely disseminated by J. R. Green, who wrote [2] that the lower portion of Erming Street did

[1] " The Four Roman Ways," *Archæological Journal*, vol. xiv.
[2] *The Making of England*, p. 49.

not exist in Roman times, the fastnesses of the forest being so impassable that the road-makers did not attempt to penetrate them. The evidence on the ground, and that afforded by the Ordnance maps, is quite against this view.

The course of Erming Street from London is direct northwards to Royston, except a bend to the east and back again to the same line. On this bend, near Braughing, three roads branched off, one eastward to Colchester, one in north-easterly direction to Chesterford, and another to the north-west. To avoid the Fen country Erming Street turns towards the north-west at Royston, crossing the river Ouse at Huntingdon, the Nene four miles west of Peterborough, and the Welland to Stamford. Then by a turn to the north it gains a ridge of high ground along which it continues through Ancaster and onwards in almost a straight line due north for 48 miles to the Humber. At Lincoln it is joined by the Foss Way, and about four miles further north a road branches off to the west-north-west by which access was given to York and the north without the necessity for crossing the wide tidal Humber. Avoiding the lower courses of the Trent, the Idle, the Don, and the Aire, the road curves round until after crossing the last-named river at Castleford it takes a northerly course. In about eight miles the road to York, apparently the more important road, curves off, but a road northwards continues on to Aldborough, Catterick, and Bishop Auckland. A few miles after the river Swale has been crossed at Catterick Bridge, a road branches off north-west, and crosses the fells to the Eden valley and Carlisle, and on to the Clyde at the west end of the Wall of Antonine. The road to the north continues on under the name of Watling Street, and after crossing the Tyne near Corbridge, and the Roman Wall about three miles further on, it takes a tolerably direct course to the north-west over the Cheviots to the south side of the Forth and on to Stirling and Perth. A little to the north of the Wall a road branches off to the north-east which is traceable to Tweedmouth. The minor branch roads will be noticed in the following detailed description.

(2) *London to Braughing.*—The course of Erming Street lies on the east of the earlier *Londinium*. It may be that it left by the east gate to avoid the marsh or fen which Sir

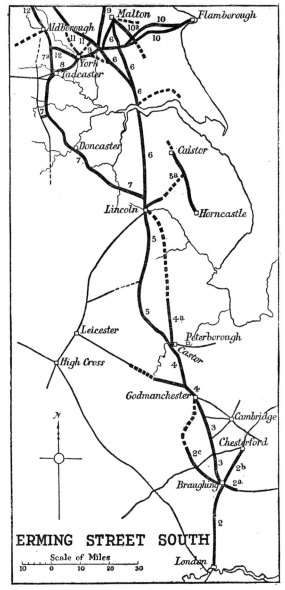

12
9 Malton 10
Aldborough □ Flamborough
11 11 6 10ª
9 10
7ª 12 York
8 6
Tadcaster
6

7

Doncaster 6 Caistor

7 7 5ª

Lincoln Horncastle

5

5 4ª
Leicester Peterborough
High Cross 4 Castor
4
Godmanchester
Cambridge
3
N Chesterford
2c 2b
3 2a
Braughing

2

ERMING STREET SOUTH

Scale of Miles
10   0   10   20   30

London

Christopher Wren discovered outside the north wall.[1]
Through the enlarged city the course is undetermined, but
there appears to be evidence that neither Gracechurch
Street nor Bishopsgate Street are on it.

On the east lies the well-known Roman burying-place
in Spitalfields, and near where Shoreditch Church stands,
Erming Street was crossed by the Roman road passing to
the north of London in the line of Old Street, to be afterwards noticed. From that point the course in a straight
line for between five and six miles is represented by Kings-
land Road and the continuation through Stoke Newington
and Tottenham to Edmonton. There are short lengths of
parish boundary along the middle of the road at Haggerston,
and Stamford Hill, and for more than half-a-mile at Stoke
Newington. The modern road turns to the east beyond
Edmonton, but Erming Street appears to have gone
straight on over Hounds Fields and Forty Hill to near
Maiden Bridge. Brickyards and buildings have effaced
what traces there were over Hounds Fields, and there is
little to mark the course further on. The line seems to
have crossed Charter Hatch Lane where a track remains
at some old houses, and to have passed to the east of the
course of the New River at Goat Lane. About half-a-mile
north of Maiden Bridge the present road takes up the line
and continues straight for nearly a mile along the west side
of Theobalds Park, which then juts out and masks the line
of the old road for a quarter of a mile. The present road
resumes the line near the north entrance to the park,
where Temple Bar has been re-erected, and continues in
the same general direction with slight windings, due to
enclosure of ground attached to houses, to near Cheshunt
Great House. The road straight on is now stopped, but a
track and footway are shown on the new Ordnance map
continuing on to a lane in the same line nearly to Cheshunt
Park. After an interval of a mile and a half the same line
is again taken up for a quarter of a mile by a lane west of
Cold Hall. Broxbourne Bury then covers the course for
a quarter of a mile, but at Martin's Green it begins to be
plainly represented for nearly two miles by a broad green
track, called Elbow Lane, through the woods to near Little
Amwell, where the modern road from Hoddesdon to Hertford

[1] *Parentalia*, p. 265.

joins it for three-eighths of a mile, and then turns off to the
west at Little Amwell. To this point (300') the general course
of Erming Street is straight from Bishopsgate for 20 miles,
and from it the high ground between Buntingford and Royston, where almost exactly the same direction is resumed, is
plainly visible. The course of the old road is continued
by lanes from where the Hertford road turns off at Little
Amwell nearly to the Ware and Hertford road in the Lea
valley. Parish boundaries which have followed Elbow
Lane and the Hertford road for more than a mile and three-
quarters to Little Amwell, continue along the lane in the
same line for a quarter of a mile, and again from the Ware
and Hertford road to the Lea, on the north of which in
Bury Fields Roman remains have been found. Gough[1]
notices a ford in the river just above Ware, and on the north
side a piece of land pointing to it called Causeway Acre.
North of Ware the Great North road takes the course of
Erming Street, and in about a mile there is a slight change
of direction on the highest ground (260'), and a straight
length begins which continues for three miles over High
Cross Hill to near St. Edmund's College (310'), pointing to
the site of the Roman camp (300') at Braughing. At
Wadesmill, where the river Rib is crossed, the road has
been altered to improve the gradient, and the straight line
has been somewhat deviated from, and the same is to be
noticed at many other places where the road has been
improved. Beyond St. Edmund's College the present
road begins to descend into the valley of the Rib, and it is
probable that the Roman road continued on in the same
course for two and a half miles to the station at Braughing.
The site of this is on the promontory formed by the confluence of the rivers Rib and Quin, on the west of Braughing.
Traces of a camp were visible formerly, but the hill is now
enclosed and planted.

(*a*) At or near this station several roads branched off.
The course of one to the east is indicated for two miles by
a parish boundary, which runs straight from the river
Rib between Puckeridge and Braughing, along hedges
and by the side of the woods to Horse Cross (379'), where
it joins the present road to Bishops Stortford. There is
no parish boundary beyond, nor anything in the present

[1] Camden's *Britannia*, vol. ii. p. 68.

road to suggest a Roman road, but beyond Bishops Stortford it is continued by the Essex Stane Street, which will be reverted to (p. 182).

(*b*) A road seems to have continued on from Braughing to the north-east, in the direction of Great Chesterford, of which the first indication, some four miles from Braughing, is a lane with a parish boundary along it pointing straight to the camp at Braughing. After an interval of a mile and a half a lane with a parish boundary continues the same straight line for about a mile and a half from near Butts Green to Coopers End, and in three-quarters of a mile the same line is taken up by a parish boundary, and then by a lane, and by a parish boundary to Elmdon Lea, together a mile and a quarter. These all lie in one straight line pointing to high ground (about 370') near Strethall, where there is a slight turn, and a lane, followed for some distance by a parish boundary, leads in two and a half miles to Great Chesterford. The Roman road continues on in the same direction, following the course of Iknild Street through Newmarket.

(*c*) There are also traces of a road branching near Braughing towards the north-west. A lane on the north side of Hamels Park is followed by a parish boundary for a quarter of a mile, and the line is taken up by a parish boundary three-quarters of a mile further on. Neither of them is very straight, but two miles from Erming Street a track begins which is continued by Back Lane, a parish boundary following both, for three and a half miles to Hare Street, and after an interval of about a mile, lanes and roads continue the line to Baldock on the Iknild Way. North of Baldock a straight road with the county boundary following it for two miles, and a parish boundary for a mile and three-quarters farther, goes on by Stratton to near Biggleswade. Bishop Bennet [1] traced a Roman road on straight to Chesterfield near Sandy, and on to Godmanchester. A dotted line on the new Ordnance map is marked Roman road for four miles from near Sandy to Crane Hill, beyond which the county boundary for half-a-mile, and afterwards a lane with a parish boundary, continue the same line, but the course of the Roman road further north seems to lie to the east of this, and to be

---

[1] Lysons, *Magna Britannia*, vol. i. p. 27.

continued by a lane with a parish boundary along it going by Weald to Toseland, where pieces of the ridge appear, and then by a lane with a county and parish boundary along it for upwards of two miles, leading to Godmanchester.

(3) *Braughing to Godmanchester.* — Northwards from Braughing, Erming Street is represented from near Coles (254′) by a straight road with a parish boundary along it for three and a half miles, through Buntingford to near Corney Bury (334′), where there is a considerable turn, and where the same straight line is taken up which was departed from south of Ware. Two lengths of straight road, very nearly in the same line, with parish boundaries nearly all the way, then extend for five and a half miles to high ground (360′) half-a-mile south of Royston. Thence a straight road runs through Royston (where Iknild Street crosses Erming Street), for eight and three-quarter miles to a point (250′) near Coombe Grove, from which another length of straight road almost exactly in the same straight line for five miles reaches to Caxton Gibbet (216′), parish boundaries following the road nearly all the way.

Five miles north of Royston a Roman road branches to Cambridge; parish boundaries follow it for half-a-mile, a quarter of a mile, and a mile and a half, to Lords Bridge, from which it is continued along a lane by Barton to Cambridge. This road will be noticed again further on (p. 195).

From Caxton Gibbet another Roman road seems to have gone to Cambridge, parish boundaries following the present road for most of the way.

Northwards from Caxton Gibbet, the present road, following the course of Erming Street, is straight for five and a quarter miles to Kings Bush. At Lattenbury Hill a section of the road showed on about five inches of earth, clay, and gravel, a foot of cobble stones and flints set in mortar, with six to nine inches of gravel and sand over. From Kings Bush (140′) which commands a view to beyond Caxton on the south, and to high ground beyond Huntingdon to the north, a straight course was laid out pointing to Green End (120′) near Great Stukeley two miles north of Huntingdon. The improvement of the gradient of the present road down the hill into the valley of the Ouse has impaired the straightness of the road, and through Godmanchester and Huntingdon the straight line of the Roman road was apparently departed from to avoid the river. In Godmanchester the foundation of the road was found in three places, consisting of flint pebbles embedded in hard black cement.

The Roman road from Sandy which joined Erming Street at Godmanchester has been noticed (p. 116). Another is plainly traceable coming from Cambridge along the edge of the Fen country; it will be noticed further on (p. 195). It is part of a road coming from the direction of Colchester to which Dr. Mason, Woodwardian Professor about 1750, gave the name *Via Devana*, supposing that it led to Chester. The name has been perpetuated on the Ordnance map.

It will be observed that the course of Erming Street, which has now been followed from London to Godmanchester, has the characteristic features of a Roman road. The general course for the first 20 miles is almost straight, and parish boundaries follow it, as they continue to do when the road turns away eastward into the valley of the Rib, where Roman roads branch from it to the east and to the north-east and to the west, and at Corney Bury the same straight line which was departed from near Ware, is again taken up for five and a half miles after an interval of 10 miles in which the road turns eastward and back again. From Royston to Godmanchester, a length of 20 miles is made up of pieces of road so nearly in the same line that no part is more than three-quarters of a mile away from a straight line, and with parish boundaries following the road for most of the way. The construction of the modern Great North Road has, however, here as elsewhere obliterated nearly all other traces of the Roman road.

(4) *Godmanchester to Castor.*—There are reasons for supposing that the site of the Roman station at Godmanchester is the rectangle on the west of Erming Street which is indicated by streets and lanes. There were remains of the walls in the middle of the eighteenth century. The wide causeway across the low ground on the south of the river Ouse in continuation of the street in Godmanchester, is probably on the line of the Roman road, but the course of the latter is uncertain until the straight line from Kings Bush is resumed on the north of Huntingdon, where there

is a quarter of a mile of parish boundary along the present road, and perhaps traces of the ridge, though the cutting down of the hill to improve the gradient has modified the original straight course. From Great Stukeley (128') a straight road two and a half miles long, with a wind to the east in the hollow beyond, and through Little Stukeley, leads to Alconbury Hill (162') where there is a change of direction of about 40° by a round turn towards the north. It seems likely that here a road branched off to the west, of which the first appearance is about two miles distant near Buckworth, where a straight road pointing to Alconbury Hill begins. A parish boundary soon joins it and follows it for a mile and three-quarters, the road continuing on in the same direction for three-quarters of a mile. In a mile and a half the same straight line is again taken up by a lane which in half-a-mile is joined by a parish boundary, and a straight road continues in the same direction for two and a half miles to Titchmarsh, parish boundaries following it for a mile and a half. Titchmarsh is nine miles from the nearest trace in the same direction of Gartree Road, a Roman road from Leicester, which at Cottingham, and one mile south of Corby, is pointing direct to Titchmarsh (p. 209).

From Alconbury Hill Erming Street takes a direct course for nine miles. Near Sawtrey the present road descends to low ground (18' to 30'), and winds slightly for about a mile until the straight line is resumed at the park of Connington Castle, and is followed to a point (91') half-a-mile north of Norman Cross and nine miles from Alconbury Hill. Hereabouts, not far from Stilton, the road was still laid with pitched stones in 1712,[1] and Stukeley[2] found the road perfect with a ridge upon the open fields for a long way together, and in some parts still paved with stone. With a turn through 25° towards north-west, the course is straight from the turn north of Norman Cross for 10 miles to a point (176') between Walcot Hall and Burghley Park. For three and a half miles the Great North Road with a parish boundary along it continues to follow the line, but to the north of Chesterton on approaching the river Nene it turns off to the west after having followed the course of the Roman road for 56 miles con-

[1] Moreton, *Natural History of Northamptonshire*, p. 502.
[2] *Itinerarium Curiosum*, 1722, p. 81.

tinuously.   The ridge of Erming Street is to be seen running
straight on, passing diagonally through what Camden
styles the evident traces of a ruined city.   It is of an irregular polygonal form, about 770 yards long from south-
east to north-west, and 400 yards broad, and is surrounded
by the remains of a rampart and ditch.   Stukeley, who
often visited it while the turnpike-road to Wansford was
being constructed along the west side, describes the
ploughing up of interments, stone coffins, urns, coins, etc.;
and the uncovering of the masonry foundations of the south
gate, and part of the wall inside a broad ditch.   The
foundations of buildings could then be traced, and many
loads of stone, tiles, and bricks were carted away every
year.   The elevated crest of the road continued to the bank
of the river Nene, which was crossed by a timber bridge on
stone piers, the remains of which were removed when the
river was made navigable.[1]   On the north of the river, to
the east of Castor railway-station, the ridge remains
conspicuous.   The sides have been dug into for the sake of
the materials, and the recesses so formed have been levelled
by the plough, but viewed from the line of the road it
presents the outline of a bank eight yards wide at the top
and as much as five feet high.   A parish boundary follows
it for 300 yards as far as the road to the station, and here
between Erming Street and the village of Castor many
Roman remains have been found, among them a milliary
dedicated to Florianus, A.D. 276, on which is M. P. L.
(or LI.), which is the distance to Lincoln.[2]   Stukeley supposed that there were traces of a Roman camp round the
churchyard at Castor, but they are not now apparent.

(a) A Roman road must have branched off hereabouts
which went due north, crossing the Welland at West
Deeping.   There is now no trace of it near Castor, but its
course is indicated from near Upton for a mile by a parish
boundary, and then by a lane, and a road in the same line
called King Street, which crosses the Midland and Great
Northern Railways one mile west of Helpston station,
and runs through West Deeping, and straight for eight

[1] Diary, April 16, and Letter to R. Gale, May 12, 1739.   *Surtees
Soc.*, vols. lxxvi. and lxxx.

[2] At Castor a black glazed pottery ware was manufactured which
is found at many Roman sites.

miles to Kates Bridge, a parish boundary following it most
of the way.   Stukeley [1] considered this to be the original
stem of Erming Street, and the road by Stamford a branch
of later date.   But so far from being a branch leaving the
former at an angle as he states, the road to Stamford runs
straight by Castor for 10 miles, and the Sleaford road
branches at an angle of 30° from it.   It seems more likely
that the road keeping to the high ground was the original
road, and that the other was made later in connection with
the Car dike,[2] and the reclamation of the Fens.   From Kates
Bridge to Sleaford King Street formed part of one of
Ogilby's principal roads in 1675,[3] and it continued to be
the road between Bourne and Sleaford until the eighteenth
century.   It is now represented by Moreham Lane, and
other highways, passing through Threckingham, between
which and Sleaford it is banked and easily traceable.   It is
supposed to have continued by Ruskington, Digby,
Scopwick and west of Metheringham and Branston, to
Lincoln.   From Castor also must have branched the
remarkable road across the fens to Norfolk, which will be
noticed further on (p. 196).

(5) *Castor to Lincoln.*—The ridge of Erming Street continues on, remaining conspicuous for more than half-a-mile,
though a good deal of it has been dug away.   In one place
the whole has been removed, and a hollow one foot six inches
deep is left in place of the ridge, which close by remains
four feet high.   It would seem that here earth, to a depth of
one foot six inches at least, was removed by the Roman
road-makers and replaced by a better material which was
worth removing with the ridge.   Professor Babington [4]
records that he saw hereabouts the foundation of the road
formed of large slabs of stones, set in mortar made with
pounded tiles.   Nothing of it is now to be seen.   Towards
the Peterborough road the ridge is eight yards wide at the
top, and four feet high.   This road, with a parish boundary
along it, takes the line of Erming Street for a quarter of a
mile, and where that is the case the ridge has almost entirely

[1] *Itinerarium Curiosum,* p. 84.
[2] A drain constructed by the Romans along the edge of the Fens
to intercept the upland waters.   It can be traced from the south of
Peterborough to Lincoln.
[3] *Britannia,* p. 241.
[4] *Ancient Cambridgeshire,* 1883, p. 54.

disappeared, after being conspicuous for a mile, affording an instructive example of the manner in which the ridge of a Roman road becomes effaced. A narrow lane with a parish boundary following it then continues the line of Erming Street on for a mile and a quarter, and then for a mile there appears to be no trace of it. On the south of Southorpe the present road is on the line for a short distance, and then, through a pasture-field, a trench four yards wide and two or three feet deep shows where the materials of the ridge and its foundation have been dug out. In the next field the line of the ridge is shown by an undulation in the surface of the pasture; and in arable land beyond all traces are lost except that a footway follows the line. A track along the west side of Walcot Hall, with no trace of a ridge, leads on to a road with a parish boundary along it, and then the ten miles of straight course ends, and there is a turn through about 35° to the west which the parish boundary follows. An undulation across arable land with a footpath on the top, and a parish boundary, mark the line of the ridge, which is hardly observable further on where a fence wall takes the middle of it. Through the plantation enclosing Burghley Park the ridge is plain, but in the cultivated land inside it is completely effaced. A footway with a parish boundary along it marks the course for a mile, and in the west of the park the ridge is plain for more than half-a-mile between the drive and the ha-ha, some four or five feet high, but cut away and narrowed. It is in the same straight line, and has a parish boundary along it. On the west side of the park there is a turn of about 30° back towards the north, and the course of Erming Street makes straight for a point (345′) north-east of Exton Park, six miles distant. Presumably this turn to the west through Burghley Park was taken to reach a convenient crossing of the river Welland about half-a-mile above Stamford. Stukeley[1] found a very high ridge on the west of Burghley Park, descending to the river, and he complains in a letter quoted by Gough[2] that " the overseers of the highways had in a sacrilegious manner digged it up to mend their wicked ways withal," and he gives a cross section of the ridge, showing a foundation two inches deep of small pebbles

[1] *Itinerarium Curiosum*, p. 84.
[2] Camden's *Britannia*, ii. 292.

and blackish stuff 20 feet wide, upon the native stony
ground, and a ridge made of stony ground three feet thick
in the middle.   Nothing now seems to remain but a parish
boundary along the course there, and there is no trace of
Erming Street across the meadows by the Welland, but on
rising out of the valley a road takes the line, and after
crossing the Tinwell road the ridge is observable under the
present road.   North of the road to Oakham the ridge was
very plain for a mile until the land was enclosed about
forty years ago, and the sides were sloped down.   It can still
be seen as an undulation in a pasture field, and on through
arable land until it approaches the road from Stamford to
the north, alongside which the ridge is almost entire for
more than a quarter of a mile between the remains of old
thorn hedges 15 to 20 yards apart; it is cut through in
several places to give access to fields from the modern road.
A section was well exhibited in 1900 in a quarry at the top
of the hill.   It showed a ridge eight yards wide at the top,
having on the west a sort of terrace or side road five yards
wide, about four feet lower than the top of the ridge, and
three feet above the surface of the field.   In the top of the
ridge was about a foot of fine rubble, under which was a
layer of packed stone nine inches thick upon one foot six
inches to two feet of light stony sand and earth resting on
one foot six inches of dark clayey soil which appeared to be
the original surface overlying the stony subsoil.   Stukeley [1]
gives a good view looking north along the road which shows
the terrace or side road on the west, and on the east the
slope of the ridge unbroken, with a road then in use along
the foot of it.   The modern North Road descends the hill
towards Casterton in a cutting, and, after it rejoins the line
of Erming Street, a county boundary follows it for more
than half-a-mile.   At Casterton, where there are some
remains of a camp, the straight line which has been followed
from Burghley Park is swerved from to avoid the river, and
is not altogether resumed until Tickencote Hall is passed.
Then the road is straight for three miles, raised four, five,
and six feet high with a width of eight yards, and with a
parish boundary along it, after which, near Exton Park,
there is a turn of about 30° towards the north, by which
the road is kept upon the high ground.   From this turn

[1] *Iter Boreale*, Plate 14.

(345') to Lincoln, 35 miles, Erming Street preserves the same general course, which though made up of many straight lengths is nowhere more than one and a half miles away from a straight line. The North Road follows it for three miles through Stretton as a wide raised road with a parish boundary along it for half-a-mile, and then leaves the line, which is shown by a hedgerow on the east of the road with a parish boundary and a county boundary along it for a mile. Horsley tells us that in 1732 High Dyke was very magnificent between Stamford and Colsterworth,[1] and the Roman ridge was no doubt incorporated in the modern road. At a point (394') about a mile east of South Witham the North Road rejoins Erming Street, and there is a slight turn more to the north. Near North Witham the North Road finally leaves Erming Street, which continues straight on as a rough track as far as the road to Bourn, and then with little to mark its course for two miles to near Easton, where it is taken up by a highway now called High Dyke, which passes a quarter of a mile east of Great Ponton rail-way-station, and with a slight turn, on to the cross roads near Somerby. It is a narrow metalled road between fences 20 yards apart, and with a slight turn near Somerby (400'), continues with a parish boundary along it to Coldharbour, where the present road turns off to the east, and High Dyke goes on for six and three-quarter miles to beyond Ancaster, parish boundaries following it. It is a wide rough grass-grown road as far as Londonthorpe, beyond which a metalled road follows it. Horsley found the ridge very high for six miles before he came to Ancaster, and traces still remain. At Ancaster Erming Street passed through a Roman camp which can be traced on the north of the cross roads in the town, measuring about 300 yards by 230 yards. From the north of Ancaster railway-station, with a slight turn, a straight wide road called High Dyke road, with parish boundaries nearly all the way along it, runs for seven and a quarter miles to near Wellingore, and then, with a very slight turn, with parish boundaries along it here and there, on for five and a half miles over Navenby Heath and Boothby Heath to Waterloo Farm, three and a half miles south of Lincoln. From Ancaster the course lies on high ground overlooking the valley of the Witham on the west and the

fens on the east.   Stukeley [1] found the road very bold and
perfect on Ancaster Heath, and Horsley [2] describes it as
very visible over most part of the heaths from Ancaster to
Lincoln.   The heaths have since been enclosed, and the
road a good deal altered, but the bank remains several feet
high near the Newark and Sleaford road and onwards.   At
Waterloo Farm High Dyke road ends, but fences continue
the line of Erming Street on in the direction of the present
road at Bracebridge Heath.   On the descent of the hill
Stukeley saw the profile of the road 10 yards wide.   In
the valley of the Witham it was joined by the Foss road
and the straight High Street seems to mark its course onwards to the Roman *Lindum*.   In a length of about 1000
yards south of the crossing of the Great Northern Railway,
a concreted causeway was uncovered in four places during
the construction of sewers.   It was from two feet six inches
to three feet nine inches below the surface, and the concrete,
eight inches to five feet thick, was on made ground from
two to nine feet thick.[3]   Further on, near the river Witham,
the swamp is said to have been crossed on a piled foundation
similar to that discovered on the north of the Medway,
at Strood on Watling Street (p. 44).   On the north of
the river a portion of the Roman road was discovered
nearly a yard below the surface, consisting of 10 to 14
inches of concrete of rubble stone on six inches of
gravel.[4]

The first Roman *Lindum*, on the hill, the enclosing walls
of which can be traced, was a rectangle of about 407 yards
north and south, and 480 yards east and west, extending
from Newport gate to the brow of the steep hill, and including the castle and the cathedral.   Another rectangle in
the lower ground, of rather larger size, was afterwards
added, extending southwards to the Stone Bow.

It is not certain that Iter V. of Antonine passes over
any part of Erming Street south of Lincoln.   Camden, from
a fanciful derivation, placed *Durolipons* at Godmanchester,
in which he was not followed by Gale or Horsley, but the
authors of the commentary on the fabricated Itinerary of

[1] *Itinerarium Curiosum*, p. 87.
[2] *Brit. Rom.*, vol. iii. p. 433.
[3] Drury, *Jour. Arch. Ass.*, xlvi. 221.
[4] *Gent. Mag.*, 1838, vol. ii. p. 181.

Richard of Cirencester adopted the site, and it appears to have been generally accepted.   But the distance from God-manchester to Lincoln by Erming Street is but 70 miles, while that from *Durolipons* to *Lindum* is 91 M. P.

(*a*) From the east gate of the upper city of *Lindum* a Roman road appears to have branched off in a north-easterly direction.   A straight road is followed for four miles from the city boundary by a parish boundary which continues on in the same straight line for another mile to Langworth, beyond which the road takes up the line again for a short distance.   It probably communicated with a road called High Street, which follows a ridge of the Wolds for 24 miles northwards   from   Horncastle   to   beyond   Caistor.   At Horncastle in Stukeley's time the remains of walls enclosing a rectangular fort, about 180 yards by 107 yards, were " manifest the whole compass round, and in some places pretty high." [1]   High Street leaves the road from Horncastle to Lincoln in about three miles, and passes by Stainton.   It is not straight, and though parish boundaries follow it con-tinuously for 15 miles to two miles beyond Caistor, it is doubtful if it follows the exact course of the Roman road. The boundaries may have followed an old track over the unenclosed wolds, that did not follow from a Roman road set out in the usual manner.   Remains of the walls of Roman Caistor are to be seen near the Church, and coins show that it was occupied until nearly the end of the fourth century, to which century most of them belong.

It has been supposed that there are traces of a Roman road across the Ancholme valley from Caistor by North Kelsey to High Street near Redbourne, but the evidence is doubtful.

(6) *Lincoln to the Humber and the East Riding of York-shire.*—From the north of Lincoln (216′) the continuation of Erming Street, under the name of High Street or Humber Street, goes on to the Humber.   For 24 miles the road runs in a straight line to near Appleby Lodge Farm (124′), one and a half miles north of Broughton, parish boundaries following it for $14\frac{1}{2}$ miles continuously.   Opposite Kirton the modern road to Brigg turns off, and the straight road onwards is a green lane for eight miles, parts of the old ridge remaining beside the present track.   Then a road from Brigg

[1] *Itinerarium Curiosum*, p. 30.

joins it, and High Street continues in nearly the same direction, and where the present road turns off to Winterton the
same line is carried on by a track for two miles further, and
the old Ordnance map shows " Old Street hedge" in continuation. At the northern end of the higher ground between
the Trent and Ancholme rivers, and between Winteringham
and Winteringham Ings reclaimed from the Humber, is the
site of the Roman station which was ploughed up about 1716,
when many antiquities were found.[1] In 1700 High Street
to the Humber was described [2] as consisting of nothing but
earth cast up where it ran over open country and heath,
but where it ran through woods as being also paved with
great stones set on edge very close together. It was thus
paved through Scawby Woods, and for a mile onwards to
Thornholme Moor, and was seven yards wide. The paving
lately remained in several places. Near Winterton a
section in low ground showed that the earth had been
excavated to a depth of 17 inches, and that there were two
courses of rough stones on edge, of a width of 12 to 13 feet,
The ordinary height of the road is three feet above the
ground, some portions higher, and near Scawby the bank is
five feet high.

From near Grantham to the Humber, except where rivers
crossed at Ancaster and Lincoln, Erming Street lies on a
high range of oolitic rocks on which water is scarce, while
the villages lie away from the road on the flanks of the ridge,
where springs break out. The consequent isolation of the
Roman road, particularly for some 16 miles north of Lincoln,
is remarkable.

From Winteringham there was a passage over the Humber
to Brough, where there are remains of a camp, and where
on Castle Hill in a field called " The Burrs "[3] numerous
coins and other Roman remains have been found. Warburton's map of Yorkshire (1720), which has been already
mentioned (p. 86), shows a Roman road visible from near
Brough eastwards to Rowley, and by broken lines to Wawne
Ferry over the river Hull, and thence, turning almost at
right angles in a south-easterly direction towards Patring-
ton. It must have crossed " carrs " and fens not much if

[1] *Itinerarium Curiosum* p. 95.
[2] De la Pryme, *Phil. Trans.*, No. 263, p. 561.
[3] Probably a corruption of Borrans.

at all above the level of the sea, and no traces of such a road now appear.

Towards the north, a Roman road followed the course of the present road by South Cave, to the north of which, at Drewton Bridge, it was found in 1851; a concrete-like layer, six inches thick, and five to seven yards wide. It was traced for nearly a quarter of a mile to Kettlethorpe.[1] The road passed by South Newbald, through Sancton, and where the present road turns towards Market Weighton, it continued on in the same direction along Humber Street and West Street to Londesborough Park. In 1853 the ridge was well defined in the fields to the west of Godmanham,[2] and in 1736 the Roman road had lately been found in Londesborough Park, " very hard and of a material very scarce in that country." [3] The paving was bared for the whole width of 24 feet, and on it were to be seen the marks of wheeled carriages,[4] and it is said that masonry is still to be seen where the road crosses the boggy ground near the ponds.[5] The ridge is marked on the Ordnance map for one and a quarter miles through the park, and for half-a-mile on the north of it over Nunburnholme Wold, from which a bridle road continues the line to Warter, where numerous Roman coins and ornaments have been found. From Warter the course is in a north-westerly direction along a wide, straight road for a mile and a quarter, and on to high ground (620') on Coldwold. It then descends into Millington Dale, where an ancient paved road remains, and Roman foundations and pavements have been found. The ridge is traceable for about a mile further on in the same direction on Millington Head, and again over Calais Wold to Garrowby Hill (805'). A survey made in 1744 for the Earl of Burlington shows this part of the Roman road with considerable accuracy. After crossing Garrowby Street (see p. 140), which leads from York towards Bridlington, the Roman road northwards follows a line of entrenchments, and then the present road seems to mark the course of it, keeping on the high ground, and passing round the head of Scotton Dale, and thence in a straight line, followed for a

---

[1] *Gent. Mag.*, 1852, part i. p. 483.   [2] *Ibid.*, 1859, part ii. p. 270.
[3] Drake, *Eboracum,* p. 32.
[4] Drake, Letter to Stukeley, *Surtees Soc.*, vol. 80, p. 359.
[5] Rev. E. M. Cole. *Trans. E. Riding Antiq. Soc.*, vol. vii. p. 44.

mile by a parish boundary, to a high point (751') on Leavening Wold. It then turns more to the north again, and
passing through Burythorpe, joins the road from Stamford
Bridge to Malton, about two miles and a half from the
latter place. This line of road from the Humber keeps on
the wolds, avoiding the low-lying moors which stretch
between the wolds and the river Derwent; and from Millington Head to Leavening Wold the course for six miles is
along the water-parting between the Vale of York and the
dales opening towards Holderness, in which tributaries of
the river Hull rise.

The general line of Erming Street northwards is taken
up by the Roman road called Wade's Causeway, extending
to the coast near Whitby. There is, however, some uncertainty as to the connexion, and it will be more convenient
not to follow the road farther until it is approached from
York (p. 137).

The course of a Roman road is shown by a dotted line
on the Ordnance map, branching from the road which has
now been followed near South Newbald, and joining the
present road from Weighton to York near Shipton. This
no doubt indicates the road described in 1852 as being very
visible in several places to the south of Market Weighton,
and as far as the Mile House on the road to Holme.[1] The
present road follows the course of the old road by Thorpe-
le-Street for five miles, having a parish boundary along it
for a mile and a half. Here at the beginning of the last
century it seems to have been raised considerably, sometimes serving as the modern road, and sometimes left on
one side of it. The course of the Roman road was traced
on in 1892 over Barmby Moor Common as a raised mound,
and towards Black Dyke a layer of concrete was found, at
a foot below the surface, 15 feet wide and nearly a foot thick.
The course onwards was marked by boulders in a straight
line across the fields, by Peacock House, Whinberry Hill,
and High Catton Common to Hunger Hill Moor, High Catton
Grange, pointing apparently to about a mile to the east
of Stamford Bridge.[2] Warburton's map marks the Roman
road as being visible, and following nearly the course of
the present road through Market Weighton to Barmby Moor

[1] *Gent. Mag.*, 1852, part i. p. 83.
[2] Cole, *Trans. E. Riding Antiq. Soc.*, vol. vii. p. 38.

I

Inn, and thence over the low-lying moors and across the river Derwent at Kexby, by Dunnington to York.

(7) *Lincoln to Tadcaster.*—With the rise of York, a way to the north without the inconvenience of a passage two miles wide across the Humber became necessary, and the road by Doncaster was made. It is followed by Iter V. (London to Carlisle) and Iter VIII. (York to London), and the Roman milliary now in the cloisters at Lincoln dedicated to Victorinus (A.D. 265–7) is supposed to give the distance, 14 M. P. to *Segelocum*, the first station on it.[1] This road, which is called Erming Street when it gets into Yorkshire, branches out of the straight Humber Street almost at right angles at a point three and a half miles north of Lincoln. Camden says that it was called Old Street, and that the ridge was very conspicuous.[2] For two miles the course is now across fields with traces of the ridge remaining, after which it joins Tillbridge Lane and continues in exactly the same line for eight miles to Littleborough, passing close to Stow Park railway-station. A causeway leads to the Trent, which was crossed by a paved ford. Gale saw it entire in the middle of the eighteenth century, a causeway 18 feet wide held up by piles. It was removed as a hindrance to navigation in 1820, and a man who was engaged in the work said that the ford was paved with rough, square stones, and on each side were oak piles 10 or 20 feet long, with timber cills across from one to the other.[3] On the west bank of the river at Littleborough, the Roman *Segelocum*, or *Agelocum*, was situated. From Littleborough there is a highway nearly in a line with Tillbridge Lane to near Sturton-le-Steeple; and between the latter place and North Wheatley, and on by Clayworth and Everton to Bawtry, there are roads which may indicate the line of the Roman road. At Bawtry the river Idle is crossed, and Erming Street turns to the north, followed by the North Road, and county and parish boundaries along this, for three and a half miles, indicate that it is on the line of the Roman road. It would seem that the Roman

---

[1] The inscription is $\dfrac{A \cdot L \cdot S \cdot M \cdot}{P \cdot XIIII}$, expanded by Bishop Wordsworth to A Lindo Segelocum milia passuum quatuor decim.

[2] *Britannia*, ii. 337.

[3] W. T. Watkin, *Archæolog. Jour.*, vol. xliii. p. 12.

road, from Littleborough here joined a road from the south at an obtuse angle. The parish and county boundary which follows Erming Street on the north of Bawtry extends a little to the south of it in the same straight line to the lake at Bawtry, and when the lake was drained in 1905 remains supposed to be those of a Roman road were found. The county boundary there turns eastward along a stream, while the parish boundary follows a ridge across a field to the Great North road, and after roughly following it for a quarter of a mile southwards, strikes across to a stream on the west. After following that for a mile the boundary returns to the same straight line and follows Green Lane, Roman Bank, and Roman Bank Lane on the east of Serlby Park, for more than two miles. The straight line of four miles from Bawtry here ends, but not far off a broad green road with a narrow metalled track in the middle, leading southward from Blythe to Ollerton, is followed by a parish boundary for five miles, except where the road has been interfered with by a canal, and the boundary goes straight on and is rejoined by the road. There seem to be no other signs of a Roman road in this direction.

After crossing the river Torne at Rossington Bridge, four and a half miles north of Bawtry, Erming Street seems to have gone straight to Doncaster (*Danum*), the North Road turning off and rejoining it. From Doncaster, where no traces of the Roman *Danum* now appear, the North Road is on the line of Erming Street for a mile and a half as far as Bodles. It is on a causeway which may be the Roman ridge widened out, and it is followed by a parish boundary. At Bodles the modern roads branch right and left, and the Roman ridge continues on in the same straight line for a mile, pointing to Leys Hill, parish boundaries following it. At first the ridge is not conspicuous, then it becomes a narrow lane raised one or two feet above the adjoining fields, and further on the ridge appears three to four feet high and 15 feet wide. There is a turn towards the north a little south of Green Lane, after crossing which the ridge appears 17 to 18 feet wide and six feet high, carrying now only a field road. Where it is cut into at Green Lane the ridge exhibited in 1899 marl and stone in thin layers. It continues as great for half-a-mile to Tithe Leys, on high ground with a rock sub-soil, and commanding

an extensive view to the north-east. On entering Woodlands at Tithe Leys the parish boundary keeps on the higher
ground to the east of the present road, apparently indicating
the course of Erming Street. Beyond Woodlands the ridge
is again very perfect, 15 feet wide and six or eight feet high,
the side slopes overgrown with bushes. At the road from
Brodsworth to Adwick-le-Street there is a turn to the north,
and the ridge continues much the same for a mile until it
approaches the Hampole road. It is a mere farm road, but
so high above the fields that cart-ways slant obliquely up
the side slopes, which are so steep that they must be built
up with stone. It is difficult to say why so high a ridge was
made on rock, on an upland overlooking everything, but
this is not a solitary instance of a Roman road raised high
in a similar situation. After crossing the Hampole road
the ridge can be traced across the fields, a parish boundary
following it, until the North Road joins it and takes the
same line for three-quarters of a mile. The road then
turns away for half-a-mile to Robin Hood's Well, and
back again in a quarter of a mile to the same straight
line. The boundary follows the road round this angle,
and on to the common on the south of the cross roads,
where the North Road quits it, and the ridge appears on
the west of the road. The line of it is soon taken by
the Pontefract road which runs straight on, with a parish
boundary along it, for a mile to the cross roads near
Walton Wood (240'). Stukeley noticed a very high and
perfect ridge hereabout.[1]

To this point parish or township boundaries are continuous from Doncaster for eight and a half miles. There is
then a turn, and the present road runs straight nearly to
the river Went, the ridge of the old road remaining conspicuous. North of the Went a parish boundary again
joins the road, and follows it for a mile and a half to Hound-
hill Hall, where the present road turns off to the north, and
the course of Erming Street is shown by a line of parish
boundaries continuing on along fences, with traces of a
ridge, for nearly two miles to Causeway Lane at one mile
west of Pontefract.

Causeway Lane appears to be a part of a Roman road
running in a westerly direction by Street House and High

[1] *Iter Boreale*, p. 76.

Street, to Riknild Street three and a half miles distant, and perhaps falling into the road by Marsden to Manchester.

The course of Erming Street continues northwards from Causeway Lane along a lane to Park Lane, where, half-a-mile east of Featherstone, the ridge is shown on the Ordnance map of 1841, but it is not now to be seen. There is no trace for two miles, and then from Round Hill, half-a-mile south of Castleford, Beancroft Lane, in a line with the road north of Castleford, marks the course to the station *Legeolium*, or *Lagecium*, supposed to be occupied now by Castleford railway-station. The river Aire was crossed a quarter of a mile west of Castleford Bridge, in the line of Rectory Street, where Stukeley saw the paved road.[1]

From Doncaster the course of Erming Street is not very direct, but from Round Hill, south of Castleford, it is straight with very slight turns for eight and a half miles. On the north of the Aire and the canal, Erming Street, here called also Roman Ridge, is joined by the present main road, along which parish boundaries run continuously for seven miles to the river at Aberford.

Camden " travelled along the bold ridge of the Roman military way," of which Leland says that he never saw in any part of England so manifest tokens of the large high crest of Watling Street; [2] and in 1731 Horsley saw it almost all the way from Castleford to Aberford. The modern road is generally 20 yards between the fences, and in some places wider, and the ridge upon which it runs is now about eight yards wide and as much as five feet high on the high ground. It would seem that the Roman ridge was widened on one side for the modern road, so that the foot of the slope extends to the fence on that side, while on the other side the original space remains between the ridge and the hedge, with trees and bushes on it in places. Across this space raised ramps give access to and from adjacent fields. At Hookmoor the modern road leaves the ridge, which continues straight on, but narrower, with the parish boundary following it. It is soon joined again by the modern road, which, it may be observed, is not raised above the ground where it is away from the Roman ridge, and the latter soon ceases to be noticeable north of Hookmoor. At Aberford

[1] *Iter Boreale*, p. 76.   [2] *Itin.*, i. 46.

there is a slight deviation from the straight line, which is resumed on rising out of the valley, and is continued to Hazelwood Schools, a mile north of Aberford. There the ridge leaves the present road and curves eastward over Bramham Moor followed for half-a-mile along the north side by a parish boundary. Gough[1] describes the road on the moor as being " in many places exceeding perfect," and quotes Leland as saying that he never in all his travels saw so perfect a Roman road as this. An engraving in 1736 shows it as still in use by horsemen and packhorses.[2] The moor is now enclosed, and the ridge is in part ploughed up, but is still plainly traceable. Where it is within the enclosure of Hazelwood it is about four feet high, with a rounded top about five yards wide. A section of the upper two feet, visible at the fence, showed it to be of pebbles and gravel in a marly clay, and loose cobble stones seemed to be remains of the paving. The ridge joins the Tadcaster road, which for a mile follows the line of the old road on the original embankment widened, and then turns off to the north, the ridge and a parish boundary continuing on for three-quarters of a mile to Stutton Moor Lane, where there seems to have been a change of direction, but no certain traces of the Roman road appear further on. At Tadcaster the remains of a roughly paved road have been found 18 inches beneath the surface of Westgate.[3]

(a) *Rudgate.*—There are traces of other ridges, one of which is shown on the Ordnance map running due west from Stutton Lodge on the road to Tadcaster, by Bramham Moor Farm to Headley Plantation. It is crossed by another, which may mark the course of a Roman road connecting Rudgate with the south. The ridge seems to fall into the highway leading to St. Helen's Ford across the Wharfe, now disused. On the south of the ford, and on the east of the road, is the site of a Roman camp, which in 1862 is described as measuring 340 yards by 210 yards.[4] From the north of the ford the road, here called Rudgate, resumes the general direction of Erming

[1] Camden, vol. iii. p. 292.
[2] Plate in Drake's *Eboracum.*
[3] *Proc. Soc. Antiq.*, March 23, 1905.
[4] *Gent. Mag.*, part i. p. 807.

Street on the south of Bramham Moor. It is a grass-grown road with a parish boundary along it, and from the turn to Thorpe Arch there is a narrow modern road between hedges about 14 yards apart. There are slight traces of the ridge further on, and the road is of varying width as it has been more or less encroached upon, and it is not very straight in general direction. From the cross roads about three-quarters of a mile south of the river Nidd at Cattal, the ridge of the Roman road is visible on the west of the present road, in line with a road on the north of the river, and the same line is continued on by the road straight for one and a half miles to Providence Green. In 1736 the Roman road was very apparent,[1] and there are still signs of the ridge, and parish boundaries follow the road for two miles from St. Helen's Ford, and elsewhere. At Providence Green the road from York to the north, followed by the Itinerary routes seems to have joined (p. 145).

(8) *Tadcaster to York.*—Tadcaster is no doubt the site of the Roman *Calcaria*, which must have been at Castle Hill on the south-west of the river Wharfe. The river was probably crossed to the north of the church in the line of an old street on the east of the river. About a mile from Tadcaster the Roman road appears half a mile north of the modern York road as a wide grass-grown farm road, at one part with a hedge on one side only, and so continues in a straight line for a mile and a half with a parish boundary along it. It was formerly called The Old Street and Street-way. At Street Houses the present road takes the line but soon leaves it, the parish boundary continuing on across fields without any other trace of the old road for a mile, and then a lane with a parish boundary along it continues the line to Queen's Arms Inn. There the present road rejoins the old road, which kept on the ridge of high ground crossed by the Great Northern Railway about two miles from York. Parish boundaries follow the road for two miles from Queen's Arms, making seven miles of parish boundaries along the nine miles of road from Tadcaster to York. Blossom Street and Micklegate Bar are probably on the line of the Roman road, pointing to Stonegate, the street which passes through the Roman city *Eburacum* on

[1] F. Drake, *Eboracum*, p. 19.

the east side of the river Ouse. The original rectangle
seems to have been about 550 yards from south-west to
north-east, and if Stonegate represents the middle street,
about 470 yards from north-west to south-east, 550 yards
by 470 yards would give *Eburacum* slightly larger dimensions than those of *Glevum, Venta* and *Isca*, with the same
proportions. The breadth from north-west to south-east
is, however, sometimes stated to be 650 yards, the position
of the Roman wall on the south-east being uncertain.

(9) *York to Stamford Bridge and Malton : Wade's Causeway.*—From the south-east gate of York a Roman road
followed the course of the present road along a ridge of
ground rising above the moors and curving round to Stamford Bridge.   Parish boundaries follow the road almost
continuously to Gate Helmsley, and then a parish boundary
runs close alongside it to the river Derwent. In 1736
vestiges of the old road remained here and there.[1] Warburton's map (1720) shows by broken lines a Roman road
turning northwards on the west side of the Derwent near
Stamford Bridge, and passing by Whitewell to the east side
of Castle Howard. There seems to be no trace of it now.

On the east side of the Derwent a Roman road is supposed to have turned northwards about a mile and a half
from Stamford Bridge, following the course of Mook Street
to Gally Gap, and continuing on to join the road which has
already been traced northwards from the Humber (p. 128),
on the high ground to the north of Thornthorpe. Thence
in two and a half miles Malton is reached, an undoubted
Roman station on the north bank of the Derwent.

From Gally Gap a road has been supposed to have
branched, crossing the river Derwent near Firby, and continuing on between Malton and Castle Howard by a course
not ascertained, to the river Rye at Newsham Bridge.
After crossing the Derwent, this supposed road would fall
into that marked on Warburton's map on the west of
that river, but there are no traces of it, nor of a road from
Malton joining it. Drake, in 1736, could find no traces of
a road either towards York or towards Malton further
south than near the river Rye, where he says the *stratum*
appeared very plain, composed of large blue pebbles, some
of a ton weight.[2] Warburton's map marks the road as

[1] F. Drake, *Eboracum*, p. 34.   [2] *Ibid.*, p. 36.

visible northwards from the river Rye, and Drake found
it discernible in places. Remains have been found near
Barugh, and Drake saw it at Riseborough. Warburton
marks it through Welton and Cawthorn; the course cannot
now be traced, but at the beginning of the last century it
was visible in Cawthorn village, and was very distinct on
approaching Cawthorn camps [1]—a remarkable group of
camps situated on a high ridge overlooking a deep valley
on the north.

The road seems to have been laid out from Riseborough
Hill (236') in a straight line, 11 miles long, by Cawthorn
Camps (654'), and over Pickering Moor to Wheldale
Gill.

At Cawthorn there are four camps; the most westerly
is rectangular, with a double ditch, and measures 133 yards
by 120 yards from crest to crest of the rampart. There are
entrances in the middle of three sides, the fourth being on
the edge of the steep slope. Adjoining is a roughly oval
camp, measuring about 280 yards by 110 yards, upon which
one angle of the westerly camp encroaches, and to the east
of it is a roughly square camp, about 186 yards by 183
yards, opening into another similar camp of rather larger
size. The entrances to all but the first-named and strongest
camp are covered on the outside by a curved prolongation
of the rampart across them. The ground is now planted
with firs, and covered up with high bracken.

The course of the Roman road northwards from these
camps is much plainer. It is called Wade's Causeway,
the story being that a giant of that name made it for his
wife's convenience in going to the moors to milk her cows.
The general course of the road for two and three-quarter
miles appears to have been laid out in a straight line from
the west of the Roman camps (650') to a point (825') on
Pickering Moor, a quarter of a mile to the north of Stape.
It descended by a steep bank on the west of the oval camp,
which appears to have been altered at the end in making
the road. Drake shows it in this position in his plan of
the camps, and states [2] that at the foot of the steep slope
the causeway was very plain, 12 feet wide, raised in some
places three feet from the surface, and paved with large

---

[1] Young, *History of Whitby*, 1817, ii. p. 694.
[2] *Eboracum*, p. 35.

stones. The paving was taken up within the memory of
man to build walls.   On the moor, to the north of the beck,
enough of the stones remain to mark the course of the road
on to the enclosures near Elleron Lodge, north of which,
where the high ground on Pickering Moor is hidden by an
intervening hill, the site of the Roman road, according to
the Ordnance map, lies a little to the west of the straight
line.   It rejoins it again when Flamborough Rigg has been
reached, and the ridge is traceable across the fields to Stape,
where, in the garth of the first house come to, some of the
paving remains, the rest having been taken up not many
years ago.   About 70 yards further on, near the chapel on
the Stape road, the paving remains entire.   There is no
trace of the road across the steep valley of the Stape beck;
it possibly bent to the west, and crossed where the present
road passes the beck.   On the moor towards the point
(825') to which the course of the road was directed, the ridge
is plain in the same straight line as before.   It is called
" The Auld Wife's Trod " (i. e. footway), and passes " The
Auld Wife's Well," and the paving is to be found a few inches
below the turf.   The road then turns slightly towards the
east, and for about 300 yards the pavement is entire at about
nine inches below the surface of the moor.   It is 17 feet
wide, and on each side are ditches.   In the enclosures near
Keysbeck Lodge the paving has been removed for building
walls, but the ridge can be traced.   The pavement was
described by a man who saw it taken up about 50 years ago,
as of flat stones gathered from the moor, laid close and
fitted together, the outside row on each side being set upright
as a kerb.   This entirely agrees with the paving which
now remains.   On the north side of Keys beck the pavement has been dug up to build the walls of enclosures,
but beyond the enclosures of Keys Beck House the ridge
again appears for half-a-mile on the moor, pointing to the
ford across Tutmoor beck at its junction with Keys beck.
Over Wheeldale Moor the course of the road can be traced,
and the paving is to be found a few inches below the surface
for about half-a-mile where it has escaped being taken up
to build enclosure walls.   Nearer to the enclosures the road
can still be traced almost on to Wheeldale Gill, which it
seems to have crossed near its confluence with Wheeldale
beck. The road must have then turned north-westward,

perhaps following about the same course as the present lane from the ford, to the high ground of Hazel Head, where traces remain. It is again traceable on the west of Julian Park House, and about a mile to the north of it. It seems to have slanted down Lease Rigg and crossed the river Esk near Grosmont bridge. On the north of the river some remains were to be seen in 1846 to the west of Grosmont Priory. It then turned more to the east and passed by Newbiggin and over Aislaby Moor. Drake in 1736 appears to have traced the road towards Dunsley Bay, but it is difficult to conceive why it should have gone there, with the more convenient harbour at Whitby close by. The supposition that it did so probably arose from the belief originating with Camden, that Dunsley Bay is the *Dunum Sinus* of Ptolemy. But if his degrees of latitude and longitude be followed, *Dunum Sinus*, in relation to York, would be at Filey or Bridlington. The last portion of the road visible in 1817 was where the Whitby road crossed it, near the third milestone. At that time several portions of the causeway were visible on Lease Rigg, and it is thus described [1]—" The foundation is usually a stratum of gravel or rubbish, over which is a strong pavement of stones placed with the flattest side uppermost, above these another stratum of gravel or earth to fill up and smooth the surface, the middle higher than the sides, which are secured with a border of flat stones placed edgeways, the elevation was in many places two or three feet, there was sometimes a gutter on each side, and the breadth exclusive of the gutters was 16 feet. The causeway preserved generally a rectilinear course, avoiding marshes, precipices, and sudden descents."

Wade's Causeway exhibits the gradual destruction of a paved Roman road in operation. On the moors, away from " intakes " or enclosures, the paving is to be found beneath a few inches of soil very much as it was when Roman traffic on it ceased. Where pieces of the moor have been enclosed, the stones of the paving have been taken up for building walls, both from the road within the intake and for some distance outside. On the unenclosed moor enough is left to be mapped as traces of a Roman road, but within the intake cultivation soon obliterates all traces. In newer

[1] Young, *History of Whitby*, p. 706

intakes an undulation in the ground shows the course of
the road, but after a time that can only be seen where walls
have been built across the ridge.[1]

(10) *Stamford Bridge to Bridlington.*—From Stamford
Bridge eastward parish boundaries continue to follow the
present road, called Garrowby Street, for nine miles and a
quarter. On Green Wold, seven miles from Stamford
Bridge, the Roman road already described from the Humber
northwards crosses Garrowby Street at the highest point
(808'), and the high wolds are entered upon, cut into by
deep, narrow dales, and traversed by long lines of intrenchments. For considerable distances Roman roads and
intrenchments follow the same course; whether the roads
took the line of older intrenchments, or have been intrenched
after Roman times, is a question which must be decided by
excavation, or by the careful observation of the evidence
afforded when the earthworks are levelled, a proceeding
continually going on. Confusion has certainly arisen in
consequence of long intrenchments having been mistaken
for Roman roads, and sometimes perhaps the reverse.
Parish boundaries follow both Roman roads and intrenchments.

On Garrowby Hill the Roman road is described as running on the top of one of a double line of British intrenchments, which subsequently accompany it for over a mile.
In about two miles the Roman road divides. The more
southerly branch, under the names of Green Lane, Low
Street, and York Road, follows a green road on the south
of Fridaythorpe, along which a parish boundary runs to
the Wetwang road, and then continues across the fields to
the green road again, and follows it for three and a half
miles. Where the Malton and Driffield Railway crosses it,
a Romano-British cemetery has been discovered.[2] About
a mile further on an intrenchment is marked on the
Ordnance map of 1898 for a mile and a half alongside the
green lane, but it has been levelled, except for half-a-mile
through the wood near Sledmere Monument. It there
consists of a double ditch and rampart, or the ridge of a
Roman road entrenched. To the east of Sledmere Monu-

---

[1] A mile and a half of the road on Wheeldale Moor was in 1913
put under protection of the Ancient Monuments Act.

[2] Mortimer, *Proc. York Geolog. and Poly. Soc.*, 1891.

ment what is in appearance the embankment of a Roman
road without intrenchment remains for nearly 400 yards,
six yards wide across the top, and as much as six feet high.
Then for about 100 yards it has been levelled, and when
it again appears it is complicated with intrenchments, which
curve round the north side of Warren Dale opening out
towards Holderness, and which the parish boundary follows.
The course of the Roman road onwards is somewhat doubtful; by some it has been supposed to have continued by
Cottam Warren House and Dane's Graves to Kilham, following parish boundaries and intrenchments, and thence
on by Wold Gate to Bridlington and Flamborough Head.
Parish boundaries follow Wold Gate for five miles from
Kilham to within two and a half miles of Bridlington.
Warburton's map seems to show the course in the direction
of a ridge which is called on a late six-inch Ordnance map
" track of a supposed raised road," and on by " Intrenchments " about a mile to the north of Kilham, which are
marked as an ascertained Roman road on Sir C. Newton's
map, prepared in 1847, and by Rudston to Bridlington.

The other road, branching near Fridaythorpe, appears
to be represented by the present road to Fimber, perhaps
continued on by the bit of ridge to be seen north of Fimber
station to what is marked " Intrenchment " on the Ordnance map, through Badger Wood. The Roman road was
found further on in Sledmere Park at the end of the eighteenth century, and there seem to be some traces of the ridge
along the road, called High Street, beyond Sledmere. In
about a mile the present road turns to the right, but the
course of the ridge can be traced on in the fields, and
more evidently where the wood has recently been grubbed;
and through the wood beyond, a Roman ridge intrenched
with ditch and rampart, or a double intrenchment, is plain.
After crossing the road from Cowlam to Lutton a ridge is
visible for about 80 yards, and the parish boundary, which
has been followed for a mile, continues on rather further
in the same line, marked " Intrenchment " on the Ordnance
map, but it is now only a straight hedge. At four miles
from Sledmere there is a slight turn in the ridge shown on
the Ordnance map, and a parish boundary for three-quarters
of a mile to the Scarborough road, and a ridge or intrenchment beyond, carry on the line in the direction of Filey,

eight miles distant.   The present road from Sledmere to
Rudston, marked " Roman road " in the latest Ordnance
map, runs parallel with the line which has just been followed,
and about half-a-mile to the south of it.   This road is followed for four miles and a half by parish boundaries, and
from a mile and a half west of Rudston to Bridlington it is
marked an ascertained Roman road in Sir Charles Newton's
map.

Drake, writing in 1736,[1] tells us that from Bridlington
Bay the Roman ridge was very apparent for many miles
over the wolds in the direction of York.   His map shows a
straight road through Rudston and Sledmere to Malton,
towards which he says the *stratum* was easily traced by
Wharram-le-Street to Settrington Brow.   A road, supposed
to be Roman, passes two and a half miles north of Sledmere
and Wharram-le-Street, and by Settrington Brow towards
Malton.   The   Ordnance   map   marks   " Intrenchments "
along it on the Wolds, and it is said to be traceable across
the fields to Norton, on the south side of the Derwent,
opposite Malton.   This is perhaps the line of the road to
Malton referred to by Drake.   His map is very inaccurate
in topography, and there is reason to think that he did not
always distinguish between the ridge of a Roman road and
an intrenchment.   In 1862 [2] a section of a Roman road
was exposed at Norton at a depth of eight feet.   It was
18 inches thick, and appeared to continue across the river
in the direction of the large camp at Malton.

(*a*) A road by Wharram-le-Street and Settrington Brow
to Malton is more in the line of an " ascertained Roman
road," on Sir C. Newton's map, from Malton to beyond
Wetwang ;   and   the   track   bearing   the   name   of   " The
Broad Balk," running northwards from Wharram-le-Street
towards Settrington Brow, may represent it.   Southwards
the present road to Sledmere and Fimber railway-station
is followed for two and a quarter miles by parish boundaries,
and bears the name of High Street.   It crosses Green Lane,
or Low Street, near the Romano-British cemetery, and
until the enclosures at the beginning of the last century, it
ran straight on from the west of Wetwang, passing half-
a-mile to the west of Tibthorpe, as a raised mound, and on

[1] *Eboracum*, p. 29.
[2] *Gent. Mag.*, 1862, part ii. p. 557.

to the west of Bainton. It can still be traced across the fields and along the hedgerows.[1]

There is much yet to be learned about the relation of the Roman roads and the earthworks of this part of the country. In the south of England, Wansdyke and other intrenchments have been proved to be post-Roman, Wansdyke plainly running for many miles along a Roman road; and it may very well be that the Roman roads on the Wolds were made use of for lines of defence against later invaders.

Iter I. of Antonine continues from York to *Derventio, Delgovicia,* and *Prætorium.* Stamford Bridge, on the Derwent, seven miles from York, is generally supposed to be the site of *Derventio,* and by distance onwards, either Malton, Warter, or the Romano-British cemetery to the north of Wetwang, would fit the position of *Delgovicia.* Twenty-five M. P. from Malton would reach Bridlington Bay, which, of the several sites suggested for it, seems to be as likely as any for the station *Prætorium.*

(11) *York to the north-east and north.*—A Roman road probably left York in a line with Stonegate, following the course of the present Malton road, along which there are some lengths of parish boundary.

It must have joined a Roman road shown on Warburton's map from the north of Stamford Bridge, through Sutton-le-Forest, Easingwold, Thirsk, and Northallerton, and joining Erming Street on the north of Catterick. It is marked by Warburton on his map as visible through Thormanby and by Thirsk to Northallerton, and he mentions it in a letter to Gale as more entire from Easingwold to Thirsk. It was faintly distinguishable at the beginning of the last century between Thirsk and Northallerton, and there seem to have been some remains between the latter town and Catterick.[2] The only trace now appears to be the road called " The Street," passing through Old Thirsk in the direction of Easingwold.

Another road left York by what is now Bootham Bar, outside which many Roman interments have been found. Boundaries run along the road for about a mile from York, and in places further on along the road and across country

[1] Cole, *Trans. E. Riding Antiq. Soc.,* vol. vii. p. 43.

[2] Gough's *Camden,* iii. p. 329.

in the direction of Easingwold, where it probably joined the road last mentioned. Drake continued the road by Newburgh to the Hambleton Hills and Teesmouth.

Another Roman road seems to have branched northwards from the Thirsk and Catterick road near Thornton-le-Street. At about two and a half miles north of the latter place a parish boundary begins to follow a lane, first for two miles, and then on in the same line for half-a-mile, then nearly the same line is taken up by a lane and a parish boundary to Bullamoor, and after a break of one and a quarter miles, boundaries continue in a straight line from Hallikeld for five miles to the Wiske river, lanes following the same line for most of the way. After a gap of a quarter of a mile the line is taken up by a lane, joined in five-eighths of a mile by parish boundaries which follow it for two and a half miles almost to the river Tees. For 13 miles the indications of a Roman road are thus evident, and on the north side of the Tees a line of highways continues on nearly due north for about eight miles, by Fighting Cocks, with boundaries along it for two miles, and on by Street House and Stanton-le-Street. This would give a road to the north on the east of the rivers Ouse and the Swale, in the direction of Chester-le-Street.

CHAPTER V

ERMING STREET AND BRANCHES (*continued*)

(12) *York to Catterick.*—The main line of Erming Street from York northwards to Aldborough (*Isurium*), near Boroughbridge, seems to have branched from the Tadcaster road on the west of the Ouse, and to have taken much the same course as the modern road; but few traces remain of it for seven miles. A parish boundary then joins the road and runs along it for two miles, crossing the river Nidd, at Skip Bridge, and continues along a track in the same direction to the cross roads at Providence Green, where a wide hedgerow seems to represent the Roman road near its junction with the road north by St. Helen's Ford (p. 135).

There appears to be no trace of a Roman road from York on the east of the Ouse, crossing that river at Aldwark, as suggested by Drake.

K 145

From Providence Green the course of Erming Street in continuation of Rudgate is due north, with two slight turns, for a mile and a half along a wide modern road, and it is then joined by the modern York and Boroughbridge road, and turns 35° towards the west. Thence to Catterick, 29 miles, the general course of the road is so straight that no part of it is more than a mile away from a straight line. Beyond Little Ouseburn the road is embanked to a height of two or three feet on the lower side on sloping ground, and on both sides in hollows; further on the ridge is strongly marked, eight yards wide between fences 20 yards apart. Several parish boundaries run along the road. About two miles from Boroughbridge the present road diverges, and the line of the old road on to Aldborough (*Isurium*) may be traced across the fields to a lane leading towards the Roman station; on approaching which the Roman road turned towards the west, and entered at the middle of the east side. From the remains of walls, and other traces, *Isurium* appears to have measured about 430 yards from east to west, and extended from ground about 100 feet high on the south, for about 630 yards towards the river Ure. It was a rectangle somewhat wider on the south, and of irregular outline towards the north. The Roman road from the south-west, which has already (pp. 97, 98) been followed from Ilkley to beyond the river Nidd, cannot now be traced towards Aldborough; but in 1712 it was laid open in Roecliff common field, two miles from Aldborough, at two feet below the surface. It was 10 feet wide, and paved with stone.[1]

Northwards from Aldborough there are now no traces of Erming Street for more than two miles. It could be discovered at the end of the seventeenth century through the meadows, bearing the name of Brig-gates, half-a-mile to the east of the present bridge,[2] and Drake mentions a tradition of a bridge, and that a beam of solid black oak had been taken out of the river not many years before.[3] In a mile and three-quarters from the river a parish boundary takes up the line, and in half-a-mile further Leeming Lane joins it, and for 13 miles is nowhere more than a quarter of a mile out of a straight line between Borough Hill, the

[1] Gale, quoted by Gough, *Camden*, iii. 300.
[2] Gale, quoted by Gough.   [3] *Eboracum* (1736), p. 25.

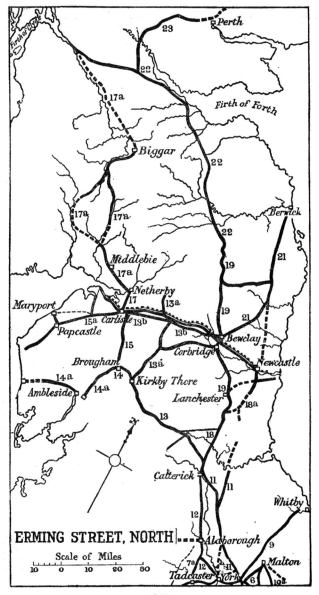

Firth of Clyde

Perth

23

22

17a

Firth of Forth

Biggar

22

Berwick

17a

17a

19

21

Middlebie

17a

19

Netherby

Maryport

17

13a

Carlisle

15a

13b

21

Papcastle

15

13b

Bewclay

Corbridge

Newcastle

Brougham

13a

14

Kirkby Thore

14a

Ameleside

14a

Lanchester

19

18a

13

18

Catterick

11

11

Whitby

12

9

ERMING STREET, NORTH

Aldborough

Malton

Scale of Miles

7a

12

11

10   0   10   20   30

Tadcaster York

6

19a

highest part of *Isurium*, and Leeming. Parish boundaries
follow the road nearly all the way to Healam Bridge,
nine and a half miles.   Stukeley [1] describes Leeming Lane
as straight and perfect from the turn to Ripon, and as " all
composed of stone and paved with large coggles which the
neighbouring inhabitants take away to build withal, and
pave their yards, etc."   The road has been modernized,
but the coggles are still to be seen in old buildings and walls
adjacent.   The course of the old road can be seen through
Leeming to Leeming Wath, 130 yards west of the bridge,
and continuing on the north of the river.   Then there is a
turn, and the road goes straight for five miles, parish
boundaries following it for two miles, to within half-a-mile
from Catterick.   The modern road then turns away from
Erming Street, and the ridge of the old road is traceable
on to a lane which continues the line to Cowsland Bridge
about a quarter of a mile west of Catterick, and a footway
continues the same straight line to Thornbrough.   There
on the south bank of the river Swale, about a quarter of
a mile west of Catterick Bridge, are the remains of a walled
camp, about 240 yards by 175 yards square, the Roman
Station *Cataracto*.   The north bank of the river is about
50 feet lower than the camp, and the river may have been,
for defence, held up by a weir which gave the name to the
station.   The road passes on the east of the station.

From *Cataracto* there is a turn in the general course of
the road towards the north.   After crossing the river Swale
a line of hedgerows marks the course to the railway, north
of which a short piece of the ridge is to be seen along a hedge.
About a quarter of a mile north of the railway the modern
road joins the course of the old road, which continues in
the same straight line between Thornbrough and a point
(488') one-eighth of a mile north of Scots Corner.   The
road, here called Watling Street and High Street, is
followed for a mile and three-quarters by parish boundaries.
For half-a-mile it is narrowed by encroachments, first on the
west and then on the east, so that the straightness is lost.

(13) *Catterick to Kirkby Thore*.—Near Scots Corner the
Roman road to Carlisle branches off to the north-westward.
It will be convenient to follow this branch before continuing
northwards along the road from which it appears to spring.

[1] *Iter Boreale*, p. 72.

According to Horsley, the road to Carlisle branched off at *Cataracto*, not far from which, he says, both branches were very conspicuous. The branching point, however, is four miles further north, near Scots Corner, where War-burton saw it, and from which point traces were lately visible branching off at an angle of 53° in a line with the present Carlisle road. The latter, followed for three-quarters of a mile by a parish boundary, runs straight for six miles to the west side of Hutton Moor (538'), parish boundaries following it for two miles. In Horsley's time the road was very conspicuous on Gatherley Moor, and generally all the way to Greta Bridge, and the ridge still carries the modern road. Towards Scots Corner the bank is now eight yards wide, having probably been widened, and is as much as five feet high in places, and beyond Melsonby Bank, where the width between the fences is 20 to 22 yards, the ridge is seven yards wide and three or four feet high, with a metalled road now four yards wide in the middle. With slight windings, and followed by parish boundaries, the same direction is preserved to Greta Bridge, where in the field between the Greta and Tutta beck, to the south of the village street, is a Roman fort (about 190 yards by 130 yards). Gough, Whitaker, and Watkin say that the Roman road ran through it from gate to gate, but there is no trace of that now, and the course of it is doubtful to the south-west corner of Rokeby Park, where there is a bend, and a straight road by Street Side for two and a half miles to Gallows Hill (800'), and then a slight turn to Bowes Cross (950'). The slightly winding course of the present road to Bowes seems due to deviations from the Roman road, of which there are some traces. At Bowes the Roman road already mentioned (p. 109) through Barnard Castle, and in the direction of Bishop Auckland, crossed. The station *Lavatræ* is on the south side of the Roman road, on the cliff over the river Greta. It measures about 140 yards square, and the ruins of Bowes Castle stand in the north corner. West of Bowes the road lies along the side of the moor on the north of the river Greta and of the railway, 1000 to 1500 feet above the sea. At Rey Cross, near the Yorkshire boundary, it passes through the remains of a camp measuring about 200 yards in each direction, and continuing on, while the modern road bends to the south to ease the gradient, in about two miles it reaches another camp about 100 yards square. Then the modern road rejoins the Roman road, and they apparently run together to within a mile and a half of Brough, where the present road makes a sharp turn towards the north across the Augill beck, while a footway goes on in the direction of the Roman station *Verteræ*. This is represented by a rectangular camp (157 yards by 113 yards) on the south-east side of the Swindale beck, half-a-mile south of the present road through Brough. It is not clear whether the latter road, or a more direct line by *Verteræ* is the course of the Roman road, probably the more direct course. In about two miles the road ascends a hill in a straight line pointing back to *Verteræ*, and with a slight turn goes on to Coupland Beck Bridge. The modern road to Appleby there turns off, and the line of the Roman road follows a footpath straight on to a wide lane, partly grass-grown, called High Street, and continues in the same direction to beyond Kirkby Thore, passing just north of Appleby railway-station. The course of the road was not long ago plain for the whole way on to Kirkby Thore, but for some distance railways now cross it and run along it. The modern road rejoins it about a mile from Kirkby Thore, after passing the remains of a camp near Crackenthorpe,[1] about 320 yards square. At the station the railway again crosses the old road, the line of which is preserved by parish boundaries along it for three and a half miles from Appleby to Kirkby Thore.

Kirkby Thore was no doubt *Brovonacæ* of Iter II., 13 M. P. from *Verteræ*. The station was on the north bank of Troutbeck, a tributary of the river Eden, and on the south of Kirkby Thore, and the site bears the name Burwens. Roman remains have been found to some extent, and quite lately coins in the Troutbeck near the Roman road, which is said to have crossed it by a bridge.[2]

(*a*) *Maiden Way*.—From Kirkby Thore a Roman road called Maiden Way branched off northwards, but there is nothing now to be seen of it for upwards of a mile. In 1845 it was visible on the brow of the hill above Hall Grange,

[1] General Roy (*Military Antiquities*) gives a plan of it under the name of Kreiginthorp Camp, 300 yards square.
[2] *Archæologia Œliana*, 1845.

and it is shown there on the Ordnance maps.   The course
onwards is over Newbiggin Moor, crossing Millburn Brook
near the corn mill, and on by Kirkland and ascending to
Melmerby Fell by Argill.   On the fell it is described, in
1845,[1] as being 21 feet wide, and two, three, and four feet
high, with a ditch on each side, and intersected by con-
duits, many of which were entire.   At the sides the stones
were two to three feet long, and one or two feet wide, and
in the middle were smaller stones.   Where the ground was
wet there were thicker stones beneath, making the road
14 inches thick.   After crossing Aglionby beck, the road
passes over Gilderdale Forest to Gilderdale beck, near its
confluence with the South Tyne, and in half-a-mile reaches
Whitley Castle, a fort, lozenge-shaped to suit the site,
about 200 yards by 130 yards.   It is then followed by
the present road on the left bank of the South Tyne, and
is crossed twice by the railway to Alston.   It is left by the
present road at Glendue Burn, and a parish boundary
marks its course for one and three-quarter miles, and then
highways take up the line.   Maiden Way passes over
Featherstone Common, and by Blenkinsop Castle, and joins
Stanegate on the south of *Magna* near Carvoran.   This
fort (143 by 120 yards) stands in a strong position commanding the valley of the Tipalt, a quarter of a mile south of
the Wall, and separated from it by a morass.   Hutchinson [2]
describes Maiden Way in Northumberland in 1776 as being
nearly six yards wide, bordered by large pebbles between
which a pavement rose to the crown.

A Roman road branched near Whitley Castle to the
Northumberland Watling Street near Corbridge.   It crossed
the South Tyne about a mile and a half north of Alston,
and its course is now followed by a highway over Willyshaw
Rigg, and a track onwards to the West Allen river, which
it crossed on the south of Whitfield Hall.   It crossed the
East Allen to Oldtown, a mile to the west of Catton, where
Warburton noticed " a portway seven yards broad all
paved with stone."   He shows the whole road on his map
of Northumberland (1716), and Horsley shows it as far as
Hexham on his map of the Pict Wall (1732).   It probably
passed through or near Hexham, which must have been

[1] Bainbridge, *Archæologia Œliana*, vol. iv.
[2] *History of Northumberland.*

a considerable Roman station, though little is known about it. At the time of Maclaughlan's survey the road seems to have been visible towards Corbridge.

Maiden Way on the north of the Wall is not connected with the Maiden Way which reaches Carvoran from the south, and the name was not applied to it before 1830. It leaves the north gate of *Ambloganna*, a fort on the Wall (198 yards by 145 yards) at Birdoswald, three miles to the west of Carvoran, and its course has been described at length by Rev. John Maughan.[1] It is perfectly straight from the north gate of *Ambloganna* to Little Beacon Tower, which is visible upwards of four miles distant in a west-north-westerly direction. It passes over Warterhead Fell, where it is raised, with a ditch on one side, and over Ash Fell, where it is 15 feet wide with an edging of stones. A section cut a little further on showed the road in excellent preservation, 16 to 17 feet wide, edged with large square kerb stones, and consisting of large and small pieces of stone and cobbles packed very tightly together in a layer eight inches thick, set on the natural clay sub-soil.[2] The road continues on in the same line for nearly a mile beyond Little Beacon Tower and then bends slightly to the top of Brown Knowe. A road then takes up the line to Bewcastle, an irregular hexagonal earthwork about 200 yards across on the north bank of Kirkbeck, where many Roman remains have been found. Maughan traced the road onwards to Skelton Pike, and across the river Kershope by Craigie Cleugh and over Tweeden Rigg to Liddel Castle, but beyond Bewcastle the road he describes is now discredited.

(b) *Stanegate.*—The Roman road, which is joined by the Maiden Way on the south of Carvoran, is not the military road along the Wall of Hadrian from end to end, and which here remains visible, but a road called Stanegate, running from two miles west of *Magna* to where the Wall crosses the North Tyne near Chesters. It has been compared to the string of a bow, and has been supposed to be a short cut from one part of the Wall to another. Stanegate is two miles from the Wall in the middle of the bow, and passes over a difficult country, and the saving in distance by it,

[1] *Archæological Journal*, vol. xi. p. 120.
[2] *Trans. Cumb. and West. Antiq. and Archæol. Soc.*, 1897, p. 196.

on the length of more than 16 miles, is not more than half-a-mile. The course of Stanegate is shown by the survey of the Roman Wall made for the Duke of Northumberland by Mr. Maclauchlan.[1]

From *Magna* eastward Stanegate can be traced for a mile, and in another two miles, after crossing Haltwhistle burn with a twist, it passes 20 yards from the south-east corner of the fort, which lies a quarter of a mile south of the *Vallum*, and was excavated in 1908.[2] The rampart was found to consist of a masonry wall with a backing of earth, with gates to the east, west, and south, but not to the north, and enclosing an area about 71 by 56 yards. A section of Stanegate revealed a foundation of cobble-stones bedded in clay, with kerbs at the sides, on which was a layer of smaller stones and gravel tightly packed, about 16 inches thick in the middle. The width was 16 feet 6 inches, and that of branch roads to gates on the east and south of the fort was nine feet. The road can be traced onwards in a straight line, with a slight turn on high ground about half-way, to *Vindolana* at Chesterholm, on the west of which Maclauchlan saw traces of it nearly in the line of the existing road. *Vindolana* (165 by 100 yards) lies five furlongs south of the *Vallum*, and a mile south of the Wall, and Stanegate passes close to the northern rampart. In about a mile the present road takes up the line through Newborough to Fourstones. Maclauchlan saw traces, and shows the road on his map, on to the North Tyne, and also by Walwick Grange to *Cilurnum* (193 by 144 yards), the largest station on the Wall except *Amblo-ganna* at Birdoswald. Stanegate has been supposed to have gone on to *Corstopitum*, and also beyond the Wall to Bewclay. There seems to be no evidence of a road in the former direction, but a continuation on the north of the Wall towards Bewclay, where the Devil's Causeway branches, is probable, and Horsley's map shows such a road. *Cilurnum* may have been at first a fort on Stanegate, guarding the passage of the North Tyne, and there are some signs of a fort earlier than that which has been excavated.

---

[1] Survey of the Roman Wall, etc., made by the direction of his Grace the Duke of Northumberland, K.G., by Henry Maclauchlan, 1857, with Memoir.

[2] *Arch. Œl.*, 3rd ser., vol. v. p. 223.

There is also a Roman fort about a furlong north of the Wall, about half-a-mile east of St. Oswalds church, and another one, about 65 yards square, three-quarters of a mile west of Bewclay and a mile north of the Wall. The remains of the Roman bridge over the North Tyne furnish other evidence of a road of early date in that direction. The bridge is 180 feet between the abutments, and the piers, the foundations of which remain in the river, show that there were four openings of 35½ feet, and that the width of the roadway was about 20 feet.[1] In the abutment which has been uncovered on the east bank, there is embedded the water pier of an earlier bridge. It measures, exclusive of the pointed cutwaters, nine feet four inches, so that it must have carried a roadway rather narrower than that. The position of this pier clearly shows that there was an earlier and narrower bridge crossing the river in the same direction as the newer bridge. At the back of the east abutment of the later bridge, and in a line with the roadway over both bridges, are the foundations of a square castle, and from the north-eastern corner of it the Wall has been traced for 60 feet, the outer face of it lining with the north side of both the bridges. Appearances suggest that the Wall on approaching the bridge was deflected northward to include the abutment of the bridge, but whether that was so, and the relative ages of the wider bridge and the Wall, are undetermined. The narrow bridge must, at any rate, be of earlier date than either, and may have belonged to a road represented by Stanegate.

Westward from *Magna* Stanegate bends northward from the south face of the fort to ease the descent to the river Tipalt, and a part of it remains. After crossing the valley it can be faintly seen, and further on more plainly about 80 yards south of the *Vallum*, passing about 50 yards to the north of Glenwhelp Camp (165 by 88 yards). Two other forts, about 90 by 95 yards, on commanding points about a quarter of a mile to the south, are passed. Recent researches have shown[2] that instead of continuing on to join the military road along the south of the Wall as it was supposed to do, Stanegate bends to the south-west

---

[1] Clayton, *Arch. Œl.*, N.S., vol. ii. p. 82.
[2] *Trans. Cumb. and West. Antiq. and Archæol. Soc.*, vol. xiii., 1911, p 380.

on nearing Poltross burn and crosses it 250 yards to the south of the *Vallum* at an angle of about 40°, passing 100 yards from, and nearly parallel to, the south-east face of Throp fort.   The ramparts of this fort proved to be of turf, partly on a foundation of stone 16 feet wide, and enclosed an area of 67 by 65 yards, with gates to the north-east and south-east.   The road was traced nearly as far as the fort, and a section of it showed stone pitching 16 feet wide, from which the outer kerb had been removed, so that the full width was 17 or 18 feet.   About a quarter of a mile to the west a ridge crosses two fields in the same direction, and 60 or 70 years ago the track was visible beyond.   Further on a trench cut 40 feet west of Bush Nook Lane revealed a road of the same section as that near Throp fort.   The road is here five furlongs south of *Amblo-ganna*, a station on the Wall, and points to Nether Denton, where a fort situated on the hill now occupied by the church and rectory was examined in 1868.   Eighty-nine coins, the latest of Trajan, were found, and " Samian " pottery of the earliest type yet found near the Wall. Similar pottery was found in 1911 in the field on the south of the rectory.   The course of Stanegate on for six and a half miles is uncertain, and then the road from Buckjumping to Crosby-in-Eden, marked " Roman Way " in Mac-laughlan's map, seems to take up the course.   Mac-laughlan gives particulars of a Roman camp, about 120 by 60 yards, not far from this line, on the south-east of Brompton old church, and a mile east of Buckjumping, and more than a mile from the Wall.[1]   About a quarter of a mile south of the road to Crosby is Watchcross camp— Horsley's *Aballaba*—resembling Throp in size and shape, seven furlongs south of the Wall.   Stanegate thus appears to have been in communication with the south by Carlisle, by the Maiden Way, and by the Northumberland Watling Street ; and to have been guarded by forts of which twelve remain, all those that have been excavated presenting features of an early date.

(14) *Kirkby Thore to Brougham.*—The present Carlisle road from Kirkby Thore, following the course of the Roman road, continues on in nearly the same line to Temple Sowerby, and then turns north round Whinfell, and after

[1] *Memoir*, p. 64.

crossing the Eden at Edenbridge, makes directly for *Brocavum*, now represented by the remains of a rectangular camp, about 134 yards by 113 yards, on the south side of the river Eamont, with the ruins of Brougham Castle close by. Until the turnpike road was made the Roman road between Stainmore and Brougham was very con-spicuous, six yards broad, formed of three courses of large square stones, or of gravel and flint as materials varied.[1]

(a) From *Brocavum* a Roman road went in a southerly direction towards Windermere. It is represented by a road which crosses the North-Western Railway at Yan-wath, a mile and three-quarters south of Penrith, and passes by Tirril and Winder Hall, over Swarth Fell (1832'), High Raise (2634'), and Kidsty Pike (2660'). It goes by the name of High Street, and is followed for four miles by parish boundaries. The pavement has been laid bare in several places at about a foot beneath the turf.[2] It passes between Hayes Water and Blea Water (2600'), and descends by Hag Gill and Long Green Head to a camp at Low Borrans one mile south of Troutbeck Church, and not far from the upper end of Windermere. The road is said to have gone on to Kendal, but it does not seem to be traceable.

Near Ambleside, about two miles and a half to the north-west, are the remains of a Roman walled fort situated on the low ground at the head of Windermere and to the east of the confluence of the rivers Rothay and Brathay. Camden describes it as the carcase of an ancient city with great ruins of walls and paved roads leading to it, and Gough[3] mentions large ruins of walls, of which little is now to be seen. The average dimensions of the fort are 141 yards by 105 yards, the walls being four feet thick backed by a clay bank. Recent sewerage works along Borrans Road, from the camp towards Rothay Bridge revealed a "corduroy road" of oak trees laid on the surface of an old morass, covered with a layer of earth and stones five or seven inches thick, and four to five feet below the surface. Large stones lay at the same level beyond.[4] There are traces of a Roman road westward from Amble-

---

[1] Gough, *Camden*, iii. p. 403.
[2] Nicholson's *Romans in Westmoreland.*
[3] *Camden*, iii. p. 407.
[4] *Pro. Soc. Ant.*, 2nd ser., xviii. p. 267.

side. It is visible six miles to the west, where near Wrynose pass the road appears to have been cut out of the rock. It is marked on the Ordnance map, on doubtful authority, along Wrynose Bottom, crossing the river Duddon three times, and then turning to the south-west along the right bank of the Duddon to Blackhall; but there seem to be no traces in that direction. The track straight on westward from Cockley Beck Bridge is marked as a Roman road after an interval of about a mile. It passes a hundred yards to the south of Hardknot Castle, a walled Roman fort about 130 yards square,[1] and not far off the road was described in 1877[2] as well paved for 150 yards, and two yards and a half wide. It winds down westward to the road which crosses the river Esk at Whahouse Bridge, and which probably follows the course of the Roman road on as far as the King of Prussia Inn, where the present road turns to the north-west. The course onwards is more uncertain. Dr. C. A. Parker, who has devoted considerable attention to the road, considers that it follows the old road along the south of Muncaster Park, where near Muncaster Head a piece of Roman paving remains, and so on to Ravenglass camp, overlooking the harbour formed by the mouth of the river Esk.

(15) *Brougham to Carlisle.*—The Roman road from *Brocavum* to Carlisle, after passing the river Eamont, seems to have turned north-west, and the present road appears to join it about one mile north of Penrith, and to follow its course to Carlisle. Gale says, in 1767, that this road on the east of the river Petterill was very well known to be the Roman road. North of Plumpton Head a parish boundary follows it for five-eighths of a mile, and at Old Penrith, five and a half miles from Penrith, a rectangular camp, 170 yards by 116 yards, on the west of the road, appears to mark the site of the station *Voreda* of Iter II. After a turn towards the east to avoid the river Petterill at Wragmire Moss, the Roman road in about three miles entered Carlisle (*Luguvalium*) on the line of Botchergate. According to Ferguson there is a well-marked Roman road called Plumpton Low Street on the west of the river Petterill and the railway, parallel to that now described.

---

[1] Dymond, *Cumb. and West. Antiq. Soc.,* vol. xii. p. 390.
[2] I. Dixon, *Trans. Cumb. and West. Antiq. Soc.,* vol. iii. p. 358.

(a) *Carlisle to Papcastle, Egremont and Maryport.*—A
Roman road left Carlisle in a south-westerly direction.
Traces of this appear in a parish boundary for a quarter of
a mile along the Cockermouth road immediately outside
the city, and again for two miles along the straight road
between Newby Cross and Nealhouse. There is then a
slight turn, and the present road, except for a mile between
Thursby and the crossing of the Maryport and Carlisle
Railway, runs straight to Red Dial, immediately to the
north of which, and one and a quarter miles south of Wigton,
is the Roman camp known as Old Carlisle. Stukeley
described it [1] as a rectangular *castrum* 170 yards by 133
yards, from the north-east gate of which a road paved with
coggles led to Carlisle, and another, paved in the same
manner, ran north as far as he could see, that is, in the
direction of Bowness. From Red Dial the Roman road
followed the course of the present road almost in the same
line straight for two and a quarter miles to near Percy Hill,
and on by White Hall and Bothel ; and afterwards pointing
for two and a half miles from Threepland Gill Bridge
straight to the Roman station in a field called Burrens,
at Papcastle on the river Derwent near Cockermouth.
The north side and portions of the east and west sides
of the camp can still be traced, the former measuring
about 226 yards, and the latter about 130 yards, as
far as they extend. The road can be traced from a gate
in the east wall. It consists of two layers of tightly
packed stones and clay, bedded on a layer of larger
stones.[2]

A Roman road, continuing southward from Papcastle,
is described in 1815 [3] as taking a straight course from the
south of Cockermouth by Street Gate, Lamplugh Cross,
Frizington, and Cleator to Egremont. Towards Cockermouth it was six yards wide, and paved with cobbles and
stone from the adjacent ground. Near Eaglesfield it was
found in 1794 as a paved way, seven yards wide, a little
below the surface, and in 1877, though the road had been
plundered of its boulders about 20 years before, the founda-

[1] *Iter Boreale*, p. 54.
[2] *Trans. Cumb. and West. Antiq. and Archæol. Soc.*, vol. xiii.
N.S., p. 131.
[3] Lysons, vol. iv. p. cxxxvii (note).

tion had lately been uncovered[1] near Lamplugh. In Frizington Park the road was found seven yards wide about 18 inches below the surface, and it could be traced near Cleator.[2]

A survey of the Roman road from Papcastle to Maryport was made by Mr. F. L. B. Dykes.[3] Leaving the camp at Papcastle, the course bends to the west along a lane and a fence, then takes a direct line across the fields to Dovenby, and then follows the road for two miles in the same line to the cross roads, beyond which it is traceable towards the river Ellen, through the grounds of Netherhall, and on to the fort on the cliff to the north of Maryport. This appears to have been about 150 yards square, with four gates.

According to R. S. Ferguson, a Roman road leading direct from Old Carlisle to Maryport was till lately distinct by Waverbridge and over Oughterside Moor. Between the latter place and Maryport a Roman road has been traced by a track of cobble stones disturbed by the plough from Crosscanonby to Bank-end Lane near the fort at Maryport, to which it points.[4]

The Roman Wall from the Tyne at Wallsend to the Solway at Bowness, with a military road on the south side of it, passed on the north of *Luguvalium*. According to Bishop Bennet[5] a Roman road continued along the coast from Bowness to Maryport, being perfectly plain at Old Mawburgh (? Mawbray), and for two or three miles north of Allonby; and a Roman road has been supposed to continue on from Maryport along the coast to Moresby, two miles north of Whitehaven, and according to R. S. Ferguson, on to Ravenglass and Bootle, south of which it is known as High Street.

(16) *Comparison of Itinerary distances and mileage.*— Iter V. of Antonine follows the road from Lincoln to Carlisle, and Iter II. passes over it in the reverse direction from *Blatum Bulgium* through Carlisle to York. Two other stations are named in the latter Iter, *Brovonacæ* and

---

[1] W. Dickenson, *Trans. Cumb. and West. Antiq. and Archæol. Soc.,* vol. iii. p. 344.

[2] I. Dixon, *Trans. Cumb. and West. Antiq. and Archæol. Soc.,* vol iii. p. 339.

[3] *Trans. Cumb. and West. Antiq. and Archæol. Soc.,* vol. i. p. 169.

[4] *Ibid.,* 1904, p. 250.   [5] Lysons' *Cumberland,* p. cxxxv.

Voreda, which the distances locate at Kirkby Thore and Old Penrith respectively, whilst *Brocavum*, mentioned in the former Iter, is omitted. Arranging the part of Iter V. north of Lincoln with the distances in M. P., and the modern names with the distances in miles, they are as follows :—

	M. P.		STATUTE MILES.
Lindo		Lincoln	
Segeloci . . .	xiv	Littleborough .	14
Dano	xxi	Doncaster . .	21½
Legeolio . . .	xvi	Castleford . .	17½
Eburaco . . .	xxi	York . . .	22½
Isubrigantum .	xvii	Aldborough . .	17½
Cataractone .	xxiv	Catterick Bridge .	23½
Levatris . . .	xviii	Bowes . . .	20
Verteris . . .	xiv	Brough . . .	13
Brocavo . . .	xx	Brougham . .	19
Luguvalio . . .	xxii	Carlisle . . .	20
	M. P. 187		Miles 188½

Reversing Iter II. from York and arranging it in the same manner :—

	M. P.		STATUTE MILES.
Eburacum		York	
Isurium . . .	xvii	Aldborough . .	17½
Cataractone . .	xxiv	Catterick Bridge .	23½
Lavatris . . .	xvi	Bowes . . .	20
Verteris . . .	xiv	Brough . . .	13
Brovonacis . .	xiii	Kirkby Thore . .	12
Voreda . . .	xiii	Old Penrith . .	13
Luguvallo . .	xiv	Carlisle . . .	13
	M. P. 111		Miles 112

It may be observed that Iter V. makes the distance from *Eburacum* to *Luguvalium* 4 M. P. greater than Iter II.

(17) *Carlisle to Netherby.*—On the north of Carlisle, after crossing the river Eden and passing through the Wall at Stanwix, where the churchyard occupies the site of the Roman station, the course of the Roman road appears to have been along a straight line about half-a-mile east of

the modern road; it is now followed by lanes and pieces
of parish boundaries for two and a half miles due north.
The modern road then joins the line and follows it for two
miles.   The Roman road continued on by Longtown and
Netherby, where Horsley placed *Castra Exploratorum* of
Iter II.   According to General Roy,[1] it went on to a station
called Liddel Moat at the junction of the Liddel and the
Esk, and seems then to have directed its course towards
Nether Woodhead, and along the east of Tarras water
towards Teviotdale, and probably on to Eildon; but there
are no traces of such a road.

(*a*) *Longtown to the Wall of Antonine.*—A road branched
at Longtown almost at right angles with the last-mentioned
road.   General Roy described it in 1790 as being conspicuous, with vestiges to be seen for many miles together.
It crossed the Esk near Longtown church, pointing towards
Gretna, and led to the camp at Birrens near Middlebie,
where *Blatum Bulgium* of Iter II has been placed.   The
camp is on the north bank of Mein Water, and is protected
by a burn on the east.   It measures about 173 yards from
the south face on the river's bank to the inner rampart on
the north, outside which there are six ditches, and 117 yards
from east to west.   The road crosses the river at the south-
west angle of the fort, and is found eighteen feet wide under
a few inches of turf.   It passes to the south of Birrenswork
Hill, about three miles to the north-west, and traces are
marked on the Ordnance map for three miles towards the
Milk river at Droveford.   It passes to the east of Locker-
bie, and crossed the Dryfe water about half-a-mile north
of its confluence with the Annan.   The road is supposed
to have divided here, one branch continuing westward
across the river Annan, to the north of Lochmaben and
by Amiesfield to Dalswinton.   It turned up the east side of
Nithsdale, where however no traces remain, to Durisdeer.
Well Path over the pass, and a road on the left bank of
the Portrail water, both marked Roman roads on the
Ordnance map, continue the course on to Elvanfoot, where,
or at Crawford Castle, it rejoined the other branch.   The
latter continuing northward on the east side of the Annan,
crossing it near Johnstone, and Evan water near Beattock.
On the west of Moffat it is visible on the ridge between the

---

[1] *Military Antiquities,* p. 104.

L

Annan and the Evan, slightly raised above the surface, and traceable as the season advances by the lighter colour of the herbage. In trenches cut in 1892, the surface of the road was found to be slightly raised in the middle, of small stones four inches deep on a layer of larger stones 11 inches deep, laid in and upon a bed of clay. The width was 21 feet.[1] The road is traceable on by a track over Black Fell to a Roman camp at Little Clyde on the north of the railway at Beattock summit, a rectangle about 480 yards by 330 yards, and onwards to the main road about a mile south of Elvanfoot. From the north of Crawford it is supposed to cross Southwood Rig, and follow the east side of the railway to join the main road to Biggar near Causeway House. General Roy found no traces on to Biggar, except in crossing Biggar Moss, and onwards he gives the probable course as by Liberton and Carstairs House, to Castle Dykes, a camp 200 yards by 187 yards, which the road passes through. Further on by Kilnkadzow to the north of Carluke he says that the road was known all along by the name of Watling Street, that between West Calder and Glasgow traces were then lately to be seen, particularly a little east of Tollcross, and that beyond Glasgow, towards Old Kilpatrick, where it joined the Wall of Antonine, remains could then be discerned.

There is no suggestion of a road in the direction of Camelon.

The Northumberland Watling Street.

The Roman road northward from Catterick Bridge and through Durham and Northumberland was surveyed for the Duke of Northumberland by Mr. H. Maclauchlan.[2] The map, engraved on a scale of two inches to a mile, gives more detailed and accurate information on matters connected with the road than the Ordnance survey, on which in the main it appears to have been based, and it is supplemented by a memoir on the part of the road in Durham

---

[1] *Proc. Soc. Ant. Scot.*, 1894, p. 314.
[2] Map of Watling Street from the river Swale to the Scotch Border from a Survey made in the years 1850 and 1851, by direction of his Grace the Duke of Northumberland, by Henry Maclauchlan.

and Northumberland. The road is called Watling Street, by which name it is known in those counties.

(18) *Scots Corner to Lanchester.*—At one-eighth of a mile north of Scots Corner, to which point the road has already been followed from *Cataracto,* there is a turn to the north-east for a quarter of a mile to a point (464'), from which the course of the present road is almost straight for 12 miles, pointing to Busselton Hill (700'), on the south of the river Gaunlees. The straight line is interrupted to pass round a small hill, Hang Bank (382'), on the east of Melsonby, the top of which is in the line and affords a view in both directions. Parish boundaries run along the road for five and a half miles to the river Tees, passing round Hang Bank. In Stukeley's time the great ridge of stone originally laid was not worn out.[1] There is a slight twist in descending to the river Tees, on the north of which at Piercebridge are the remains of a camp (253 yards by 200 yards), on the west of the road. The course of Watling Street is then in a straight line for four miles to Legs Cross 660'), pointing to Busselton Hill. It is soon joined by the modern road, on both sides of which traces of it appear, and it continues on in nearly the same line for two and a half miles from Legs Cross to the river Gaunlees, east of Shildon Bridge. At Royal Oak the traces are evident for 150 yards on the west of the modern road, and thence continue on to the river. Parish boundaries follow the course of Watling Street continuously for upwards of three miles to the south side of the Gaunlees. Maclauchlan's map shows a Roman road joining Watling Street on the south side of the river, which is probably the road from Barnard Castle by Streatlam before-mentioned (p. 109). North of the river there is a turn towards the east, and the modern road, on the site of the Roman road, goes straight through Bishop Auckland in a line from Busselton Hill to the station at Bincester. To follow that course now to Bincester would involve crossing a loop of the river Wear, and there has perhaps been an alteration of the river course since Roman times. On reaching the station, *Vinovia,* the road appears to have turned to the west and entered the south-east front and gone out by the north-east front of a camp (200 yards by 154 yards), on the brow

[1] *Iter Boreale,* p. 72.

of the east bank of the river Wear.   In the 21 miles from
Catterick to Bincester no part of the Roman road is half-a-
mile away from a straight line joining those points.

From Bincester onwards the course of the road is somewhat obscure; it appears to have crossed the river Wear
soon after leaving the station, pointing north-west, and
Maclauchlan says that it was visible on the north of the
river until it entered a lane, and again where the lane
quitted the line of the road, and on between Hunwick and
Hunwick railway-station down to the brook, beyond which
the raised bank remained on one side or the other of the
road to Willington.   At Willington burn the present road
turns to the east, but Watling Street goes straight on and is
visible on both sides of the burn.   Here a Roman road
turned off north-east by Hollin Hall; it was traced to
Brancepeth Park, and was supposed by Horsley [1] to have
gone on to Chester-le-Street.   Watling Street passes over
Brandon Hill (875′) where Maclauchlan describes it as
nearly perfect.   A remarkable change in the direction of
the road there takes place.   The general direction from
Catterick is nearly due north, and for four miles to the
north of Brandon Hill it points a few degrees east of north.
It then, for no obvious reason, turns 65° to the west, and
the direction of the road, thus far pointing to Newcastle,
changes to Lanchester and Corbridge.   Maclauchlan traced
the road from the turn down to the river Deerness, and the
Ordnance map shows it for a mile and a half in the same
direction and again for a mile and a quarter to the camp
near Lanchester (200 yards by 157 yards) on the west of
the road.

There is no evidence that the road over Brandon Hill
continued on in the same direction, pointing to Newcastle,
though four miles to the east there are evidences of a Roman
road running north and south through Chester-le-Street.
There the hard and compact surface of the Roman road
was met with in 1902 at the depth of a yard, and the
road northwards, formerly called Streetway, is straight for
four miles to Leybourne Hold.   The course of the Roman
road seems to follow a lane for another mile to Wrekenton,
and thence to go straight on over Gateshead Fell and
through Gateshead to the Tyne.

[1] *Brit. Rom.*, p. 399.

At Wrekenton a Roman road called Wrekendyke crossed from south-west to north-east. It is visible on the south-west of Wrekenton, and it is said to have been formerly traceable on in that direction to the north of Kibblesworth and beyond in the direction of Lanchester.[1] To the north-east, the course is followed by a parish boundary for nearly a mile, and is then continued by Leam Lane, straight on for another three miles to Fell Gate, and on thence to the south side of Jarrow Slake, now Tyne Docks. It probably continued to the walled camp at The Lawes, South Shields, which was traceable in 1870, 205 yards by 120 yards.

The Roman bridge over the Tyne, *Pons Ælii*, occupied the site of the present low-level swing-bridge. The piers of it were incorporated in the mediæval bridge, and the foundations of one of the piers were removed when the present bridge was built.

North of the Tyne the Roman road apparently followed the same course as the present road, straight over Town Moor, and on by South Gosforth, Stannington, and Morpeth, probably joining the Devil's Causeway, but nothing appears certain.

From Lanchester, Maclauchlan marks a road to the north-east, as the probable course of Wrekendyke.

(19) *Lanchester to Chew Green.*—Watling Street, leaving Lanchester on the east, passes by Low and High Woodside, where there are a few traces of it, and on to the west of the high ground on which Iveston stands. A road then takes up very nearly the same straight line, pointing from the high ground near Iveston, for two miles through Leadgate, and on nearly straight to the west of Ebchester (*Vindomora*), a camp 133 yards square, on the east side of the Derwent and on the north of a tributary burn. Warburton [2] describes the road hereabouts as one of the most entire, regular, and large ways he ever saw, the ridge being for the most part two yards in height, full eight yards broad, and all paved with stone that is at present as even as if new laid. Watling Street curves down the burn to cross the Derwent and then turns more to the west, the line being taken up after three-quarters of a mile by a lane, straight for a mile to Whittonstall, and on with a very slight turn

---

[1] Horsley's *Britannia Romana*, p. 451.
[2] Letter to Roger Gale, 1717.

to a square camp on Castle Hill on the south of Stocksfield burn. There is a turn down to the burn, and after curving up the north side of it, Watling Street takes a new line and is soon left by the present road, the course being traceable until the latter rejoins it in a mile and a quarter. In three-quarters of a mile it seems to wind down into the Tyne valley. There are traces of it between the present road and the railway near Riding, and then the modern road seems to occupy the site of it for half-a-mile, beyond which the ridge is visible on the south of the road. After being joined by the Roman road from Whitley Castle (p. 151), Watling Street crossed the Tyne about half a mile to the west of the present bridge at Corbridge by a bridge which crossed the present river course at an angle of about 40°, the Tyne having swung to the south since Roman times. The south abutment is visible, and the foundations of five piers have been found in the river. The piers are 29 feet long to the end of the cutwater, and 15 feet 4 inches wide at the foundation course. Other piers have been traced by boring beneath the north bank of the river by Messrs. J. E. and R. H. Forster,[1] from which it would appear that there were ten piers, and eleven spans of about 20 feet. The superstructure was probably of timber.

Not far from the north end of the bridge a remarkable section of the Roman road has been revealed, showing two if not three roads superimposed. The lowest road, the surface of which was five feet below the ground level, was 35 feet 9 inches wide between the kerbs, four feet thick in the middle, and two feet six inches at the sides. The kerbs were of square stone as much as two feet seven inches high, rising from the subsoil to the surface of the road, and nine inches thick, and were backed up by rough stones piled against them. The body of the road consisted of six layers : (1) a layer of a hard yellow sandy substance six inches thick lying on the clay subsoil, (2) a course of rough quarry stones eight inches thick, (3) eight inches of very hard yellow gravel with occasional patches of lime, (4) eight or nine inches of rough quarry stones, (5) six inches of sand, and (6) a surface layer one foot thick of rubble stone and gravel rammed together. The layers thinned out so as to give a fall of one foot six inches from the middle

[1] *Jour. Archæol. Ass.*, 1906, p. 205, and 1907, p. 125.

to the side of the road.   Over this, apparently the Roman
road, were two other road surfaces, one foot, and three feet
above the surface of the Roman road, as if that had been
raised, perhaps to keep it above flood level.   In a section
about 80 yards more to the north the road resembled the
upper layer of the earliest road above described, of cobbles
and gravel so tightly rammed together that it was difficult to
get a pick into them.   It was 36 feet wide and 18 inches
thick, and there was no other road over it.[1]   The Roman
Corstopitum at Corchester, now being carefully excavated,
stood on rising ground (149') near the north bank of the
Tyne, and was protected on the west and north by the
Corburn; it was roughly oval in shape, about 440 yards by
352 yards in diameter.   The road from the south appears to
have entered it on the south-west, and left it on the north-
east side.   There are evident traces of the ridge for half-a-
mile north of the Corburn, and then the same line is taken up
by the present road pointing to Stagshaw Bank, 180 yards
south of the Roman Wall.   Here there is a camp, and, with
a slight turn to the west, the road, of which there are traces,
runs for a mile and a quarter to Bewclay hill (700') in a
straight line which crosses the Wall obliquely, as if the
laying out of the road had no relation to an existing wall.
Across Stagshaw common a township boundary runs along
the straight modern road for a mile, the first instance of a
boundary along the Roman road since the river Gaunlees
was crossed.

On the south side of the Wall the military way, which
followed the Wall from end to end, was no doubt communicated with.   In Horsley's time it was very plain, but it was
destroyed not long after to make General Wade's road from
Newcastle to Carlisle, and there is now no trace of it until
that road leaves the Wall near Sewingshields, beyond which
it is evident for many miles.   Bruce [2] described it as being
usually about 17 feet wide, of rubble stone, raised in the
middle   18 inches   above   the   adjoining   ground   and
bounded by kerb stones on each side.   Sections were made
at White Moor and at Brunstock Park a few miles east of
Carlisle in 1912.[3]   At the former, peat four inches thick, lay

[1] *Archæol. Æliana*, vol. iv. p. 208.
[2] *The Roman Wall*, p. 76.
[3] *Trans. Cumb. and West. Antiq. and Archæol. Soc.*, vol. xiv. p. 403.

on the sandy subsoil, and on it was a layer of sandy clay six inches thick and 27 feet 6 inches wide, and then a double line of larger stones on edge in the middle of the road and kerbs at the sides, the spaces between being filled by stones and gravel 10 inches thick, the larger stones being at the bottom. The top width was 23 feet, and there was a ditch on each side. The whole was covered by two inches of peat. At Brunstock Park the road was 21 feet wide, of loose sandstone fragments with large stones at its axis and edges, those in the middle being decidedly higher than those at the sides. On the west of Poltross burn trenches cut in 1912 showed the road 50 feet from the wall, 19 feet 3 inches wide, with the kerbs in position, and with a foundation of flat stones, where it was on peat moss.[1]

On the north of the Wall a parish boundary follows the road for three-quarters of a mile, and on reaching Bewclay, a mile from the Wall, the road divides into two branches, one with a turn towards the north-west, and the other called the Devil's Causeway taking a north-easterly direction (p. 170). The former runs straight for four miles in the direction of high ground (532') between Swinburn Castle and Colwell. The present road then leaves the course of the Roman road ; and the ridge of the latter can be traced nearly down to the Swinburn, and up on the north side of the burn, where the modern road rejoins it and follows it in a straight line for one and a half miles to Long Crag, and on in almost the same line for two and a quarter miles to a ridge (950') near Hill Head. With a slight turn to the east another piece of straight road one and three-quarter miles long, followed by township boundaries, succeeds, passing Swinehills camp, 173 yards square, on the west. The modern road then turns off to the east to Redesdale, but Watling Street, marked by a track and traces of the ridge, continues straight on for half-a-mile, and then, pointing to High Leam, across the moor for two miles to the river Rede, on the east of which, and on the north of a tributary burn, at Risingham is a rectangular camp (180 yards by 157 yards), marking the site of *Habitancum*, as an inscription proves.

After crossing the river Rede there are traces of the Roman road in a northerly direction straight to Woodhouse, where the present road joins and follows it for five miles

[1] *Trans. Cumb. and West. Antiq. and Archæol. Soc.*, vol. xiii. p. 390.

in straight lengths of about a mile, except near Troughend, where for half-a-mile it leaves Watling Street to the east. After passing Dargues Camp (308 yards by 263 yards), the modern road turns to the east at Blakehope to cross the river Rede, and the course of the Roman road, of which there are evident traces, continues on to cross the Rede higher up where there are said to be the remains of a Roman bridge.   There are some traces of the ridge after the Rede is crossed, but the course is uncertain on to High Riechester, *Bremenium*, a square camp (133 yards by 133 yards), with the remains of masonry walls.   Horsley [1] describes the road, in 1732, as being visible for almost the whole way from Risingham.

From *Bremenium* a Roman road may be traced eastwards, winding over the fells and along valleys north of Greenwood Law and Dod Hill to the river Coquet at Holystone, and on by Sharperton, and close under the hill on the north of Callaby Camp to join the Devil's Causeway near Thrunton.   Here, when taken up at the beginning of the last century, it was 14 feet wide. [2]

Watling Street, proceeding northwards, slants down to cross the Sills burn, and then goes in a straight line, past a camp at Bellshields (572 yards by 374 yards) for three miles to Featherwood, where there is another camp (550 yards by 396 yards), and winds on over the fells (1200' to 1400'), a parish boundary following the track for a mile.   At Chew Green, on the Cheviots near the source of the river Coquet, there is a complication of camps.   A camp, about 330 yards square, is overlapped by another camp, 330 yards by 200 yards, and encloses three smaller camps, one of which, about 110 yards square, is more stongly intrenched than the others. The name *Ad fines*, from the Itinerary of Richard, was given to the camps at Chew Green by the authors of the commentary on that fabrication, and it has unfortunately been perpetuated on the Ordnance maps.

Maclauchlan describes the road as visible for nearly the whole way from Riechester over the moors, where the side ditches are fully eight feet wide in most places, forming a total width of nearly 50 feet.   Towards the Border the road is not so plain.

[1] *Britannia Romana*, vol. ii. p. 396.
[2] *Gent. Mag.*, 1825, part i. p. 39.

It is to be noticed that from the Wall northwards to the Cheviots the road is more generally laid out in straight lengths than it is from the river Wear to the Tyne; though the country is wilder, it was perhaps in Roman times more open in the northern part.

(20) *Comparison of Itinerary distances and mileage.*— Iter I. of Antonine passes over the road from *Bremenium* to *Cataracto.* Reversing the Iter with the distances in M. P., and arranging it in parallel columns with the modern names and distances in miles, they appear as follows :—

	M. P.		STATUTE MILES.
Cataractoni		Catterick Bridge	
Vinovia	xxii	Bincester . . .	21
Vindomora . . .	xix	Ebchester . . .	18
Corstopito. . . .	ix	Corbridge . . .	9½
Bremenio	xx	Riechester . . .	24
	M. P. 70		Miles 72½

The distances agree with the sites usually given for the stations except the last, which would rather place *Bremenium* at the large camp at Dargues, but it has been placed at Riechester on the evidence of an inscription there in which *Bremenium* is mentioned.[1]

(21) *The Devil's Causeway.*—The Roman road, branching off at Bewclay about a mile north of the Wall, called the Devil's Causeway, was also surveyed by Mr. Maclauchlan for the Duke of Northumberland.[2] The first trace of it is at Cob Causeway, two and a quarter miles from Bewclay, beyond which it appears for a mile. The track for three miles near Tongues is in a line with Chickmire Hill, and near Ferney Chesters a parish boundary follows it for half-a-mile, and the course is straight on for four and a half miles to near the Hart, a quarter of a mile west of Hartburn. It is plain for one and a half miles south of the Wansbeck, and can be traced on the high ground between

[1] Horsley, vol. i. plate 192.
[2] Map of the Eastern Branch of Watling Street from Bewclay to Berwick-on-Tweed, together with a branch from High Rochester to Whittingham. From a survey made by direction of his Grace the Duke of Northumberland, in the years 1857-9, by Henry Maclauchlan, with a Memoir.

the North British Railway and the Hart.[1] It winds down and up across the Hart valley, on the north of which there is a slight turn to the east, and the course, along Harpath Lane, points for three and a half miles to High Trewitley, and there are traces here and there all along. The road then turns nearly due north, and the track is visible for three-quarters of a mile, and then for a quarter of a mile, on to near Todburn (482'). The river Coquet is crossed at Todstead ford, and then a lane takes up the line north of the Coquet to Long Framlington, and after an interval of a mile a road follows it for one mile. Then the causeway quits the road and ascends Framlington Moor, where it is traceable, and crossing the road three-quarters of a mile east of Moorhouse Inn, bends towards the west of Edlingham, and round to near Thrunton. There it is joined by the Roman road from Riechester (p. 169) and enters upon a straight course of four miles nearly to the river Breamish, crossing the river Alne close to the Alnwick and Coldstream railway. Near Glanton, in a field called Deer Street,[2] where the old road was taken up at the beginning of the last century, a paving of large flagstones, 12 feet wide, was found under about 6 inches of soil.[3]

After a turn more towards the east, and crossing the Beamish river, a straight line continues on for eight miles to the river Till, near Fowberry Tower, and on to Horton, following the line of the railway as far as Wooperton Station; roads, lanes, and tracks indicating the course nearly all the way to the Till. This straight line of eight miles appears to point southwards to Glanton Pike. There are traces of the road on the north of the Till, and at Horton a lane takes up the line for five miles to Lowick, with parish boundaries along it for two miles. From Lowick the course can be traced pointing straight to Berwick Castle nine miles off. From the river Beamish to the Tweed, 22 miles, no part of the road is more than a quarter of a mile out of a

---

[1] Maclauchlan.

[2] Deer Street or Dere Street is an old name for Watling Street between Corbridge and Melrose. It appears in several places in the Black Book of Hexham (A.D. 1479) as a land boundary to the north of Corbridge, and it is mentioned as the western limit of the territory between the Wear and the Tyne given to St. Cuthbert. *Jour. Archæol. Ass.*, 1906, p. 205 (note).

[3] *Gent. Mag.*, 1825, part i. p. 40.

straight line. Maclauchlan considered that on nearing the Tweed the road turned to the north-east to a ford half-a-mile below Berwick Bridge. General Roy thought that it crossed the Tweed near West Ord, but he found no traces in Berwickshire, or beyond.[1] It probably went no further.

Warburton shows this road with considerable accuracy in his map of Northumberland (1716). He describes it in a note as 22 feet in breadth, and paved with stone. It is between 50 and 60 miles long, and no part of it is mentioned in the Itinerary of Antonine.

(22) *Chew Green to the Wall of Antonine.*—Beyond Chew Green the Roman road keeps on the crest of the Cheviot Hills for two miles, and then descends by the pass of Woden Law. It crosses the Kalewater at Towford, where there are remains of a camp, of which Roy gives a plan, about 583 yards by 366 yards, having in the south-east corner a camp of stronger profile, 330 yards by 166 yards. The road onwards is somewhat winding to keep on high ground; it is followed by a parish boundary for four miles to the south of Shibden Hill, and then it turns to the north-west, pointing to the Eildon Hills 14 miles distant. At Cappuch and Oxnam Water, two miles north of Shibden Hill, are the remains of a camp with clay ramparts and a double ditch on two sides. The road crosses the river Teviot near the confluence of the Jed, to which point it is again a parish boundary for three miles and a half. In about two miles the road appears again in the same line, bordered by trees for three miles, and followed by a parish boundary for a mile and a half, until the Ancrum road falls into it, and follows it for a mile and a half. On nearing the Eildon Hills it turns to the east of them, and remains were very distinct in 1803 [2] where the road crossed the Bowden burn near St. Boswells Station. It crossed the Tweed a mile and a quarter east of Melrose, where at Newstead the Roman station has lately been systematically explored. On the higher ground a quarter of a mile south of the Tweed, a camp 530 by 446 yards, enclosing about 49 acres, was found, and on the west of it the foundations of a later walled fort, 270 by 240 yards.[3] A causeway leading to the river was laid bare

---

[1] *Military Antiquities*, p. 103.   [2] Chalmer's *Caledonia.*
[3] For details of the excavations see *A Roman Frontier Fort*, by J. Curle.

about the year 1820, and the foundations of a bridge were described by Milne in 1743 as being very evident,[1] but there is no trace of it now.   After crossing the Tweed the course inclines to the west, and continues along the high ground between the Allan and Gala waters towards Soutra Hill. General Roy considered that the course then inclined more to the west, but he found no traces until the river Gore is crossed near Borthwick Castle.   He supposed that the South Esk was crossed at Dalhousie, and the North Esk near Mavis Bank, and that the road continued by Loanhead and under the east of the Pentland Hills, where there were vestiges a few years before 1790, and also traces on to Cramond on the Firth of Forth.   The Ordnance map shows the course of the Roman road on the north-east end of the Pentland Hills for more than a mile northwards from Lothianburn, four miles south of Edinburgh, followed by a parish boundary.   From Cramond the Roman road is supposed to have passed by Queensferry and Abercorn to Carriden at the east end of the Wall of Antonine.   Warburton, who rode over the road, found " the paving very entire and the stones large." [2]

From this point on the Forth, about seven miles west of Queensferry, the Wall of Antonine passed by Falkirk, and then on the south of the Bonie burn and the Kelvin river to Old Kilpatrick on the Clyde.   There are still remains of the wall, and at the end of the eighteenth century the military road behind it could be traced almost throughout the whole length.   It lay 40 or 50 yards to the south of the *Vallum.*   Sections of it made lately showed a base of fairly large stones, with a layer of smaller stones over it rising to a rounded crown in the middle.   The kerbs were not squared, and hardly distinguishable from the other stones of the base.   It is usually 16 to 18 feet wide, and at only one place did anything like a paved surface appear.[3]   Near Bar Hill a considerable length was uncovered.   The foundation there was of fairly large stones resting on a bed of wrought clay, and above was a convex layer of smaller stones.   The width was 17 feet.[4]

(23) *Camelon to the Tay.*—At Camelon, to the west of Falkirk, a Roman road runs northward from the Wall for

[1] Wilson, *Prehistoric Scotland,* vol. ii. p. 50.
[2] Letter to R. Gale, 1723.   [3] Antonine Wall Report, p. 114.
[4] *Roman Forts at Bar Hill,* p. 18.

about three-quarters of a mile to a double camp overlooking the river Carron. The ramparts of the northern rectangle enclose an area 177 yards by 163 yards, and those of the camp adjoining on the south, an area 180 yards from north to south and 203 to 228 yards from west to east. A Roman road continued on north-westward by Larbert, and it was formerly visible to the south of Torwood, and traces are shown on the Ordnance map on the west of the Stirling road from near Bannockburn House to St. Ninian's. It passed to the west of Stirling, by a Roman camp of which some remains exist, and by Craigforth Causeway, which a parish boundary follows, to the Forth, and on to Dunblane.[1]

The straight road running north-east to Greenloming is probably on the line of the Roman road, and perhaps so is the road to the north to Ardoch after crossing Allan Water. The fort and camps there are on the east bank of Knaick Water. A remarkable fort, about 320 yards by 230 yards to the outside of the ramparts, has six ramparts and five ditches on the south and east sides, and five ramparts on the north side; on the west, where it is protected by Knaick water, there is a single fosse. The inner area is about 160 yards by 140 yards. On the north is a kind of camp called by General Roy a *procestrium*, 353 yards by 300 yards, and beyond it is a large rectangular camp having a mean length from north to south of 933 yards and a mean breadth of 650 yards. The west side of this large camp is intersected by the rampart of another camp, 630 yards by 446 yards, lying about half within and half without the larger camp.[2]

The Roman road is plainly indicated along the east side, and excavation revealed the old road surface a few inches below the sod, of compacted gravel 26 feet wide. Further north it is traceable in uncultivated land, and opposite Kaims it was found to consist of a pavement of rough flags upon which was a layer of broken stone surfaced with gravel. A considerable portion of the road constructed in the same way had been removed. Kaims fort, about two miles north-east of Ardoch, is a rectangle much rounded at the corners, triple ditched, 66 yards by 60 yards outside, and

[1] Maitland's *History of Scotland*, vol. iii. p. 169.
[2] *Roy. Military Antiquities.*

28 by 27 yards from the crest of the inner rampart.[1] About three and a quarter miles farther north the road turns to the east, and in less than a quarter of a mile enters Strageath Camp, 160 yards by 140 yards, overlooking the river Earn.

The road, continuing eastward from the fort, crosses the river Earn to the north of Innerpeffray. For nearly two miles it is effaced by cultivation, and then it is traceable to where the Perth road takes the line of it. A quarter of a mile north-west of Gask House are the remains of a rectangular camp, 167 yards by 137 yards, and not far off the road was found to be of rough stones closely laid together, and 20 feet in width.[2] About two miles further on, near Dupplin, Pennant in 1770 found the road visible in many places, formed of great stones, and 24 feet broad. He also noticed[3] near Gask two small circular entrenchments about half a mile apart, and two others like them between Gask and Innerpeffray. These and other similar entrenchments along the road were examined in 1890.[4] Eight of them were found between Innerpeffray and Dupplin, two in the first five miles, one of which was entirely ploughed down, and six in the three miles on to Dupplin. Seven of them were circular, and all much alike, 80 to 108 feet in total diameter, comprising an inner area surrounded by a rampart and ditch. In the largest, 108 feet in outside diameter, the inner area is 44 feet in diameter, the rampart and ditch, the latter six feet deep, occupying a width of 30 feet. In the middle were four holes at the corners of a rectangle 11 feet by 9 feet, 18 inches in diameter and two feet deep, filled with dark-coloured earth with some charred wood. It is supposed that the holes held timber supports of watch towers, at intervals of from half a mile to nearly a mile. The most easterly entrenchment near Dupplin was oval, and larger than the circular ones, being 100 feet by 75 feet to the crest of the rampart, and enclosing 75 feet by 50 feet of level space. The resemblance of these small entrenchments to the Hügel of the German *Limes* is remarkable. Traces of the road beyond Dupplin appear now to be lost, but Maitland continues it over Tibbermuir and across the river Almond

---

[1] *Proc. Soc. Antiq. Scot* vol. 35, p. 18.   [2] *Ibid.*, vol. 32.
[3] *Tour in Scotland.*
[4] *Proc. Soc. Antiq. Scot.*, vol. 35, p. 16.

near its confluence with the Tay, two and a half miles above
Perth.   He describes the remains of a rectangular camp
situated at Bertha on the north of the Almond and the
west of the Tay, of which about 226 yards of the north
rampart and 150 yards of the south rampart on the
brow of the bank of the Almond still remained.   The
western and eastern ramparts he describes as having been
demolished by the plough and the river Tay.   He says that
the military way ran along the verge of the northern ditch,
an arable ridge called the Causeway ridge, " the pavement
whereof is still to be seen leading to the river Tay," across
which was a Roman bridge of which the remains could be
seen when the water is lowest.   He also says that a number
of Roman stones and bricks had been dug up.[1]   It can hardly
be doubted that Maitland before 1757 had seen these remains
of a camp.   They seem to show that there was here a fort
larger than those at Gask, Strageath, or Kaims, situated at
the upper end of the tidal estuary of the Tay, and so in communication with the sea, and reached by a road protected
by frontier posts at short intervals as well as by forts.   The
co-operation of the fleet with Agricola's army in his sixth
year's campaign [2] is thus recalled to mind.   Maitland continues a Roman road on the east of the Tay by Cambus
Michael and Couper to Battle Dykes, and other so-called
Agricola's camps in that direction, but evidence of any
Roman road north of Perth is very doubtful.   The Roman
origin of the most northern camp, near the sources of the
Ithan in the north of Aberdeenshire appears, however, to be
proved.[3]

The Itinerary of Antonine extends no further than to
Blatum Bulgium at Middlebie, and *Bremenium* at Riechester ;
the names of Roman stations more to the north than these
are all derived from the forged Itinerary of Richard of
Cirencester, in which there are Roman roads extending to
the Moray Firth.

[1] Maitland, *History of Scotland*, 1757, vol. i. p. 198.
[2] Tacitus, *Agricola*, c. 25.
[3] *Proc. Soc. Antiq.*, 1913–1914, p. 244.

CHAPTER VI

EAST ANGLIA, IKNILD STREET, AND AKEMAN STREET

(1) EAST ANGLIA. *General Course.*—In the greater part of this district the course of the Roman roads are very imperfectly known. The Roman road, from London to Colchester by Chelmsford, and that from Erming Street through Dunmow to Colchester, can be followed without difficulty, but north of that important Roman city there is an area in which few remains of Roman roads are known to exist, and where parish boundaries afford little help in tracing them, or in verifying the courses which have been suggested between supposed Roman stations. From Cambridge a road can be traced to within about 20 miles of Colchester, and then it is lost. Peddars Way is easily followed from the Norfolk coast near Hunstanton for 48 miles pointing to Colchester, and more doubtfully for

another 14 miles in the same direction, and then there is little trace for the remaining 17 miles to Colchester. The course of the Roman road from Caister St. Edmunds, near Norwich, to Colchester is uncertain for the 12 or 13 miles south of the river Gipping; and very little is known of the roads to the east, which must have communicated with the Roman station on the coast near Dunwich, the site of which has been destroyed by the sea. The same may be said of the communications with the Roman stations on the Norfolk coast, Burgh Castle, and Castor; and in fact from Peddars Way eastward the Roman roads of Norfolk are almost unknown.

A like uncertainty prevails with respect to the stations in this part of the country named in the Itinerary of Antonine. In Iter V. the localities of all the six stations between *Colonia* (Colchester) and *Lindum* (Lincoln) are undetermined, and the distance according to the Itinerary between those places is 204 M. P., while the actual distance is less than 140 miles by way of Cambridge and Godmanchester. In Iter IX. the distance between *Camolodunum* (Colchester) and *Venta Icinorum*, generally placed at Caister, three miles south of Norwich, is 75 M. P. compared with 55 miles by the direct road, and the localities of the three intermediate stations are unknown. There is thus a good deal of scope for conjecture in the placing of these nine stations; this has been freely exercised, and Roman roads, of which there is little or no evidence, have been supposed to connect the localities chosen for them and for other stations of more doubtful authenticity.

The rough map known as the *Tabula Peutingeriana* gives seven names in this part of England, of which six can without much doubt be identified with names in the Itinerary; and the stations marked *Baromaci*, *Caunonio*, and *Camuloduno* may be placed with some certainty at Chelmsford, Kelvedon and Colchester. The name not in the Itinerary, *Ad taum*, appears from the *Tabula* to be near the Suffolk coast, and from it, on a line drawn to *Ad Ansam* on the coast more to the south, are marked *Sinomagi* and *Convetoni*, supposed to be the same as *Sitomago* and *Combretonio* of Iter IX. Without throwing much light on their proper positions, the *Tabula Peutingeriana* gives no support to the sites often assigned to these stations.

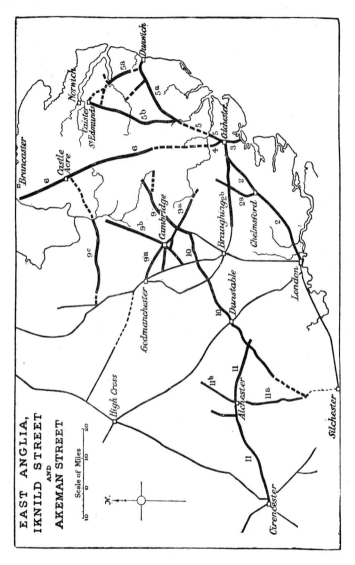

EAST ANGLIA,
IKNILD STREET
AND
AKEMAN STREET

Scale of Miles

N.

(2) *London to Colchester.*—The earlier Roman road to Colchester was probably a continuation of the line of Oxford Street by Old Street to Old Ford, where it crossed the river Lea. The course on from Oxford Street is more apparent on the older maps. Portpool Lane, in line with Old Street, is shown on Aggas' map (1580), and other maps of later date, extending westward from Charterhouse through open ground now occupied by Gray's Inn Gardens, Red Lion Square, etc., to the north of Oxford Street, and Old Street, extending eastward from Goswell Road to Finsbury Fields, and on as far as Shoreditch. Aggas' map shows no road east of Shoreditch, but a straight hedge or bank can be seen in the same line onwards, and the same appears on old maps of the parish of Shoreditch (1720–1755), extending to Bethnal Green. At the west end of Old Street two Roman road surfaces were found in 1867,[1] and in making the Middle Level sewer the Roman road was found 11 feet below the surface of Old Street Road, near Shoreditch.[2] A Roman burial in Camden Street on the south of Bethnal Green Road, and another in the same road near its junction with Cambridge Road, may be some indication that the Roman road was near. Green Street, an old green lane for which a footbridge was provided over the Regent's Canal at the beginning of the last century, is marked on Ogilby's map (1677) " Roman Road," and east of Three Colts Lane it is marked " Roman Walk." In the middle of the last century it was about nine feet wide, with ditches and banks on each side, and was then known locally as the Roman road, a name lately again extended to it from a street so named near Old Ford.

There can be little doubt that the river Lea was crossed at Old Ford, and the place seems to be at Iceland Wharf, to the south of the northern outfall sewer, where large lumps of herring-bone masonry such as would form part of a paved ford, were brought up in dredging undertaken by the Lea Conservancy some years ago.[3] Old Ford continued to be the Roman crossing-place over the Lea, after the traffic had been diverted through *Londinium.* The causeway of gravel 16 feet wide supported by walls seven feet six

[1] *Jour. Soc. Art.*, Dec. 16, 1910.
[2] *London and Middx. Arch Soc. Trans.*, vol. iii. p. 563.
[3] *Proc. Soc. Antiq.*, 1910, vol. xxiii. p. 230.

inches high outside the earlier city pointing towards Aldgate
has been already mentioned (p. 58), and in the same line
Aldgate Street, High Street Whitechapel, and part of Whitechapel Road, point direct to Old Ford. It is probable that
the Roman road was cut through in constructing the railway
beneath Whitechapel High Street. Five road surfaces were
met with, the lowest one of large flints set close together and
very difficult to break through. Unfortunately, no parti-
cular attention was attracted to it. Where the two lines of
road, from Old Street and from Aldgate, come together near
Old Ford, many Roman interments have been found, which
may have been near either or both roads. Old Ford continued to be the crossing-place over the Lea until the building
of Bow Bridge by Matilda, Queen of Henry I. It is stated
by Daniel Defoe in 1772 that there had been lately
found the remains of a stone causeway across the marsh
between Old Ford and a place called the Wick.[1] After crossing the river Lea at Old Ford, the road continued through
Stratford and Great Ilford, and by Chadwell Street to
Chadwell Heath (70'), where there is a change of direction
towards Romford and the high ground (325') above Warley.
At Romford the present road curves round to the south,
and is not straight until at Haroldwood Hall (105'), two
miles from Romford, a straight road on the line of the
Roman road begins, and with a parish boundary along it for
two miles, runs for four miles through Brook Street to the
west side of Brentwood (300'). The modern road through
Brentwood, and on to Mountnessing, is somewhat winding;
but there a straight road begins pointing back to the high
ground at Brentwood (300'), and continues for two and a
half miles through Ingatestone. A winding road then
begins, which a parish boundary follows for a mile down
the hill to Margaretting, and again for half-a-mile by
Hylands. The course of the Roman road through Chelmsford was probably along Moulsham Street and Springfield
Road, crossing the river at Old Bridge.

There is some reason for thinking that the Roman station
Cæsaromagus was near Widford on the south-west of
Chelmsford.

(a) *Chelmsford to the North.*—A Roman road turned
off to the north at Chelmsford, the course being along New

[1] *Tour through the Eastern Counties in* 1772.

Street and Bishop's Hall Road, and then along a footway
which a parish boundary follows for a mile.   The present
road then continues in the same straight line through
Broomfield to Little Waltham, where there is a turn towards
the north-east and the road runs straight, except where
streams are crossed, for four miles to high ground (240')
near Chatley, parish boundaries following it for a mile and
a half, and for a quarter of a mile.   The straight road,
almost in the same line, continues on for eight miles, crossing Stane Street at Braintree, to Gosfield, with parish boundaries along it here and there.   There is no trace of the
road further; it perhaps joined a road from Colchester by
Haverhill to Cambridge.   In 1790 [1] two pieces of the ridge
of the latter road were very visible on the west of Ridgewell,
eight miles north-west of Gosfield, and remains extended
further in that direction; and from Streetley, four miles
west-north-west of Haverhill and nine miles from Ridgewell, it can be followed on to Cambridge.   This road will be
reverted to (p. 193).

(b) Stane Street, which is crossed by the road from
Chelmsford to Gosfield, branches eastwards from Erming
Street near Braughing, and has already been noticed as far
as Bishops Stortford (p. 115), to the east of which it continues for eight miles, with county and parish boundaries
along it, to Dunmow.   After crossing the valley of the
Chelmer, a straight road begins, which in two and a half
miles is succeeded by another straight road almost in the
same line for a mile and a half, parish boundaries following
both.   The road then winds, but parish boundaries follow
it continuously for seven and a half miles through Braintree,
on the east of which the ridge formerly appeared for a
quarter of a mile or more,[2] to Bay Tree Farm.   A piece of
straight road then succeeds, two and a half miles long, and
another length of straight road continues through Cogges-
hall to Marks Tey, where it joins the Roman road from
London to Colchester.

On the north-east of Chelmsford the present Colchester
road probably occupies the site of the Roman road through
Hatfield Peverel and Witham, passing close to the east of
Kelvedon, and on to Marks Tey, where Stane Street joins.

[1] *Archæologia*, vol. xiv. p. 62.
[2] *Gent. Mag.*, 1864, pt. i. p. 357.

The course continues along the present road to beyond
Stanway Bridge, from which it has been traced on by Dr.
Laver.[1] It turns away from the modern road towards the
south end of Lexden Heath, following a thick hedge-bank
for some distance, and then goes across the fields, where
under 15 inches of soil remains of the road were found about
14 yards wide, consisting of about one foot of stones mixed
with chalk or lime, and rammed.   The original surface
soil beneath had been removed.   With a turn northward
the road, of which remains were found in several places, ran
straight to the the Balkern gate of Colchester, crossing the
present London road on the west of the hospital.

There is a complication of roads and earthworks near
Lexden Heath which led Sir Richard Colt Hoare and the
Rev. H. Jenkins to suppose that it was the site of *Camolodunum*, the British capital, while Colchester two miles to
the east was *Colonia*, the Roman city.

The area enclosed by the Roman walls of Colchester,
of which a good deal remain, is about 1000 yards from west
to east, and 530 yards from north to south, the Balkern
gate being near the middle of the west face.

(3) *Colchester to the South.*—The course of the road from
Colchester to the south, as described by Dr. Laver, agrees
with that shown on Mr. Jenkins' map.[2] It leaves by St.
Botolph's Gate, from which a parish boundary follows the
street alongside St. John's Abbey wall, and continues on in
the same direction.   The ridge is visible in the fields towards
Monk Wike, the stackyard of which is on the line of the
road.   Further on, the ridge is two or three feet high, in
line with the raised road on the east of Berechurch Hall,
and along it is a right of way to the Roman river.   There
are traces in the road near Abberton Church, which is on the
line of the road, and then the course is lost; but Dr. Laver
conjectures that it went on by Peet Tye to the Strood, a
causeway supposed to be of Roman origin, leading to Mersea.

By others it is thought that a road went south from
Head Gate, by Head Street and Butt Road, alongside which
on the west side there was a Roman cemetery.   Parish
boundaries give support to this view, following Head Street
and Butt Road, and continuing south across the fields for

[1] *Trans. Essex Soc. Arch.*, N.S., vol. iii. p. 123.
[2] *Archæologia*, vol. xxix.

a quarter of a mile at the south of the Cavalry Barracks. The line is taken up by the road on the west of Berechurch Hall, and is continued by a parish boundary for one and a quarter miles from Roman river to Layer Brook.

The *Tabula Peutingeriana* seems to show that *Ad Ansam*, mentioned in Iter IX. of Antonine, was on the coast in this direction. *Ansa* appears to have the meaning preserved in the Italian *Ansa*, and the French *Anse*, namely a shallow bay such as may very likely have existed in Roman times near the mouths of the rivers Colne and Blackwater on the west and north of Mersea, where Roman remains have been found. It must be admitted that placing *Ad Ansam* here does not help to explain Iter IX.

(4) *Colchester to the North.*—The road from Colchester to the north, according to Dr. Laver, did not follow the course of North Street, because the remains of a villa were found in the middle of that street. A parish boundary however follows the street northwards from the river for three-eighths of a mile to beyond the railway-station, and then follows the Bures Road. A road in continuation of North Street runs due north through Mile End, beyond which it is said that the *agger* formed a conspicuous object for three miles before Horkesley Heath was enclosed;[1] and the road, bearing the name of Horkesley Causeway, goes on straight to Nayland. Dr. Laver traces the road northwards from Rye Gate, Colchester, across the river at Middle Mill Ford and so to Mile End. Beyond Nayland there was perhaps a road communicating with Peddars Way through Woolpit, but no traces of it appear for 13 miles, beyond which to the north of Hitcham there are indications of a road due north.

(5) *Colchester to the North-east.*—The Roman road from Colchester to the north-east appears to have left by the East Gate, turning off after crossing the Colne and following the course of the present Ipswich road to Stratford St. Mary. The road, although not in a straight line, is followed by parish boundaries for more than half the distance, and for upwards of three miles continuously to the river Stour just above Stratford Bridge. The parish boundary runs straight on to the river where the present road turns to the east to the bridge, and on the north side of the river the course of the Roman road lies to the west of the present road.

[1] Jenkins, *Journal Arch. Assoc.*, vol. xix. p. 275.

From Stratford St. Mary a Roman road is supposed to have gone north to Hadleigh, and on to Woolpit, but there is no evidence of it on the map, except the name Stone Street north of Hadleigh, until the indications already referred to of a Roman road due north from Hitcham are reached.

To the north-east from Stratford St. Mary a parish boundary follows the present Ipswich road for a mile on the north of Capel St. Mary, and except that there is no trace by parish boundaries or otherwise for 12 miles. Then on the north-east of the river Gipping and on the west of the road, seven miles from Ipswich, there was found in 1823 a solid structure of stone and gravel, six or seven yards wide, which was traced through a meadow called Sharnford to a former ford across the Gipping, on the south of which was Causeway meadow. It pointed towards Great Blakenham Church.[1] Onwards there are indications of Roman roads in two directions, to the north-east and to the north.

(a) That to the north-east seems to be represented by a parish boundary in Shrubland Park, and by a highway between Coddenham and Pettaugh, which is straight for three miles, and then, when the road is no longer straight, it is followed for a mile by a parish boundary. The present road continues on for four and a half miles in a straight line, except where the river is crossed at Earl Soham, and there is half-a-mile of parish boundary along it near Creting-ham Lodge. At Saxtead Green the present road turns off to Framlingham, but in two miles the same straight line as before is resumed by a lane with a parish boundary along it for five-eighths of a mile, and one and a quarter miles further on the present road takes up the same straight line for two miles. A portion, presumably of this road, is described by Suckling[2] as existing in an extremely perfect state just to the north-west of the abbey grounds at Sibton, about two miles further on. The road is supposed to have led to the Roman station on the coast near Dunwich, from which a road is supposed to have gone to the north-west and to have crossed the Waveney near Harleston. This may be represented by highways in a straight line from Peasenhall by Ubbeston and Cratfield to Weybread.

[1] *Gent. Mag.*, 1824, pt. i. p. 261; 1825, pt. i. p. 291.
[2] *History of Suffolk*, 1848, p. xviii.

A Roman road is said to have been distinctly traced from the heaths which surround Dunwich to Bury St. Edmunds.[1] According to Gardner [2] it went to Wenhaston and Blythford Bridge, where it parted, one branch going to Bungay, and the other to Bury St. Edmunds, called the King's Road or the King's Highway; and he mentions a grant in the ninth year of Henry VII. of land near Bramfield, abutting northwards on the King's Highway leading from Dunwich to Bury St. Edmunds. There appears to be now no trace of it, and the maps afford no clue.

There is little trace of a road northward towards Bungay for some miles, but north of Halesworth a straight length of road called Stone Street begins, and is followed by a parish boundary for a mile. The straight road continues for three miles, a parish boundary again following it for a quarter of a mile, and then there is a slight turn. About two and a half miles farther on the present road turns off to the north-west to Bungay, but the course of the Roman road appears to be straight on along the line of a parish boundary which runs in a direct line for a mile and three-quarters from near Mettingham Castle across the Waveney to Ditchingham railway-station. The parish boundary then turns to the north-east over Broome Heath, and there is a bit of parish boundary beyond, but the Roman road is supposed to have continued on north-westward by Hedenham, Brooke, and Poringland, to Caister, with a branch from Woodton to Tasburgh.[3] The crest of the road was formerly clearly visible over Ditchingham Common.

Burgh Castle, the Roman fortress on the east of the marshes near the confluence of the Waveney and the Yare, seven miles further north, was probably approached from the east end of Oulton Broad, and by Flixton, and along the road followed by a parish boundary to Hopton, and on by Jew's Way. The Roman walls of Burgh Castle still remain on three sides, about nine feet thick, enclosing an area about 230 yards by 108 yards, on the edge of a low cliff.

(b) The course of the Roman road northward from the river Gipping towards Caister St. Edmunds appears to be

[1] *History of Suffolk*, vol. ii. p. 230.
[2] *History of Dunwich*, etc., 1754, p. 38.
[3] *Norfolk and Norwich Arch. Soc.*, vol. vi. p. 153.

followed by the present road, which runs in nearly a straight line for 10 miles, with parish boundaries along it near Stonham, and again for two and a half miles from Waltham Hall to Brockford Street. At Stoke Ash it curves towards the north-east, parish boundaries following it near Thornham, through Yaxley, near Goswold Hall, for a mile and a quarter on the south of the Waveney river at Scole Lodge, for a mile near Tivetshall, and for two and a quarter miles between that and Long Stratton. The road, called Pye Street on old maps, is in straight lengths from Yaxley as far as Upper Tasburgh, where there are remains of a rectangular camp, and where on no good authority *Ad taum* has been placed, a station of the *Tabula Peutingeriana*, but which would seem from it to have been near the coast. The present road crosses to the west side of the river Tas at Saxlingham Thorpe, and then points straight for two miles to the Roman fort at Caister St. Edmunds, with a parish boundary along it for a quarter of a mile. The road then turns off, and straight on, one and a half miles further north, on the east bank of the river Tas, and not much above it, is the fort, a rectangle about 450 yards by 370 yards, with ruins of the walls remaining. It is generally supposed to mark the site of *Venta Icinorum*, though it is but 55 miles from Colchester by the road which has been now followed, compared with the Itinerary distance of 75 M. P.

(6) *Peddars Way.*—The indications of a Roman road from the direction of Colchester towards Woolpit have been referred to as appearing on the north of Hitcham ; and it has been mentioned (p. 185) that of a supposed road from Stratford St. Mary by Hadleigh to Woolpit there is little evidence until the same indications of a Roman road are reached. On the north of Hitcham, about 16 miles from Colchester, the present road turns towards Stowmarket, and Hitcham Street continues on, and then a lane pointing due north is followed for three-quarters of a mile by a parish boundary, which runs on across country for a mile to a highway, and follows it for a mile to Pay Street Green. At Clopton Green, a mile and a quarter further north, a lane takes up the same line for a mile, to within a mile of Woolpit, which has been supposed to be the site of a Roman station. About four miles north of Woolpit in the same direction is Stowlangtoft, where Roman remains have been found, and three miles

further is Stanton, on the west of which the most southerly
trace of Peddars Way is shown on the old Ordnance map.
This remarkable road can be traced hence for 45 miles
to the north coast of Norfolk.   It has been called British,
but it has all the characteristics of Roman laying out,
and is indeed the best preserved Roman road in East
Anglia.

The old Ordnance map shows Peddars Way crossing
the road from Honington to Barningham, one mile west of
the latter place, and passing by Street Farm on the west
of Coney Weston to the Little Ouse.   It was formerly
plain on Barningham Common, and on Knittishall
Common to the south of the river.   A parish boundary
continues in the same straight line for three miles to Brettenham Heath, crossing the river Thet four miles east of
Thetford.   Over Brettenham Heath Peddars Way appears
as a green track through the ferns and gorse, five or six
yards wide, and raised one or two feet above the adjoining
ground.   Wheel-ruts cut through the turf, but go no
deeper, and the ferns on each side seem to mark out the
width of the Roman gravel coating.   On Roudham Heath,
north of the Norwich railway, the ridge continues plain,
worn narrower by the present cart-track, which is generally
on one side or other of the ridge.   A mile further, where the
Swaffham railway approaches it, a line of old firs growing on
the ridge renders it conspicuous, and further on the Way
becomes a lane alongside the railway, which crosses it a
little south of Wretham Station.   It continues on in the
same direction, with a parish boundary along it, to Galley
Hill, Hockham Heath (156'), where there is a turn, and then,
except for the five miles to be presently referred to, the
remaining 33 miles of the course of the Way, wherever it
can be traced, is almost absolutely straight.   A lane and a
parish boundary mark its course for nearly three miles to
the Thetford and Watton road, and there is a parish boundary onwards in the same line for a mile through Merton
Park, on the south of which it was described in 1788 as
being high-crested and very visible.   The straight line is then
lost, and a crooked lane to the west of it, with a parish
boundary along it for two and a half miles, is called Peddars
Way, and no other trace appears for five miles.   Hereabouts
a road may have turned off communicating with Caister

St. Edmunds, of which there are said to be traces near Saham, two miles from Peddars Way, and at Hethersett,[1] five miles from Caister, which is 22 miles from Peddars Way. Near North Pickenham the straight line lost near Merton is resumed, and a green lane, and then a narrow metalled road between hedges, and towards the Swaffham and Dereham railway a green road 10 to 15 yards wide, takes up the straight line of Peddars Way, with parish boundaries all along. There is no trace through arable land on the north of the railway, but through the meadows south of Palgrave Hall the track is plain, the ridge and its foundation having been removed for the sake of the gravel, leaving a shallow hollow. It is traceable on the north of Palgrave Hall, and then for two miles to Castle Acre no trace appears. The line appears to be straight for the entrance on the south face of the Roman camp, a rectangle 300 yards by 170 yards, on the west of the Norman earthworks. The road which leaves Castle Acre, apparently from the north-east corner of the Roman camp, in the course of Peddars Way, is in the same line, showing apparently that the site of the Roman camp, which was the beginning of the vast earthworks afterwards thrown up, was determined by the course of Peddars Way.

On the north of Castle Acre Peddars Way is now a metalled road 20 feet between the fences, but in a mile or two it becomes a green lane, and then a cart-way along-side the fence of arable fields; and further on it is wide between the fences, but overgrown with gorse, leaving but a narrow track in the middle. Near Little Massingham the ridge is apparent for a short distance. From Massingham Heath the course continues straight for eight and a half miles, parish boundaries following it for the last six miles to beyond Fring. It is generally a green road overgrown with gorse in places, with the ridge remaining plain here and there, more particularly to the west of Houghton and on towards Fring. Lanes, footways, and parish boundaries continue the line on to Ringstead and, with a slight turn towards the east, to the shore of the Wash at Holme-next-Sea, two miles north-east of Hunstanton, and four miles west of Brancaster, where there are remains of a Roman walled fort, which appears to have been a square of about

[1] *Archæologia*, vol. xxiii. p. 369.

190 yards with rounded corners, and where *Branodunum* of the *Notitia* has been placed. In 1600 the walls, 11 feet thick, remained 12 feet above the ground.

Peddars Way has been said to pass through neither town nor village, and it is true that from Ringstead southwards as far as it can be traced, about 45 miles, Castle Acre is the only village upon it, and those near it are but small. In this respect it resembles the Foss Way.

(7) Iter V. and Iter IX. of Antonine both pass through East Anglia, the first from London through Colchester and Lincoln to Carlisle, and the second from *Venta Icinorum* to London. *Colonia* in Iter V., and *Camolodunum* in Iter IX., both represent Colchester, the distance of which from London is 51 miles compared with 52 M. P. in each Iter. *Cæsaromagus* becomes Chelmsford by distance from London and from Colchester, and *Canonium* by distance becomes Kelvedon. *Durolitum*, 16 M. P. from *Cæsaromagus* and 15 M. P. from London, must according to distances be placed near Romford. Gale, to bring *Durolitum*, to the river Lea, altered the numerals of the Iter to 26 M. P. and 5 M. P.

Beyond Colchester the course of Iter V. as far as Lincoln is obscure, there being no station on it fixed with any certainty, and the distances in the Itinerary between *Colonia* and *Lindum* amount to 204 M. P., while a direct route by Cambridge and Godmanchester would not exceed 140 miles. The Itinerary distances from London to Colchester agree with the mileage, and for that part of the Iter from Lincoln to Carlisle the total distance and the distances apart of the nine intermediate stations between *Lindum* and *Luguvalium* all agree with the actual mileage. The total distance prefixed to the Iter also agrees with the sum of the intermediate distances, and the obscurity between Colchester and Lincoln must be attributed to ignorance of the course of the Iter between those places.

The course of Iter IX. is also obscure beyond Colchester. By the direct road through Stratford St. Mary to Caister St. Edmunds the distance is 55 miles, compared with 75 M. P. between *Camolodunum* and *Venta Icinorum*, and it is quite uncertain where the intermediate stations mentioned in the Itinerary were.

(8) IKNILD STREET. *General Course.*—It has already been said that roads bearing the name of Iknild Street or

Way under various forms extend from the borders of Norfolk into Dorset, and as far as North Wilts there is a continuous line or lines of roads so designated. From its first appearance for some 10 miles, there is little trace of the Roman manner of setting out the course in straight lines, and then that manner of setting out is evident for 16 miles, and traces of the ridge appear in the modern road which now follows its course. From Worstead Lodge the road is straight for five and a half miles nearly to the Roman camp at Chesterford, and points straight to Strethall, two miles south of Chesterford camp. At Stump Cross, half-a-mile from the camp, Iknild Street turns off from the straight road at an angle of 50°, and passing through Ickleton goes on to Royston and Baldock in a winding course not at all suggestive of Roman laying out, while from Strethall, indications of a Roman road are plain in one straight line for seven miles in the direction of the station near Braughing on Erming Street (p. 116).

Iknild Street continues on beyond Baldock without any characteristics of a Roman road, by Wilbury Hill north of Hitchin (where perhaps Ashwell Street, which branched off at Worstead Lodge, rejoins), passing through Dunstable to Beacon Hill near Ivinghoe, where it again divides, the principal branch continuing on through Wendover and along the flank of the Chiltern Hills under the name of Ickleton Road, crossing the Thames near Streatley, and going on along the edge of the chalk escarpment overlooking the vale of White Horse, where it now bears the name of Ickleton Street, and the Ridgeway.

It is to be remarked that after it leaves the straight Newmarket road at Stump Cross, Iknild Street through Hertfordshire, Bedfordshire, Bucks, Oxfordshire, Berkshire, and Wiltshire bears but little likeness to a Roman road, either in the laying out of the course or in construction. Dr. Guest considered it to be a British track; he observes [1] that there are no ancient towns on its course, Royston and Dunstable, where Erming Street and Watling Street are crossed, dating from the twelfth century, and that there are no Roman remains on it, but British in abundance. Whatever may be the age of Royston, distances however prove that Dunstable represents the station *Durocobrivæ*, on

[1] *Archæological Journal*, vol. xiv. p. 99.

Watling Street.   Dr. Plot observed,[1] in 1705, that Iknild
Street was "not cast up in a ridge bank or laid out by a deep
trench."   Bishop Bennet, who described a large part of its
course early in the last century, observed the absence of
straightness, and that it did not appear to have been ever
paved or raised, and he endorsed the opinion that it was a
British trackway.   Where it has not been modernized it still
remains a grass road or track, winding along the flanks of
the chalk hills for most of its course, quite unlike a Roman
road except between Newmarket and Chesterford, where
it seems to have been reconstructed after the Roman
manner; and for this 16 miles Iknild Street constitutes part
of a Roman road from Erming Street near Braughing to
Newmarket (p. 116).

Iknild Street, although it generally has little claim to
be considered Roman, is connected with several Roman
roads besides those which have been referred to.   One
which comes from the direction of Colchester crosses it at
Worstead Lodge and leads on to Cambridge, and from
Cambridge other Roman roads radiate to the north-east,
the west, and the south-west.

(9) *Lackford to Worstead Lodge.*—The first certain traces
of Iknild Way appear near Lackford, about 10 miles west
of the most southern trace of Peddars Way, and 32 miles
from Caister St. Edmunds, the supposed *Venta Icinorum,*
but, according to Professor Babington, in 1882 it could
be traced from near Thetford.   A broad green lane bearing
the name leads from Lackford to near Kentford, where it
joins the road from Bury St. Edmunds to Newmarket.
The latter road is followed by parish boundaries for more
than half the distance from Kentford to Bury, and may
represent a Roman road to the latter town, where Roman
remains have been found.   The county boundary runs
along the road from Kentford to the north of Bury Hill,
on the east of Newmarket, and after turning off to enclose
an almost detached piece of Suffolk, continues on from Bury
Hill in the same direction, passing through Newmarket,
and along the London road nearly to Devil's Ditch.   A
deed, temp. Hen. III., mentions Iknild Way through
Newmarket, and for six miles the course seems to be indicated by the county boundary.   The present road con-

[1] *Natural History of Oxfordshire.* p. 323.

tinues on in the same line for three miles farther, and then leaves it, rejoining it in four miles at Fleam Dyke, where a straight road with a parish boundary along it runs for two miles to Worstead Lodge.

(a) *Haverhill to Cambridge and Godmanchester.*—At Worstead Lodge Iknild Way is crossed by a Roman road, the *Via Devana* of Dr. Mason already mentioned, which, coming from the south, now first appears near Haverhill, though it was formerly traceable five miles further in the direction of Colchester. Near Horseheath a section was made in 1909. At the bottom was rammed chalk, clay, and gravel, above that a layer of large flints and stones, then one foot six inches of packed earth with small flints and stones, and then another layer of large flints and boulder stones. The roadway was 12 feet wide, with a ditch three feet deep and four feet wide, in which coins, glass, Roman pottery and oyster shells were found.[1] From Streetley by Mark's Grave to Worstead Lodge it is a green lane with a ridge along the middle, and it continues on in a straight line for three miles to a point on the north-west of Gogmagog Hill (230′), three miles south-east of Cambridge, the ridge being prominent all the way. Near Worstead Lodge it is six yards wide, and quite five feet high; further on in lower ground it is not so marked, but on Gogmagog Hill it is six yards wide and four and five feet high, topped with pebble gravel. Where the green lane turns to the north to join the Fulbourne Road, the ridge can be traced straight on through arable land to the road at the top of the hill leading down to Red Cross. A parish boundary follows the ridge to this road, which is called Wort's Causeway, and continues along it down the hill to Red Cross. There is a turn of about 30° at the top of the hill, and the road points to Grantchester, to which a Roman road continued straight on. The course is described by Bishop Bennet.[2] From Red Cross it descended into the fen and disappeared, but as the ground rises the road appeared in the old line going just north of Trumpington, where in 1882 it was still to be traced as a raised bank.[3] It followed an old lane down into Trumpington Fen nearly opposite Grant-

---

[1] *Proc. Camb. Ant. Soc.*, Jan. 1910, p. 162.
[2] Lysons' *Cambridgeshire*, 1808, p. 45.
[3] Babington, *Ancient Cambridgeshire*, p. 26.

chester Church, and was found again on the west of the fen
in the same course in an old lane which passes through
Grantchester, where a rectangular camp (about 127 yards
by 75 yards) adjoins the road. It followed a road on to
Barton, where it fell into the Roman road leading from
Cambridge to Erming Street.

At Red Cross the parish boundary which follows Worts
Causeway down the hill turns 45° to the north-west along
the road to Cambridge. It may be that the turn to the
west at the top of the hill towards Red Cross, and thence
back again to the north-west, had no other object than to
keep the road on the higher ground between Cherry Hinton
and Trumpington Fen, but it is suggestive of a road across
the Cam to Grantchester in the first place, before the station
on the north of Cambridge was established. Towards
Cambridge the Roman road has been traced on the west
of the Hills Road in the grounds of Homerton College, and
the ridge was well marked through Perse School playing
fields in 1910, when a section was exposed, showing (1) nine
inches of chalk; (2) two feet three inches of gravelly earth,
and (3) chalk again, the upper surface having been removed.
The road was 12 to 15 feet wide, with ditches at the sides.[1]
Further on, Regent Street and other streets seem to be
approximately on the line. In 1823, in making a sewer in
Bridge Street, the pile-work of what was supposed to be a
Roman causeway was found between the church of the
Holy Sepulchre and Great Bridge. It consisted of wooden
piles upon which rested squared beams, 14 feet below the
surface of the road. The causeway was again seen in 1894
during the construction of a sewer. In a shaft sunk to
the south of St. Clement's Church, the Rev. E. G. Wood
observed a platform of logs laid transversely with gravel
between them, at a depth of about 14 feet below the street
surface, and about eight feet wide. In another shaft to
the north of the church similar remains are said to have
been met with at the same depth. The level of the causeway as given by Babington in 1823 is thus confirmed.
From levels obligingly furnished by the Rev. E. G. Wood,
it appears to have been rather more than a foot above the
natural water-level in the river before it was raised by the
construction of the lock below Cambridge. The causeway

[1] *Proceedings of the Cambridge Antiq. Soc.,* vol. xiv. p. 166.

probably led to a ford, and appears to have been in construction like those found at Strood, Lincoln, and Littleborough.

On the north of the Cam a good deal of three sides of the Roman station may still be traced. Within it is Castle Hill, a mound of considerable height, probably of British origin, to which several Roman roads converge. That from Erming Street, passing through Barton, could be easily followed in Bishop Bennet's time in the fields at the back of the colleges until it fell into the road from Cambridge to Barton. Soon leaving this, it passed through Barton churchyard, and following a green lane, rejoined the road again near Lord's Bridge. The ridge was to be seen beyond in 1808, and on by Orwell to Erming Street. The road was cut through near Barton, and plans were made, in 1908, by the Cambridge Antiquarian Society.[1] It is 12 feet wide, with side ditches four feet wide and three feet deep. Under one foot six inches of soil, etc., was found one foot six inches of earth, sand and chalk, then a layer of cobble stones, and then two feet six inches of chalk and gravel on the gravel subsoil. The road surface, of boulder and flints, had been removed to make up a new road.

The Roman road to Cambridge from Godmanchester points straight to Castle Hill for four and a half miles from near Lolworth Hedges, where there is a very slight change of direction to Fen Stanton, but for 10 miles there is hardly any deviation from a straight line. At Fen Stanton there is a turn more to the west, and the road then makes straight to Godmanchester on Erming Street. Parish boundaries follow the road for nearly all the way from Cambridge, and the ridge remained in places in Stukeley's time. Two milliaries from this road are now in the Fitzwilliam Museum, apparently dating from A.D. 305 to 353.

The continuation of the Roman road from Cambridge in the same straight line to Erming Street, across a field on the east of Godmanchester, where the modern road bends to the south, has been found by the Rev. F. G. Walker. A section revealed on a subsoil of gravel and clay, (1) six inches of gravel and clay; (2) a concrete of stones two to four inches in diameter, one foot thick; (3) six to nine inches of rammed sand and gravel, the top of which was two feet below the

[1] *Proc.*, vol. xiv. p. 159.

present surface. The road was 12 feet wide with ditches at the sides extending to the subsoil.[1]

(b) *Cambridge to Ely and Denver.*—Another road can be seen from Castle Hill radiating in the direction of Ely. It could be traced over the open fields in 1882 to a camp at King's Hedges, two miles from Cambridge (738 yards by 295 yards), the longer side bounded by the Roman road.[2] A country lane, raised in some parts, called the Mereway, then takes up the line to Landbeach, beyond which, near the Ely road, the crest was plainly to be seen in the beginning of the last century, and it could lately be faintly traced. The Ely road follows it for two miles to Chittering, the same straight line having been preserved for seven and a half miles from Cambridge, and then there is a slight turn, perhaps to an easy crossing of the river Ouse, a parish boundary following the road. On the north of Chittering the Roman road was found in 1910, about 15 feet wide, of gravel with ditches on each side.[3] The road is supposed to have gone through Stretham, by Bedwell Hay Farm to Ely, where it was found in 1905 at a depth of eight feet, and on through Littleport to Coldharbour Farm, where Bishop Bennet says it was visible in 1808, and then with a turn across the Little Ouse to Southery, and northwards to Denver.

(c) *The Fen Road.*—From Denver westward went the Roman Fen road which was described by Dugdale[4] as " that long causey made of gravel of about three feet in thickness, and 60 feet broad (now covered with the moor in some places three and in others five feet thick), which extendeth itself from Denver (near Salter's Lode) over the great Wash to Charke; thence to March, Plantwater, and Eldernell, and so to Peterborough, in length about 24 miles." In 1853 this road was traceable across a ploughed field on the west of Denver, and it was cut through in 1850 about a mile from Salter's Lode Sluice, near Denver; it was of gravel set very hard and upwards of three feet thick, very much barrelled, and the middle about three feet below the present surface.[5] The course can be traced across the fens

[1] *Proc. Camb. Antiq. Soc.*, 1910, p. 164.
[2] Babington's *Ancient Cambridgeshire*, p. 14.
[3] *Proc. Camb. Arch. Soc.*, vol. xiv. p. 155.
[4] *History of Imbanking and Draining*, 1772, p. 174.
[5] *Norfolk and Norwich Archæological Society*, vol. iii. p. 425.

to the north of March and Westrey, and then again across
the fens for four miles to Eldernell. It was plainly visible
30 or 40 years ago as a causeway three feet above the fen
between March and Eldernell, and on the north of the road
towards Whittlesey it was one or two feet above the surface
of the land, and very hard, but the gravel ridge has since
been removed. The line appears to be continued by a
straight road for two and a half miles on the west of
Whittlesey, pointing to Peterborough. According to
Bishop Bennet it had been traced through Milton Park to
Castor. The length through the fens of this remarkable
road is 11 miles between Denver and March, four miles
between March and Eldernell, and one and a half miles
between Whittlesey and Horsey. The purpose no doubt
was to afford a direct communication between East Anglia
and Erming Street and the west and north; and the shortest
course from Downham Market (100'), jutting like a promontory into the fens, to Peterborough was skilfully chosen.
It must be remembered that the fens were embanked by
the Romans far to the north of this road, as the Roman
bank on the north of Holbeach testifies. A careful examination appears to have shown that the causeway was
carried over a very considerable thickness of peat on boughs
and branches of trees.[1]

The course of the Fen road eastward is doubtful; some
traces of it to the north-east of Denver were seen in 1853.[2]
It may have joined Peddars Way south of Castle Acre,
where from Bartholomew Hills a lane passing over Swaffham
Heath with a parish boundary along it for two and a half
miles leads to the Downham Market road, pointing in the
direction of Denver 12 miles distant.

(10) *Worstead Lodge to Chesterford, Dunstable, etc.*—
Returning to Iknild Street; at Worstead Lodge one of those
branchings characteristic of Iknild Way there begins. The
London road, following one course, turns 27° towards the
south, but a lane continues on in the same direction as before
to Babraham, and the same general line is taken up in a
few miles by a lane through Thriplow and Foulmire, and
by Ashwell Street to Stotfold, two miles north-west of
Baldock, keeping parallel to, and two or three miles distant

---

[1] Marshall, *Cambridge Antiquarian Communications*, **iv.** 205.
[2] Babington, p. 68.

from, the more usually recognized Iknild Way for 21 miles and rejoining it, perhaps, at Wilbury Hill, where there is a camp.

The London road runs straight on for five and a half miles towards Chesterford, pointing to high ground (400′) near Strethall, three miles further on.   It is a wide road 20 yards between the fences, with evidence of the ridge of the Roman road, which is very apparent south-west of Pampisford Station, where it is some three feet high with the slopes inside the fences, which are 25 yards apart.   For one and a half miles to Stump Cross the county boundary follows the road and then turns off at about an angle of 45° along a green road to Ickleton Ford, while the road continues on for a quarter of a mile in the same line.   The county boundary probably shows the line of Iknild Way, and the road straight on led to the great Roman fort at Chesterford, described and measured by Stukeley in 1719,[1] when the foundations of the walls were apparent all round, forming a rectangle 555 yards by 333 yards, with rounded corners.   There are now no remains visible above ground.

From Chesterford a Roman road led in a south-westerly direction by Strethall to Erming Street.   The course of it from Erming Street, near Braughing, has already been described (p. 116).   It is almost in the same direction as the road through Chesterford to Newmarket, which has just been followed; whereas Iknild Street turns off to the west at Stump Cross at an angle of 45° to Ickleton.   It would seem to run by Ickleton Farm, near which Bishop Bennet found it very manifest, but where no traces now appear, to Chrishall Grange, from which a green lane leads in four miles to the Royston road.   A parish boundary, and a county boundary, follow the lane for two miles, and the latter boundary runs along the Royston road for another two miles to that town, and through it, and on for five miles further.   Marks of the course of Iknild Way were evident in 1808 on the downs east and west of Royston, and the present road which now follows it continues on between the railway and the downs on the south to Baldock, followed by parish boundaries after the county boundary leaves it. The course is then along a field track on the north of the

[1] *Itinerarium Curiosum*, p. 78.

railway for three miles to Wilbury Hill, from which a lane with a county boundary along it leads to Ickleford. It seems to continue by the road to Punch's Cross, and by a lane with a parish boundary along it to Telegraph Hill (600') and on to Brays Ditches on the north of Warden Hill, followed for a mile and a quarter by a county boundary. Then, according to Bishop Bennet, the Way again divides, a branch to the north going through Houghton Regis to Maiden Bower, while the principal road continues on by Limbury and joins the present road from Luton, which, with a parish boundary along it, enters Dunstable by Church Street. At Dunstable, Iknild Street crosses Watling Street, turns south-west, and winds round the north of Beacon Hill (762') near Ivinghoe. It then divides : Lower Iknild Way wanders through Ivinghoe to Aston Clinton, Little Kimble, and Chinnor; and Upper Iknild Way winds north of Tring, through Wendover, by Princes Risborough, and along the flank of the Chiltern Hills. The course here-abouts, as described by Bishop Bennet, is doubtful; it seems to continue on under the name of Ickleton Road or Icleton Street to the south of Lewknor, Watlington, and Ewelme, to near Streatley, where it crosses the Thames, and then along the edge of the chalk escarpment overlook-ing the vale of White Horse, where it becomes the Ridgeway. Iknild Street, as already stated, is mentioned in a charter of the tenth century as far west as between Blewbury and Weyland Smithy, and in the tenth and eleventh centuries Icenhilde Strete was the name of the road leading to Avebury.

(11) AKEMAN STREET *to Cirencester*.—A road bearing the name of Akeman Street crosses Iknild Way near Tring, and is supposed to have come from Verulam. From half-a-mile west of Tring it lies for five miles in a straight line through Aston Clinton to a mile east of Aylesbury, pointing between a high hill (680') between Tring Park and Wiggington, and high ground (340') near Waddesdon, and the same line is taken up for a mile by the present road on the west of Aylesbury. On to Waddesdon there is nothing to show the course, but further on short lengths of parish boundaries along the present road seem to indicate that it follows generally the course of Akeman Street. Across the low ground of the valley of the Ray the general course is straight

for five miles to Blackthorn Hill (252'). Dr. Plot [1] says
that there were tracks of a stony ridge visible and useful,
and that the Ray was crossed at Steanford. The ridge is
now merged in the modern road, and the Ray is crossed by
Gallows Bridge south of the old ford, near which a parish
boundary follows the road for a mile. From Blackthorn
Hill the modern road turns north-west to Bicester, but
the course of Akeman Street continues in the same line
along a lane, and on to the brook at Langford, on the west of
which a parish boundary and a lane leading to Chesterton
mark the line for a mile. To the south is the Roman
station at Alchester, through which a Roman road passes,
making a turn when it crosses Akeman Street, and continuing
northwards. This road will be reverted to (p. 202). At Chesterton there is a slight turn to the south-west, and a straight
road runs for four miles to the north-west corner of Kirtlington Park (355'), with parish boundaries along it for a mile
and three-quarters. From this point a road called Portway
runs due north, past Heyford, Somerton, and Souldern, to
Aynho, on the east of which it was still pitched with stones
in 1712; [2] the course beyond is unknown.

From Kirtlington Park, Akeman Street makes a slight
turn more to the south-west, and the course is straight for
three miles across the valley of the Cherwell along the south
side of Tackley Park, marked by lanes with parish boundaries. A lane then takes up the line to Stratford Bridge,
and on to the Wootton gate of Woodstock Park, through
which and for some distance on there are traces of the ridge.
A section cut in Woodstock Park showed that the foundation of the road was of flags of the local stone called Stonesfield Slate, about an inch thick, and from 14 by 12 inches
to half that size. They were laid sloping in the direction
of the road at an angle of 20° to 25° and upon this foundation was a layer of six inches of gravel under the sod. The
width was 17 feet. [3] The course is indicated by parish
boundaries to the south of Stonesfield, and on to Ramsden
(450'), where there is a turn more to the south-west, and a
straight line to Bradwell Grove, eight miles distant, begins.
For two miles a lane marks the course, and then for three

[1] *Nat. Hist. of Oxfordshire*, 1705, p. 319–321.
[2] Morton's *Nat. Hist. of Northamptonshire*, p. 502.
[3] Dr. Haverfield, *Proc. Soc. Ant.*, xvii. p. 333.

miles across the Windrush valley there are apparently few traces, but beyond Asthall a parish boundary takes up the line for one and a quarter miles to Shill brook. At the north side of Bradwell Grove (420′) there is a turn towards the west, and for 11½ miles the general course appears to be straight for Cirencester, and the high ground (450′) beyond. A lane and a parish boundary mark the course for two miles from Bradwell Grove, and traces of the ridge remain. After the valley of the Leach is crossed, a lane takes up the line to Williamstrip Park, in which it is shown by two bits of parish boundary. After the river Coln is crossed a road follows the course for three and a half miles, with a parish boundary along it for most of the way. The ridge is visible in the valley where the modern road leaves the old road, and then the course onwards is un-defined for two miles; it is crossed by Cherry Tree Lane, a prolongation of the Foss road from Hare Bushes Lodge with a parish boundary along it, which continues on for a mile to the local Ermin Way. The road from Ampney then seems to take the line, and it bears the name Akeman Street to the north-east gate of Cirencester, by which the Foss road also entered *Corinium*, the *Durocornovium* of the Itinerary.

According to Dr. Plot, about 1705, Akeman Street was a raised bank from Chesterton to Stonesfield, for a short length near Whitley Green, and from Bradwell Grove to the boundary of Oxfordshire.

There is a great contrast between the laying out of Akeman Street and the winding course of Iknild Way. It may be noticed that the name Iknild Street is sometimes given to Akeman Street on the east of Cirencester, and that the Foss to the south-west of Cirencester is sometimes called Akeman Street. They both led to Bath (Akemancester).

(a) *Alchester to Dorchester.*—The camp at Alchester, a quarter of a mile south of Akeman Street, is 330 yards square, and from the east gate the ridge of a road is visible as far as the railway, as if to give a direct access to the camp from the east. The Roman road southwards ran straight for Shotover Hill (520′). Across Otmoor the ridge was very conspicuous for some miles in Camden's time, though often under water in winter floods.[1] It was still

---

[1] Camden's *Britannia*, vol. ii. p. 5.

paved in Dr. Plot's time, stone being found on and about the ridge and nowhere else on the moor.[1] On leaving the moor the direction changes slightly, and the course lies by Beckley and Headington Quarries to Bullingdon Green, from which a lane with a parish boundary along it for two and a half miles runs to Toot Baldon (300′). There is then a slight turn, and the course is straight to Dorchester, and a hill (340′) on the south of the Thames. It follows a lane with a parish boundary along it to March Baldon, where the paved ridge formerly was to be seen, and then a track, a lane, and a road take up the line to Dorchester. The road has been traced by the Rev. J. E. Field in the same line across the Thames and in Wittenham Wood.

From Dorchester a Roman road probably ran to the Iknild Way along the line of the present road to Benson ; and from this road, about half-a-mile from Dorchester, a parish boundary strikes across the Thames to the hill (340′) already mentioned one mile south of the river. From that the straight line on the north of Dorchester is resumed by a lane, with a parish boundary along it for a mile through Mackney, pointing to the road south of Cholsey and to the road through Moulsford to Streatley. There is no trace beyond this, but the Roman road probably continued on by Streatley to Silchester.

(b) *Alchester to the North.*—North of Alchester the modern road to Buckingham seems to occupy the line of a Roman road which passed to the west of Bicester, to the north of which parish boundaries follow the road for four miles to Fringford, pointing to Finmere Plantation (400′). There is then a slight change of direction, and a parish boundary, and then the county boundary, follow the modern road for three-quarters of a mile to Finmere. The county boundary continues in the same line across country to Water Stratford, indicating the course of the Roman road, which is taken up by a lane in the same line on to Stowe Park, across which the old road can be traced in the same direction, but not beyond it. It no doubt joined Watling Street, but in the intervening five miles there are apparently no vestiges of the road.

[1] *Nat. Hist. of Oxfordshire,* 1705, p. 326.

CHAPTER VII

THE FOSS WAY

(1) *General Course.*—The Foss Way or Foss Road is remarkable for its direct course. From Lincoln, to the most southern traces of it beyond South Petherton in Somerset, no part is more than six miles away from a straight line about 182 miles long joining the extreme points, Leicester and Bath being on the line. There are not many marked changes of direction. Between Lincoln and Cotgrave Gorse it bends only two miles out of a straight line in 30 miles, and then there is a turn through 25° towards Leicester, from the north of which town the general course is the same for some 60 miles to the south of Stow-on-the-Wold, with a slight turn at the crossing of Watling Street. A turn through 25° on the south of Stow-on-the-Wold does not alter the general direction of the road as far as Cirencester so much as the angle would suggest. The Foss road enters the east gate of Cirencester with Akeman Street, and its course both in entering and quitting that town suggests that it was laid out with reference to *Corinium* already existing on the Roman road from Speen to Gloucester. From four miles south of Cirencester there is a straight course pointing to Bath for 17 miles, and then a turn keeps the road on high ground till it descends from Banner Down to join another Roman road

before reaching Bath. Bath is left in the same general direction, which is not much departed from until Ilchester is reached, where there is a turn of about 20°. The characteristic Roman setting out is plain throughout. On a map Lincoln, Leicester, Cirencester and Bath lie nearly in one straight line. Of these Leicester may have arisen on the Foss road, but not the others, and the straightness of the general course must be due rather to chance than design. The course lies across the general direction of the Roman advance, and it has been thought that it may have been laid out when the Roman province was bounded by the Severn and Trent, but there is nothing to suggest a defensive purpose. One camp only, or name suggestive of a camp, is to be found on it in the 74 miles between Leicester and Cirencester.

There was probably a branch joining Erming Street about 10 miles north of Leicester, and at that town two Roman roads joined it, but to the south of Watling Street it seems to have had but few connexions with other roads. Riknild Street must have joined it somewhere near Bourton-on-the-Water, and at Cirencester it joined Akeman Street and crossed the Gloucestershire Erming Street. It crossed the road from Speen to the mouth of the Avon at Bath, and another Roman road on the Mendips, and at Ilchester there is a branch to Dorchester. It no doubt communicated with the Roman road from Dorchester to Exeter, and it is possible that to the latter town there was a more direct road, branching near South Petherton.

There are comparatively few towns or villages on it. Leicester, Cirencester, Bath and Ilchester are Roman, the last-named now not more than a village. Between Lincoln and Leicester, Newark, which is not Roman, is the only town on it. From Leicester through Warwickshire it is now an unimportant road, for 41 miles mostly grass-grown, or little more than a lane or a field road. Further south the small town of Moreton-in-the-Marsh has arisen on the road, apparently since Roman times. Between Cirencester and Bath, 29 miles, there is not a village on it, and for long distances it is a farm road, or grass-grown, and south of Bath, though the road has been modernized for the most part, there are no towns, and hardly a village on it.

Many places on its course derive their name from the road. There are Foss Farms, Foss Bridge, Foss Mill, Foss Knowl, Foss Lane, and a Street-on-the-Fosse, and several Strat-tons-on-the-Fosse.

The only part traceable in the Itinerary of Antonine is that between Lincoln and High Cross, where Iter VI. and Iter VIII. turn on to it from Watling Street, and of the five stations named, *Ratæ* is the only one of which there is a modern representative.

(2) *Lincoln to Leicester.*—The Foss Way left Lincoln with Erming Street and branched off from it near Bracebridge. Between Erming Street and Brace-bridge some of the pavement, of flagstone set edgewise, remained in Stukeley's time.[1] On the west of the river Witham the present road, occupying the course of the Roman road, is straight for eight miles to Potter Hill (120′), between which and some point on the high ground near Lincoln the course was probably laid out, but trees now shut out the prospect. Stukeley, who travelled over the road in 1723, found the straight ridge preserved, much overgrown with gorse, the moor but thinly so, and " the common road going round about." By this he probably means that the track was sometimes on one side and sometimes on the other of the ridge, as is still to be seen where no modern road has been

FOSS WAY

Scale of Miles

5 0 5 10 15

---

[1] *Itinerarium Curiosum*, p, 103.

constructed on the line of a Roman road. At Potter Hill
there is a slight turn, and another straight line of six
miles begins. The road appears to have been fenced
in 20 to 30 yards wide, and to have been since encroached
upon in many places, by which the general straightness
is disguised. The county boundary follows the road
for a mile, and four miles north of Newark, at Brough,
the station *Crococalana* of Iter VI. is placed. The road
continues straight through the town of Newark, and
then there is a slight turn, and another piece of straight
road two and a half miles long reaches to near the bank
of the river Trent near East Stoke, where the station *Ad
Pontem* must have been. Remains of a Roman bridge are
said to have been found in the river Trent here. The road
then ascends the higher ground between the Trent and the
Devon, and another straight line eight miles long ends near
High Thorpe (200′), crossing the railway just west of Bing-
ham Station, one mile due north of which, at Castle Hill,
Barrow Field is the site of the station *Margidunum*. Excavations made in 1910 show that the camp was an irregular
rhomboid enclosing about nine acres, through the middle
of which the Foss way passes, and that the earthworks
were older than the road. From the south side of the camp
Bridgeford Street, in part a footway, and in part a grassy
lane, followed by a parish boundary, runs straight to an
old ford across the Trent near Stratford Manor. Pottery
of the second half of the first century was found.[1] A slight
turn at High Thorpe is followed by another straight length
of three and a half miles ending at Cotgrave Gorse (250′),
where there is a turn through 28° to the south, but of the
29 miles from Lincoln to Cotgrave Gorse no part of the road
is more than two miles out of the direct straight line.
Until it turns off to Cotgrave a modern road occupies the
middle between the fences, but beyond that the Foss road
is a wide rough track, not appearing very straight because
of encroachments. It continues so for most of the way
to the Nottingham and Melton road, beyond which for a
mile a narrow metalled road runs along the middle between
fences 20 yards or more apart, and then turns off. Until
lately a wide green road continued for four miles and a
quarter to Six Hills (447′), but the road has now been

[1] Dr. Felix Oswald, *Margidunum*.

modernised between the Nottingham road and Six Hills. From Cotgrave Gorse the general course is straight for eight and a half miles to Six Hills. The straight line is deviated from for two miles in the lower ground near Willoughby-on-the-Wolds, but parish and county boundaries follow the road continuously from Cotgrave Gorse for 14 miles to Ratcliffe-on-the-Wreak. Near Lodge - on - the - Wolds, two miles south of Cotgrave Gorse, Stukeley describes the pavement of the road as " of great blue flagstones laid edgeways very carefully," and he says that all the way thence to Willoughby-on-the-Wolds the road was paved with red flints laid with the smoothest side upwards upon a bed of gravel, and the report then was that the Foss was thus paved all the way from Newark to Leicester.[1] This paving still exists about a mile to the north of Six Hills. Near Willoughby-on-the-Wolds the station *Verometum* was situated.

At Six Hills a Roman road is supposed to have branched off to join Erming Street near Ponton.[2] A straight road is followed by a parish boundary for three miles to the high ground (511'), near Dalby tunnel. It continues on with a slight turn, and the line of highways passing to the north of Croxton Park may perhaps follow the course of the Roman road.

From Six Hills (445') the Foss road makes straight for six and a half miles to beyond Syston railway-station (194'), where the modern road from Melton Mowbray to Leicester joins it. To this point from Cotgrave the Foss is now an insignificant road, and the course is in places not very well marked except by the parish boundaries following it. From this point (194'), near Syston railway-station, a straight modern road four miles long extends to the middle of the present town of Leicester.

About three miles north of Leicester, a Roman milliary was found in 1771 by the side of this road. It is a short column three feet six inches high, and one foot nine inches in diameter, which apparently stood on a square base, close to which it was dug up. It was appropriated as suitable for a roller, and after some time it was claimed by the road trustees as material for mending the road, but the inscrip-

---

[1] *Itinerarium Curiosum*, p. 106.
[2] Nichols, *Leicestershire*, p. cxlviii.

tion having attracted notice, it was set up in 1773 as " the centre of a neat obelisk surmounted with a lamp." [1] It is now in the Leicester Museum. The ends of the lines of the inscription are defaced, and several readings have been suggested, but of the important part there is no doubt. The inscription commemorates the Emperor Hadrian, in the fourth year of his reign, and third consulate, corresponding to A.D. 120, when Hadrian was in Britain. At that date therefore the Foss Way north of Leicester was in existence. It also gives the distance *a Ratis III.*, confirmatory of the Roman name of Leicester. It is the oldest known milliary in Britain,[2] and also the most perfect.

The Roman *Ratæ* occupied a rectangular area on the east bank of the river Soar. In 1722 the walls could be traced, and Stukeley made a plan,[3] which modern maps show to be fairly accurate, except that he omitted the west wall. From the north to the south gates it was about 860 yards, and from the east gate to the west about 580 yards, and the Roman town is still marked out by streets outside the line of the walls. High Cross Street represents the street from the north to the south gates, and High Street, the principal street at right angles to it, by which the Foss passed through *Ratæ* from the east gate, crossing the river Soar a little north of Bow Bridge, and then turning south along the course of Great Holmer Street and Narborough road. The road now called Fosse road, more to the west, may possibly represent a Roman road connecting the Foss with a road leaving *Ratæ* by the north gate, crossing the Soar at North Bridge, and then turning west. A parish boundary follows Anstey Lane for two and a half miles north westward from Fosse road, and other boundaries further on confirm the supposition of a Roman road in that direction.

---

[1] Nichols' *Leicestershire,* 1795, vol. i. p. 5.
[2] The legible portion of the inscription is thus given by Nichols, and by Gough, Camden, ii. 315—

IMP. CÆSAR
DIVO. TRAIAN PARTH. F. DIV.
TRAIAN. HADRIAN. AUG.
POT. IV COS III. A RATIS
H

[3] *Itinerarium Curiosum,* plate 92.

A straight road, joining Watling Street near *Manduesedo,* and pointing to Leicester, has been mentioned (p. 65). Towards Leicester there are said to be some traces of a Roman road on the north of the Hinkley road in the direction of the road through Peckleton to Kirkby Mallory.

(*a*) *Gartree Road.*—A Roman road left the south gate of *Ratæ* in an east-south-easterly direction. From near the Midland railway-station a boundary seems to indicate its course, crossing the London road at the north corner of Victoria Park, from which it is followed by a footpath for more than half-a-mile. The footpath continues on to Stoughton Grange, where it joins Gartree Road, which continues on in the same straight line for four and a half miles to a high ridge (500′) near Burton Overy, and on in nearly the same line for three and a half miles further, a parish boundary following it for three and a half miles. Further on there are traces of the ridge, and from Medbourne, lanes and roads follow the same line to Cottingham, beyond which the present road takes up the line for two miles, and the ridge is traceable. In the same direction, after an interval of nine miles, is the line of the road which has already been mentioned (p. 119) as being indicated from Alconbury Hill on Erming Street, to Titchmarsh. Gartree Road has got the modern name of *Via Devana* as the continuation of the road so called in Cambridgeshire, which has already been mentioned (p. 118).

(3) *Leicester to Cirencester.*—After leaving Leicester the Foss road is nearly straight for 11 miles, with a very slight turn on high ground (300′) near Narborough. For three and a half miles the present road occupies its course, and then leaves it for two miles, but there are traces of the old road in the interval. South of Narborough, parish boundaries follow it continuously for six miles to High Cross, on approaching which it is a grass-grown road through fields. The ditches on each side are traceable, about eight yards apart, and a paving appears to remain beneath the surface in places. Stukeley [1] mentions " a visible pavement of great round coggles by Sharnford," two miles north of High Cross.

At High Cross (450′) (*Venonæ*), where there are only a few houses, the Foss crosses Watling Street, the four roads

[1] *Itinerarium Curiosum,* p. 110.

O

diverging in different directions. From *Venonæ* to *Lindum* Iter VI. and Iter VIII. of Antonine pass over the Foss, making the distance 63 and 64 M. P.; the distance from High Cross to Lincoln measuring 62 miles. The intermediate distances agree with the sites which have been given above for the stations between *Ratæ* and *Lindum.*

The Foss leaves Watling Street for the south 50 yards to the west of the point at which it meets it from the north, and turning 15° to the east, runs straight towards Dunmore Heath for eight miles. It is a narrow lane for a mile and a half, and the contrast between Watling Street and the Foss Way in both directions is remarkable. A parish boundary follows the lane, and then a road for three and a half miles, and the same straight line is continued by a track to near Stretton, and then the course of the road is not traceable for a mile. It appears to pass by the east of Brinklow mound, a parish boundary from Smite brook running to, and continuing along, the road to the east of Brinklow, indicating the course of it. At three-eighths of a mile to the south of Brinklow, almost exactly the same line as that from High Cross is resumed, the road for two miles pointing straight for the mound. The old fences, 20 or 25 yards apart, remain, with long strips enclosed, on the sides of the present road. On the north side of the Avon the Foss is now a narrow grass field leading to the old Bret-ford, on the east of the present road and Bretford bridge. The general course of the road lies between High Cross and high ground (350') on Dunsmore Heath, long since enclosed. It is bent to the east in the Avon valley to avoid the river on the south of the ford, and the old road has been narrowed, is not very straight, and is little better than a lane.

There is a slight turn to the west on Dunsmore Heath, and for twenty miles the general course of Foss Lane is straight to Halford, apparently in the direction of high ground (800') near Bourton-on-the-Hill ten miles still further on. Nothing but the trees now prevent some prominent object or mark there being visible from Dunsmore Heath. A good deal of the original straightness has been lost, but it would seem that in the lower ground, when the distant marks were lost sight of, it never was quite straight. The width between the fences has been encroached upon on one side and the other, and it now varies from twenty or twenty-five yards down to as many feet. In parts the road is little more than a field road or a lane, but the ridge or embankment of the Roman road is still to be traced here and there, particularly when broad green sides remain, as near Compton Verney.

Near Chesterton the road passes through some remains of a camp; and near Eatington a Roman road from Strat-ford-on-Avon seems to have joined, but there are now no traces of it. On the north of Halford, Foss Lane ends, and the modern road from Warwick takes the line and follows it to Cirencester. The course is generally straight for four and a half miles, then there is a slight bend, and between Knee Brook and Lemington there are slight windings on high ground, followed for two miles by a county boundary, which seems to indicate that the line of the Foss road is occupied by the modern road. It is nowhere quite straight for any considerable length on to Moreton-in-the-Marsh, and where it crosses valleys there are twists, some-times due in part to improving the gradient for the modern road. It is 20 to 25 yards between the fences, where it has not been encroached upon.

The main street of Moreton-in-the-Marsh occupies the course of the Foss road, which makes a slight turn to the east to a point one mile south of Stow-on-the-Wold, where there is a considerable turn to the south-west in the direc-tion of Cirencester. There are several lengths of straight road of from one to four miles, nearly in the same straight line, with windings where coombes in the oolitic tableland (440' to 660') are crossed. The road generally turns up the coombes and back again to the same line. Parish boun-daries, which run along the road nearly all the way, follow these windings into and out of the coombes, except at one a mile to the north of Northleach, where the boundary keeps a direct course, and marks the line of the Foss where it has been quitted by the modern road. Beyond Foss Cross the straight course is deviated from to pass round the upper ends of several coombes, and after about a mile and a half of straight road, a round turn leads to a straight road nearly north and south. The modern road is hereabouts considerably banked up, near Bramston Farms, about three miles from Cirencester, as much as six feet, and there are deep side ditches outside the embankment. To what extent the embankment represents the Roman ridge, and how far the side ditches are owing to the excavation of materials for the modern road is uncertain. Such hollows along the sides of roads, made for the purpose of getting road materials, are common in this stony tableland. The parish boundaries that have followed the Foss continue to follow Cherry Tree Lane, in prolongation of the Foss, for half-a-mile past the turn to Cirencester at Hare Bushes Lodge, as far as the course of Akeman Street. Whether the Foss road joined the latter road there, or had an independent course from Hare Bushes Lodge, is uncertain, but the two roads entered Cirencester together by the north-east gate.

The walls of the Roman *Corinium* of Ptolemy, or *Durocornovium* of the Itinerary of Antonine, form a rough rectangle through the longest diameter of which the course of the Roman road from Speen to Gloucester runs in a straight line for nearly a mile. The principal cross street at right angles with it, the *Via principalis* of a Roman camp, has been found to have been in the line of Lewis Lane and Queen Street from the north-east gate, by which Akeman Street and the Foss road entered, and to have led straight to the amphitheatre outside the south-west gate.[1] The width from wall to wall in this direction is about half-a-mile.

(4) *Cirencester to Bath.*—The Foss road leaves the Roman town on the line of Castle Street, a quarter of a mile to the north-west of the principal cross street, and makes straight for high ground (442′) on the tableland on the north of Jackments Bottom, with a very slight turn north of Thames Head. The way in which the Foss road enters and leaves *Corinium* suggests that the Roman town had grown up upon the course of the Speen and Gloucester road before the Foss road was laid out. South of Cirencester the Foss road, or Acman Street as it is also called, is now a wide modern road, along one side of which the county boundary runs, for a considerable distance in a deep hollow, for two and a half miles to Jackments Bottom. The boundary may possibly show the original line of the Roman road, which was broken up, and with the addition of the stone dug out, went to make the modern road along the side. The road

[1] W. Cripps, *Proc. Soc. Antiq.*, vol. xvii. p. 201.

probably followed the line of the county boundary into
Jackments Bottom and out again, but there are now no
traces of it there.

From the south of Jackments Bottom (400') the course
of the road is so straight for 16½ miles that no part is more
than half-a-mile from a straight line. It is made up of
straight lines from point to point, only deviated from in
crossing valleys, after which the line is resumed. The
general course must have been laid out from several
intermediate points on the tableland. The high ground
(500') in the park one mile west of Cirencester is visible
for some distance along this part of the Foss, and may have
been one point of direction.

The county boundary continues to follow the Foss road
for two miles from Jackments Bottom, and then parish
boundaries follow it for another two miles, and after an
interval of half-a-mile, again for one mile, when a county
boundary again joins the road for a mile and three-quarters,
and parish boundaries then follow the road for eight miles.

From Jackments Bottom onwards the Foss road is now
a green road for 10 miles, used only for farm traffic, but it
is a highway available as a bridle-road, and it can be
travelled over in a two-wheeled vehicle. It is 20 yards
wide between the fence walls for long lengths. Near
Culkerton Down Wood there is an embanked ridge five
or six yards wide, and raised three, four, or five feet, the
sides sloping about one in five, or one in six. It is described
at the end of the eighteenth century as " showing its bold
ridge sided with ditches." [1] Sometimes the width has been
encroached upon, leaving the level top of the ridge and one
slope, and perhaps a small part of the other between the
walls. There is no trace of a paving or a stoned surface
where the ridge is deeply cut into by cart ruts. Further
on the road is wide in places with high hedges, and timber
trees shading it, and in other places it has been narrowed,
and is overgrown with bushes, and there is little or no trace
of a ridge. In the valley of the Anton at White Walls,
about two and a half miles west of Malmesbury, are the
Roman remains, foundations and tesselated pavements, to
which the name *Mutuantonis* (from the Ravenna list) was
given by Sir R. C. Hoare. A little further on, at Littlefield,

[1] Collinson's *History of Somerset*, vol. i. p. 100.

the Foss road is stopped up for a quarter of a mile, one of the very few places where that has taken place. At Lords Wood Farm the green road ends for a time, a parish highway taking the course, and about one and a quarter mile further on this was cut through in making the railway to the Severn Tunnel, without anything indicative of a Roman road being found, or indeed any evident traces of a made road on the stony subsoil. Hereabouts there is very little evidence that the old road was raised above the surface. A narrow modern road runs between hedges 20 yards apart where there is no encroachment as far as the turn to Grittleton, near Dunley Farm, and then a green road is entered upon, 18 or 20 yards wide between the hedges, but in places overgrown with ferns, briars, and nut-bushes, so that a dog-cart can hardly pass. This continues for one and a quarter miles to Foss Gate, where a modern highway from Grittleton joins, and three-quarters of a mile further on, after crossing the Gatcombe Valley, the parish and county boundaries which have followed the Foss for nearly 11 miles cease to do so for a mile and a quarter. Sir R. C. Hoare relates that hereabouts, at the beginning of the last century, labourers were destroying the Foss, and had " cut through a bold and lofty ridge by which a favourable specimen of its original construction was rendered visible," but unfortunately he did not describe it.[1] Near North Wraxall (490'), three and a half miles further on, the south end of the 16½ miles of nearly straight road is reached, and there is a slight turn towards the east, and a straight road for a mile to the Duncombe valley, which is crossed by a narrow winding road. A county boundary follows the road from the south of the stream for two and a quarter miles, and on regaining the tableland near Ashwick Park (546') there is another bend towards the east by which the road is kept on the high ground, and it runs straight for three miles to Banner Down (600'), overlooking Bathford, followed by a parish boundary in continuation of the county boundary. Sir R. C. Hoare, in 1820, observed a ridge of fine appearance, and a high raised *dorsum*, which was then being broken up,[2] and the road in its modernized form is banked up about three feet. Near the fourth milestone from Bath the parish boundary and the modern road part,

---

[1] *Ancient Wilts, Roman Æra*, p. 102.   [2] *Ibid.*, p. 103.

the former continuing straight on and rejoining the road in about a quarter of a mile. In another quarter of a mile the main road turns to the west, and the boundary follows Morris Lane down to the London road, which it joins not far from where the Great Western Railway crosses the road to Bathford. Sir R. C. Hoare makes the present road leave the Foss near the fourth milestone, the course of the latter lying, he supposed, through the quarries and down Foss Lane. Collison also makes it descend by Foss Lane, which he described in 1791 [1] as deep, narrow, and overhung with hedges, and joining the London road at a bridge over a little stream. This lane, a quarter of a mile nearer Bath, still bears the name, but the evidence of the boundary is against it.

The London road from Bathford to Bath is on the line of the Roman road from Silchester and Speen, and the Foss road joins it at right angles. From Batheaston the course is straight for two miles to Walcot, and according to Scarth it continued by Guinea Lane to the top of Russell Street before turning southwards to enter the Roman city, but it may have bent southward, and approached the North Gate more on the line of Walcot Street.

The mediæval walls of Bath were on the foundations of the Roman walls of *Aquæ Solis* (or *Sulis*), and they can still be followed in the modern streets. They enclosed a pentagon approaching an irregular rectangle about 400 yards east and west by 388 yards north and south. The north gate was at the north end of High Street, not far from Pulteney Bridge, the west gate at the end of Westgate Street, and the south gate at the south end of Stall Street, near St. James' Church, on the slope of the ground rising above the low-lying land on the north of the river Avon.

(5) *Bath to Ilchester.*—By the south gate the Foss road left *Aquæ Solis*, along what is now Southgate Street, and crossed the river Avon by a ford, of which there were vestiges at the beginning of the eighteenth century.[2] It then ascended by Holloway and Devonshire Place by a winding course, the modern road joining and following it after the first half-mile.

It was suggested by Scarth[3] that there was possibly a

[1] Collinson's *History of Somerset,* p. 99.
[2] Collinson, vol i. p. 100.   [3] *Aquæ Sulis*, p. 110, 1864.

road from the Foss hereabouts to the road from Bath to
Silchester, avoiding Bath, the ridge of which was to be
seen on the north of Claverton road pointing to Warleigh
Ferry over the Avon.   In 1906 this ridge was cut through
by Mr. G. Gray.   In the middle, at four inches below the
surface, a bed of large and moderate-sized stones, 20 inches
thick, was found lying on the rock subsoil, and at nine feet
from the middle, the same was found at a few inches deeper.
In the following year, the ridge in the same line between
the canal and the river was cut into near the railway, and
at 10 feet from the middle a bed of fairly large stones was
met with four inches beneath the surface, and to the south
of the ridge numerous fragments of Roman and British
pottery, bones, and a coin of Constantine were found.[1]
According to Scarth the road from Warleigh Ferry to the
Dry Arch on the Bradford road was then known among the
peasants as the old Roman road.   The lane now ends at
the road to Sheephouse Farm, but a footway continues on
by Bay House Farm to a road leading to Monkton Farleigh,
from which a lane and an old track leads on to the Roman
road near Ashley Wood.

On Odd Down a straight road begins, which at Vernham
Wood is joined by a parish boundary.   On the high ground
one mile north-west of Coombe Hay the modern road
diverges to the west, and the line of the Foss is along a
narrow lane, with remains of the ridge, which the parish
boundary continues to follow down into Dunkerton Bottom,
a descent of about 400 feet, and up again on the south of
the valley.   The modern road rejoins the line of the Foss,
and after again quitting it for a quarter of a mile, follows
it past Huddox Hill to near Clandown, parish boundaries
continuing along the road.   The modern road then turns
off to Radstock, and the Foss runs straight on to Smallcombe, down into which parish boundaries are continuous
for five miles from Odd Down.

In Smallcombe a cottage, which is actually on the Foss
road, is freehold, and is said to be the only freehold in
the hamlet.   From Smallcombe the course of the Foss is
straight for three miles in a line between high ground (555'),
near Camerton Park, and (538') near Stratton-on-the-Foss.
The road, which the parish boundary follows, is rather

---

[1] *Proc. Bath branch, Somerset Archæol. Soc.*, pp. 110, 151.

winding up out of Smallcombe, between which and the Somer valley is a spur of high ground, over which, as the gradients up and down are too steep for modern wheeled traffic, the old road remains in almost its original state. It is a ridge about three feet six inches high and six feet wide across the top, between two old hedges, outside of which are ditches. In 1884, Mr. McMurtrie had a trench cut across near the lane leading to Welton, and described the section.[1] The original soil was met with at a level corresponding with that of the adjacent fields, and upon it is a layer of rubble stone five inches thick in the middle, and thinning off towards the sides, next is a bed of concrete about one foot three inches thick, then a layer of finer material composed of limestone pounded fine and mixed with lime and well rammed, ten and a half inches thick in the middle, and rounded off at the sides. On this was laid a course of paving stones, four or five inches thick, from the lias beds of the neighbourhood, of all sizes and shapes fitted together and grouted with lime mortar. This, the ancient surface of the road, was laid bare for a length of several yards, and two distinct ruts were exposed, three feet apart from centre to centre, one about two inches wide, and two or three inches deep, and the other wider and shallower. The ancient road surface has been covered with stones and earth, exclusive of which the thickness is two feet eleven inches. Another section was made by Mr. McMurtrie in 1904, 108 yards south-west of the former one. On black soil was six inches of rubbly stone, then two inches of pebbles in a red matrix, and then 16 inches of stone mostly of small size, covered by five inches of finer material, on which was a layer of flat rubbly stones of irregular size about four inches thick, apparently lias, making a total thickness of two feet eight inches, thinning towards the sides. The paving was eight feet wide, showing wheel-tracks three feet apart from centre to centre. The width at the base was 16 feet.[2] Sir R. C. Hoare [3] notices a very similar section of the Foss near Radstock, which was observed by Mr. Skinner, the foundation consisting of a layer

[1] *Proc. Somerset Archæol. and N. H. Soc.*, vol. xxx. p. 76.

[2] *Proc. Somerset Archæol. and N. H. Soc.*, 1904; *Bristol and Gloucester Archæol. Soc.*, xxvi. 326.

[3] *Ancient Wilts, Roman Æra*, vol. ii. p. 77.

of large flat stones, then one and a half feet of earth and rubble, afterwards a course of small stones, with pavement or pitching stones on the surface.

There are remains of the ridge on the steep south side of the Somer valley, and then the modern road through Radstock takes up the line. Near Stratton-on-the-Foss, where a rough paving of large stones on clay was found 18 inches beneath the surface of the road in 1910, there is a slight turn, and the road points to high ground (920') on Beacon Hill, near the east end of the Mendips, to which the Foss also points from the south for five and a half miles. After two miles in this direction the road winds down to cross the deep valley at Nettle Bridge, the parish boundary following it. A smaller valley is crossed near Ashwick Grove, where the main road turns off and then a straight lane followed by a parish boundary leads in a mile to the above-mentioned point (920') on Beacon Hill.

(a) *Road to Uphill.*—At this point the Foss road is crossed by a Roman road from the south-east to the north-west. The ridge is traceable for a mile to the eastward, and further on the line is thought to be indicated by Rough Ditch dividing the parishes of East Cranmore and Downhead. To the west of the Foss traces of the ridge are shown on the old Ordnance map for two and a half miles to the cross roads beyond Masebury Castle, and then a highway in nearly the same straight line, followed for two miles by parish boundaries, occupies the course for two and a quarter miles to Green Ore. Further on the ridge is shown on the old Ordnance map for a mile on the south of Castle Comfort Inn. Sections made by Mr. McMurtrie between Green Ore and Castle Comfort, where the ridge was 15 to 18 inches above the adjoining land, showed a bed of rubble stone 5 to 11 inches thick, and 11 to 17 feet wide on layers of dark brown earth.[1] Traces continue over Ubley Warren, and on nearly to Charterhouse, where there are Roman remains, and evidence of lead-mining at a very early period of the Roman occupation.[2] Sir R. C. Hoare saw the ridge

---

[1] *Trans. Bristol and Gloucestershire Archæol. Soc.*, vol. xxix. p. 30.

[2] A pig of lead from the mines at Charterhouse Hinton now in the Bristol Museum bears the stamp of the Emperor Vespasian, A.D. 70, and another, mined in the Mendips, bears the name of Claudius and his son, A.D. 49 (Hodgkin).

of the road for a mile along the south of Black Down, beyond
which the course seems to be followed by a lane from the
north of Shipham, and to have continued along the south
side of Banwell Hill, and along the north side of Bleadon
Hill, where it is marked by a green track passing to the
south of Hutton wood, and on to the south of Oldmixon
and Uphill.   Sir R. C. Hoare found traces of a square
circumvallation and pottery at Borough Walls (? Wal-
borough) on the south of Uphill near the mouth of the river
Axe, and there he placed a Roman station to which he
gave the name *Ad Axium*.[1]   There is no other authority
for the name, but it has been perpetuated on the new
Ordnance maps, which, however, place the camp a quarter
of a mile to the east of the railway, above Oldmixon.

It is very probable that there was a port at the mouth of
the Axe from which lead from the Mendip mines was
shipped, and the position of *Ischalis* as given by Ptolemy's
degrees in relation to *Aquæ Calidæ* (Bath) is there, and not at
Ilchester.   It is much more likely that a port at the mouth
of the Axe should have been known to Ptolemy than an
inland and unimportant place at Ilchester.   The name
Ischalis too appears to be connected with the Axe.

The Foss from the point (920') on Beacon Hill takes a
straight course to Easton Hill (462'), between Ditcheat and
East Pennard, five and a half miles distant, parish boundaries following it nearly all the way.   After descending the
hill a lane takes up the line, which passes through Charlton
on the east of Shepton Mallet, to Cannard's Grave, where
the Ilchester road joins it.   At Easton Hill there is a considerable turn to the south-west, and a somewhat winding
road leads down (462' to 200') to Wraxhill in a mile and a
quarter, and then a straight road succeeds, four miles long,
pointing between high ground (460') near Easton Hill and
Cross Keys (110'), with parish boundaries along it for most
of the way.   There is a slight turn at Cross Keys, and
one and a half miles further on the modern road diverges
from the Foss to descend the hill, and rejoins it in half-a-
mile, the Foss continuing in the same straight line for three
miles and a quarter from Cross Keys, and with a very
slight turn, on for two and a quarter miles to Ilchester,
parish boundaries following the road for two miles.

[1] *Ancient Wilts, Roman Æra*, p. 44.

The Foss road crossed the river Yeo by a ford, which Stukeley describes as being made with great flagstones, to the Roman station, the walls and ditch of which he traced nearly all round. He gives a plan of it, and describes it as an oblong square 500 paces by 300 paces,[1] the longer side of which lies along the south bank of the Yeo. The supposed sites of the gates make it 533 yards by 326 yards. Ilchester has been supposed to be the *Ischalis* of Ptolemy, whose latitudes and longitudes would however put that station nearly as far north as Bath, and 27 miles to the west of it, that is, near the mouth of the Axe.

(*b*) A Roman road branched from Ilchester to Dorchester. For nearly three miles the straight modern road indicates the course to Vagg (400′), where the direction changes to high ground (800′), near Frome St. Quentin, 11 miles off, on which line there are traces here and there of the old road. The Dorchester end of the road will be noticed further on (p. 257).

(6) *Ilchester to Axminster.*—The Foss road continues straight through Ilchester, constituting the principal street of it, on the line of the cross street of the Roman town. At the site of the south gate there is a turn to the south-west, and the road for four and a half miles is in a straight line with a point in high ground (700′) near Cricket St. Thomas, 13 miles distant. Stukeley,[2] in 1723, saw the original paving of the road in many parts, " composed of the flat quarry stones of the country, of a good breadth, laid edge-wise, and so close that it looks like the side of a wall fallen down." The road appears to have retained its original state until the beginning of the last century, when the modern road took the course of it to near Petherton Bridge. Parish boundaries follow the present road nearly all the way. There is a slight change of direction on high ground about a mile south of Martock, and half-a-mile further on the modern road turns away from the Foss to Petherton Bridge, the course of the latter road apparently continuing straight on to high ground (220′), beyond Over Stratton. Bridge House is on the line, which is taken up by lanes, with a slight turn beyond Over Stratton, as far as Dinnington. The course of the Foss, which can be followed to this point from Lincoln without difficulty, then becomes un-

---

[1] *Itinerarium Curiosum*, p. 154.   [2] *Ibid.*, p. 155.

certain.   The early descriptions take it to Exeter, but there
seems to be no evidence of it for many miles in that direction.
A road has been traced from near South Petherton on somewhat inconclusive evidence, westward by Hurcot, Broadway, and Street Ash, and in the spring of 1900 a paved road
was exposed by a flood at Donyatt Mill, near Ilminster,
one and a half miles to the south of this line lying in the
direction of a road through Crock Street, which a parish
boundary follows for one and a half miles.

Near Dinnington, the narrow lane worn deep in the sand,
which represents the Foss, branches right and left, and there
is no trace onwards over the hill and through the valley
beyond for three miles.   Then from a point (600') near
Cricket St. Thomas the present road, followed by a parish
boundary, and with some traces of the ridge, runs straight
for a mile, and when, near Street, it bends to avoid a hill,
there are traces straight on, and in rather more than half-
a-mile the straight line is resumed by the modern road,
which a parish boundary again follows for half-a-mile at
Monkham Down.   The present road, probably following the
line of the Foss, bends to the west to avoid the valley of the
Axe, and at Tytherleigh turns more to the south again, and
takes a straight course.   It crosses the Axe at Weycroft,
formerly called Stratford, and from Millbrook, where the
Axminster road turns off, Stony Lane continues the line
to the Dorchester road a quarter of a mile east of Axminster.
The Foss there met the Roman road from Dorchester to
Exeter by Honiton, and there are no evidences that it crossed
it and continued on to the mouth of the Axe near Seaton,
where Camden and others placed *Muridunum*, and according
to distances from Dorchester and Exeter *Muridunum* must
have been seven miles further west.   The Foss has been
said to have gone to Exeter and Devon, and that may be
so if the Roman road from Axminster through Honiton to
Exeter may be looked upon as a continuation of the Foss
rather than as part of a road from Dorchester to Exeter.
For convenience the latter view will be here taken.

CHAPTER VIII

(1) *General Course.*—From early times a Roman road bearing the name of Riknild Street, or something like it, has been known, but it has been confused with Icknild Street, and its course has been somewhat uncertain. Apart from Higden's general description that it began at St. Davids and continued to the Tyne, the course he gives by Worcester, Birmingham, Lichfield, Derby and Chesterfield, can be traced now, but not beyond in either direction. Southwards it probably communicated with Caerleon, the headquarters of Legion II., and so originated; but northwards on getting into Yorkshire there is confusion. This appears to be due to the rise of York to be the military capital of Britain in the second century, and to the alteration of traffic, and the new roads which followed.

(2) *Worcester to Selly Oak.*—From Worcester towards Droitwich a street and road seem to follow the course for two miles and a quarter, and then the same straight line is continued by a parish boundary across Hindlip Park, along the line of a shallow trench from which the Roman road materials have probably been removed. The main road then follows the same line to the south of Droitwich, pointing to a gap (700′) [1] in the Lickey range. There is then a slight turn towards a point (900′) more to the east,

[1] Nash, *Hist. of Worcestershire*, 1781–89, vol. ii. p. cvii.

near the Obelisk, and the present road follows a straight course in that direction for seven miles, deviated from at one place. From Droit-wich a road called Salt Way runs straight for three miles in the direction of Alcester, followed for a mile by a parish boundary. The course of Riknild Street on-wards is uncertain. The road through Bromsgrove may follow it for a mile and a half, but it then turns off. Towards the end of the eighteenth century there was a high raised road on the Lickey Hills pointing directly to Bromsgrove, and from the north of the Lickey Hills the present road lies in a straight line to Selly Oak, except for half-a-mile near Northfield.

(3) *Bourton-on-the-Water to Derby.*—The road now bearing the name of Riknild Street appears to have joined the Foss Way near Bourton-on-the-Water, about two miles north of which, and two miles west of Stow-on-the-Wold, a lane in a straight line northwards past Con-dicote to Hinchwick appears to indicate the course, point-ing to high ground (about 840′) on Bourton Down. It is not clear how the ascent of 250 feet from Hinchwick

RIKNILD STREET
Scale of Miles

to the down was made, but on the down a lane from Spring-hill, with a county boundary along it, takes up nearly the same line for a mile and a half to near the Evesham road (950'). About a hundred yards north of the road from Chipping Camden to Snowshill a section of the ridge showed that under the turf was a layer of small broken stones and earth upon about six inches of flat stones bedded on beaten earth over the local rock.[1] From the Evesham road a parish boundary over Saintbury Hill seems to mark the course down the north side. On the west side of Weston Park, a line seems to be taken up lying between high ground (940'), two miles to the south, and Alcester, 12 miles to the north. A road in this line, passing on the west of Weston-sub-Edge, leads on to a highway with a parish boundary along it called Riknild or Icknield Street. It is crossed by the railway at Honey-bourne Station, near which county boundaries follow it for a mile and three-quarters. It continues northward under the name of Buckle Street to Staple Hill, one mile south of Bidford, where there is a slight turn, and a straight line begins, pointing to the west of Alcester, four and a half miles distant. There is nothing to indicate the line for about a mile north of Bidford, when a lane called Icknield Street joins it and continues nearly to Alcester.

From Alcester a Roman road ran eastward, along the course followed for six miles by the straight modern road, to Stratford-on-Avon, and a parish boundary along the road for two miles south-east from Stratford-on-Avon seems to indicate that the latter occupies the line of a Roman road on towards the Foss near Eatington.

North of Alcester the line of Riknild Street is followed by the present Birmingham road, called Haydon Way, through Studley and to one mile beyond, where the latter road turns off to the north-eastward and there is no trace of Riknild Street for a mile and a half. At Ipsley a lane called Icknield Street exactly in a line with Haydon Way is reached. This line appears to point from Alcester to high ground (about 480'), one mile east of Rowney Green, and a mile and a half north of Beoley. There is here a slight turn, and lanes follow the line of the old road by Forhill to near Headley Heath. Hutton [2] gives the course onwards by Stirchley Street, crossing the Bromsgrove road at Selly

[1] G. B. Grundy, *Proc. Soc. Antiq.*, 1913–1914, p. 208.
[2] *History of Birmingham*, p. 142.

Oak, leaving Harborne a mile to the west, by the observatory in Lady Wood Lane, crossing the Dudley Road at Sandpits, and along Worstone Lane, passing five furlongs north of the Navigation Bridge in Great Charles Street, Birmingham. He saw the section of the road where the inhabitants attempted to pull it up for the sake of the materials, 20 yards wide, and one yard deep, filled up with stone cemented with coarse mortar, and he says that the course was discoverable by its barren track through uncultivated meadows. Birmingham and its suburbs now cover the old road for about four miles.

Stukeley says [1] that he found Rigning Street very broad by Moseley, over a heath on the east side of the river Rea, but that appears to be away from this line.

On the north of Birmingham the place of crossing the river Tame is shown on the old Ordnance map by the name Holdford Farm (? Old Ford); and onwards the county boundary marks the line of the road for about a quarter of a mile to Gorsey Bank. Then a road continues it, passing a quarter of a mile to the east of Oscott, and it can be traced along a track shown on the old Ordnance map to near the Royal Oak Inn on the west side of Sutton Coldfield Park. In the park the ridge appears very plainly, of a rounded profile, eight or nine yards wide over all, and three to four feet high in the middle. It has been described [2] as presenting one of the best examples of a Roman road, 60 feet wide with a ditch on each side. It has little claim to be so considered, and the ditches where they occur appear to be connected with modern drainage. At the south of the park, holes rather than ditches at the sides seem to show where the material for the mound was got. Further on in lower ground the ridge is not so prominent, but it is again more marked towards Streetley Hill. It is plainly traceable all through the park for a mile and a half, overgrown with gorse and heather, except where two golf putting-greens have been made in the course of it. The old Ordnance map shows it as the county boundary through the park. The coating of gravel can be seen here and there, and it was cut through by a new road near the Streetley gate. The railway crosses it about 100 yards east of Streetley station. To the

---

[1] *Iter Boreale,* p. 21.
[2] *Journ. Archæol. Assoc.,* 1873.

north of the park it can be traced for about half-a-mile on
the west of the drive through Birmingham Wood to Little
Aston Hall.   A short length of road north of Little Aston,
and another length to the west of Shenstone, mark the
course of the road in a straight line from Streetley Hill to
high ground (450′) on the north-east of Wall.   From near
Birmingham to Wall (*Etocetum*) for nine miles the road is
not perceptibly out of a straight line, which may very well
have been set out from intermediate points at Streetley
Hill, and the high ground (500′) south of the Royal Oak
Inn.

Riknild Street seems to have reached Watling Street
at about half-a-mile to the east of Wall, and left it northwards still more to the east.   Another long straight line of
22 miles succeeds, inclining 24° to the east of the course to
the south of Watling Street.   A lane following the course of
the old road for most of the way from near Wall, is crossed
by the North-Western Railway just east of Lichfield
station, and joins the Lichfield and Burton Road at Street-
hay.   The latter road occupies the line of Riknild Street
nearly as far as Branston.   In Stukeley's time " part of
Rigning Way north from Wall was very fair with a high
straight bank." [1]   The same straight line appears to have
continued through Burton-on-Trent, and on to high ground
(340′) near the Knoll, Littleover, two miles from Derby.
The modern road from Burton to Derby occupies the course
of Riknild Street from the middle of the former town to
near the river Dove, where the straight line is deviated from
for a mile in crossing the river, and then resumed.   Onwards, parish boundaries follow the present road in places
for about half the way to Derby.   In the beginning of the
eighteenth century the road on Burton Moor was paved; [2]
in Stukeley's time it was the common road, and in 1769 a
considerable length appeared on Egginton Heath, [3] but it
has since been obliterated by the making of the turnpike
road.   Stukeley notes that " upon the hill south of Littleover, Rigning is under the eye as far as *Etocetum*, and the
hills beyond it." [4]   It is perfectly straight from Watling
Street for 22 miles.

[1] *Iter Boreale*, p. 21.   [2] Plot's *Staffordshire*, p. 400.
[3] S. Pegge, *Roman Roads in the Country of the Coritani*, p. 5.
[4] *Iter Boreale*, p. 25.

At Littleover the modern road turns to the east, and the course of Riknild Street onwards is said by Stukeley[1] and Pegge to be over Nuns Green and down Darley Slade to a bridge over the Derwent, on the east of which a gravelled road in continuation passed on the north side of the Roman station at Little Chester. Stukeley describes the river there as being broad and deep, with steep banks, and impracticable for a ford. His plan shows the piers of a bridge, the foundations of which he and others say were visible under favourable conditions, and could be felt with a staff.[2] It is doubtful, however, if Riknild Street originally crossed the Derwent by a bridge at an unfordable place. Half-a-mile farther down the river, in the heart of Derby was an ancient ford, superseded by St. Mary's Bridge, but kept in remembrance by Ford Street and Ford Lane, to which the principal roads on both sides of the river converge. The ford there seems to be a more probable crossing-place for Riknild Street, superseded perhaps when the fort and the bridge at Little Chester were constructed, and again reverted to after the Roman bridge fell to ruin. There seems to be no trace of the Roman road from Littleover either to the ford or to the bridge at Little Chester. The Roman fort was between the river and the Great Northern Railway, and according to Stukeley, who traced the walls all round,[3] it measured 200 yards by 166 yards.

(4) *Roads from Little Chester.*—Bishop Bennet mentions as uncertain a Roman road from Little Chester to Lawley Ferry on the Trent,[4] the ridge of which is said to have been visible some thirty years ago near the north-east of Derby race-course, pointing towards the angle of the enclosure at Chaddesden Hall.[5] It can still be traced there, and the course onwards towards Chaddesden may, it is said, be distinguished in very dry weather by the colour of the herbage. A section of the road in a line with Old Chester Road was cut in 1910 by Mr. W. Smithard[6] between the race-course and the Derby Canal. Beneath eight inches of turf was a bed of coarse sandstone boulders, 12 feet wide

---

[1] *Iter Boreale*, p. 25.   [2] *Itinerarium Curiosum*, p. 54, pl. 86.
[3] *Iter Boreale*, p. 25.   [4] Lysons, *Derbyshire*, p. ccxiii.
[5] Watkins, *Derbyshire Archæol. and Nat. Hist. Trans.*, vol. viii. p. 213.
[6] *Derbyshire Archæol. and Nat. Hist. Jour.*, vol. xxxiii.

and about 10½ inches deep, covered by a layer of gravel
three inches thick. There is a bend southward on the
north of the race-course, and the traces across it, and on
towards Chaddesden, lie in the direction of a highway which
begins about a mile from Little Chester and lies in a straight
line for seven miles to the river Trent at Sawley, except
for half-a-mile where the straight line is continued by
hedgerows. It points to the steep north side of West Leake
hills, twelve miles distant, rising 200 feet above the Trent
valley, but there are no traces in continuation beyond
that river. The Rev. S. P. Potter [1] connects a " street
way " in an old terrier with a road, not in the same line,
which he supposes to be a Roman road in the direction of
Six Hills on the Foss road, but the identification is not
clear.

Reference has been made (p. 80) to a possible continuation of a Roman road from Sandbach by Chesterton,
Meir and Rocester to Derby. Bishop Bennet [2] makes it
cross the river Dove a little below Rocester, and pass by
Marston Montgomery and Longford, and then follow Long
Lane, a straight road more than four miles long pointing
to the Roman Station at Little Chester, four miles farther
on. There are no parish boundaries along it on the 25 miles
from Meir to Little Chester, nor are any definite traces of
a Roman road or other Roman remains known ; but it is
an old road, made up of straight lengths, interrupted by
crooked portions, the straight lengths changing in direction
slightly on high points, as is common in Roman setting out.
It is called Rickmilde Streete (the *m* should probably be *n*)
in a charter of 1257.[3] Local antiquaries have considered
it probably Roman, and Mr. J. Ward, F.S.A., who has
walked along most of it, has no doubt of its Roman origin.

(5) *Derby to Buxton.*—A Roman road went from Derby
to Buxton and Manchester, of which there are now few
traces for 14 miles from Derby. Bishop Bennet described [4]
it, in 1817, as branching at Darley Slade, and passing
between Kedleston Park and Duffield, and close by Hopton,
where a part of it had lately been opened, and over Bras-

[1] *History of East Leake.*
[2] Lysons, *Derbyshire*, vol. v. p. ccxiii
[3] Duignan, *Notes on Staffordshire Place Names*, p. 33.
[4] Lysons, vol. v. p. ccxiii.

sington Moor, where it was visible.   From near Slipperlow
Farm a parish boundary runs straight for a mile and three-
quarters past Minninglow, and here two sections have been
opened by Mr. W. Smithard.[1]   They were on slightly
sloping ground, on which the road was raised.   In one
section the middle five feet of a road 12 feet wide consisted
of limestone pitching 10 inches deep, laid on the original
surface, with earth at the sides, both covered with three
inches of limestone rubble.   In the other section a bank of
earth one foot six inches high on the lower side of the slope
was supported by stone blocks, and a layer of angular
limestone six inches thick and 12 feet wide overlaid the
earth bank.   The road is now covered with turf.   For half-
a-mile onwards a road in the same straight line as the
boundary leads to Pike Hall, half-way between Hartington
and Winster.   After a gap of half-a-mile a parish boundary
in the same line marks the course of the road over Smervil
Moor, Middleton Common, and by Benty Grange, to
Henmoor (1140').   In Bishop Bennet's time the road was
visible from Pike Hall to Henmoor on the east of the
modern road, and there are still traces of it.   Half-a-mile
further the parish boundary joins the road and follows it
to Street House.   The modern road then turns to the west,
and the course of the old road, indicated by traces and by
the parish boundary, continued on, apparently crossing the
modern road near Brierlow.   At two miles from Buxton
the track of the Roman road appears as an irregular hollow
followed by a parish boundary, which leaves the present
road, and continues for more than a mile on the south-
west of it.

At Buxton remains of Roman baths and other buildings
were formerly found, and it is probably the *Aquis* of the
Ravenna list.   On the north-west of Buxton a Roman
road seems to have followed the course of the old Manchester road, as already noticed (p. 88), by Withan Lache
and Whalley Bridge to Stockport and Manchester.

(6) *Batham Gate.*—From Buxton a Roman road called
Batham Gate or Bath Way led in a north-easterly direction.
About one and a quarter miles from Buxton on the Chapel-
en-le-Frith road a lane branches off to Peak Forest railway
station, with a parish boundary along it.   The boundary

[1] *Jour. Derbyshire Archæol. and Nat. Hist. Soc.*, 1910.

continues on, but there seem to be no traces of the old road for a mile, and then a straight lane takes up the line for a mile to Dam Dale, which is crossed by winding down and up again.   Towards the Bakewell and Chapel-en-le-Frith road, at the back of the High Peak Inn, the road appears as a grass-grown ridge, but slightly raised above the ground and about 20 feet wide, with a layer of gravel at about three inches beneath the surface.[1]   Traces appear onwards for more than a mile across enclosed fields, and then a lane begins.   Here, at the boundary between Tideswell and Bradwell, Bishop Bennet described it in 1817 as visible for a mile on the Buxton side of the stone fence dividing the moors, and quite plain near the fence, 18 or 20 feet wide.[2]   It is still visible on Bradwell Moor, in places cut out of the slope and banked up on its outer side.[3]   The road appears to have descended by Cresswellport Lane, and through Smalldale, and Streetfield.   In 1769 it was plain for a mile onwards to Brough,[4] where the remains of the Roman fort were excavated in 1903 by the Derbyshire Archæological and Natural History Society.   It is a rectangle with rounded corners 112 yards by 92 yards inside the walls, which are six feet thick.   It appears to have been built, or more probably rebuilt, about A.D. 158, and it is probably *Nanone*, next to *Aquis* (Buxton), in the Ravenna list, as a Roman milliary found at Higher Buxton is inscribed *Anaviona* **x**.   Beyond Brough the line of Batham Gate is lost for two miles, but from the river Derwent it ascends in a straight and very steep course, and above Bamford remains in much perfection.   It crosses the moors between Stanedge and Redmires, where the large paving-stones remain in many places.   It there bears the name of " Long Causey," and continues on through Lydgate, over Crookesmoor, and along Camp Lane, and is then lost in the suburbs of Sheffield.[5]   It probably joined Riknild Street near Swinton.

Mr. J. Ward, F.S.A., has observed traces of a Roman road northwards from the point where Batham Gate turns

---

[1] W. Smithard, *Jour. Derbyshire Archæol. and Nat. Hist. Soc.*, vol. xxxiii. p. 95.

[2] Lysons, vol. v. p. ccviii.   [3] W. Smithard, *loc. cit.*

[4] Pegge, *loc. cit.*, p. 12.

[5] Guest, *History of Rotherham*, 1879, p. 593.

off from the Chapel-en-le-Frith road. A low ridge appears
on the west side of that road, and continues for about
three-quarters of a mile to the refuse mounds of the lime
works, and again beyond them more faintly for about a
third of a mile to a small stream near Doveholes. A section
at the side of a ditch showed that the *agger* was of millstone grit which must have been brought there. At the
stream mentioned above, near Ashpiece Farm, the road
seemed to have been embanked as if to cross by a bridge.
No traces were found beyond.

(7) *Derby to Aldborough.*—The course of Riknild Street
onwards is uncertain as far as Beardsall, north-east of
which the present road seems to occupy, or be close to
the line for a mile and a half past Breadsall Priory. At the
east corner of the latter (434´) there is a turn to the north,
and a parish boundary follows the road for a quarter of
a mile, and then traces of the ridge appear in the fields
on the east of the present road for half-a-mile. In 1769
it was visible quite across Morley moor,[1] and Bishop Bennet
noticed a large fragment of the ridge in 1817.[2] The line
can be traced on in the direction of Horsley Lodge, near
which it was very high and covered with furze early in the
last century,[2] and west of Horsley Woodhouse to Ticknall
Lane and Street Lane in the same line for four and a half
miles, the last three-quarters of a mile being followed by
a parish boundary. On the north of Horsley Woodhouse,
where Riknild Street passes between Kilbourne and Denby,
the ridge is conspicuous for a quarter of a mile on the west
of the present road. Mr. J. Ward, F.S.A., writes that it
is eight yards wide and as much as four or five feet high.

Just beyond, near Upper Hartshay (450´), there seems
to have been a turn; there is now no trace onwards for
three miles, but in 1769 the ridge was visible in places all
the way to Oakerthorpe, pointing to Coneygre House.[3]
Farther on, on the west of the road, is a square camp with
a double vallum, noticed by Pegge in 1769, and still discernible. Trenches were cut in 1909. No traces of walls
were found, but a paving about an inch thick of small
stones without mortar and Roman pottery were discovered.

[1] S. Pegge, *Roman Roads in the Country of the Coritani*, p. 6.
[2] Bishop Bennet. Lysons, vol. v., *Derbyshire*, p. ccviii.
[3] S. Pegge, *loc. cit.*, p. 6.

The inner *vallum* is 50 paces long in each direction.[1] The road at the south of Oakerthorpe seems to be on the line for a quarter of a mile, and the road on the north also, and there are traces of the ridge about a mile north of Wingfield Station, between the road and the railway, where in 1817 the ridge was visible for a mile.[2]

The present road through Higham and Stretton to Claycross seems to follow the course. Bishop Bennet, in 1817, described it as being quite plain for 300 yards through enclosures and over Tupton Moor three miles south of Chesterfield,[3] where it was formerly called Bignal Street.

A few miles north of Chesterfield the course of Riknild Street is shown on John Warburton's map of Yorkshire by Eckington to Beighton. There is a note on the map, " Here Rikenild Street enters from Darby," and that is confirmed by the discovery in 1847 of a paved road crossing the railway obliquely on the north of Beighton railway-station.[4] Warburton marks the road on by broken lines, as not visible, to a Roman camp at Templebrough, on the south side of the river Don, about a mile to the south-west of Rotherham. The camp (about 200 yards by 120 yards) can still be distinguished, and important remains have of late years been discovered there. On the north of the Don more than one line of ridges could formerly be traced, and are marked on the Ordnance maps as Roman, and it is far from certain which of them, if either, represents Riknild Street. One line marked " Roman ridge " runs by Meadow Hall, Kimberworth, Greasborough, and just below the dam of the lowest pond in Wentworth Park. On the north of the pond the ridge remains tolerably perfect, with a ditch and counter-scarp on the south-east side, and has all the appearance of a defensive work. It can be traced on to Upper Haugh, and a lane seems to connect it with a ridge which is visible on the north of Birch Wood. The Ordnance map continues it for a mile farther. Another line of " Roman ridge " is marked close to this one about half-a-mile on the north of Meadow Hall; it passes half-a-mile to the west of Kimberworth, and crosses Dog Kennel pond

---

[1] W. Smithard, *Jour. Derbyshire Archæol. and Nat. Hist. Soc.*, vol. xxxiii. p. 111.

[2] Bishop Bennet. Lysons, vol. v. p. ccix.

[3] Lysons, vol. v. p. ccxi.   [4] Hunter's *Hallamshire*, p. 23.

in Wentworth Park. On the south of the pond the ridge is visible without ditch or counterscarp, and it is shown onwards for a mile and a half by Hollen Hall to Hoober Hill, where it turns nearly eastward by Abdy and through Wath Wood, to the north of Swinton. Parish boundaries run along the line for the greater part of the way, and the ridge lately remained in many places.

If either of these ridges represents a Roman road, which is doubtful, it would seem to lie more in the course of Batham Gate from Buxton onwards to join Riknild Street, than in that of Riknild Street itself. The connexion of the ridges with the camp at Templebrough on the other side of the Don is not clear, nor is there any trace known of a Roman road to Templebrough from the direction of Beighton.

It is possible that Riknild Street followed a more direct course northwards from Beighton. A road following Warburton's line through Eckington and Beighton continues on to Aughton, and then turns more to the west to Guildthwaite, from which place tracks continue the same line to Alpha Place, and then, with a slight turn, roads, tracks, and a parish boundary carry the line on to the river Don at Aldwarke in the direction of Swinton; but from Aldwarke to Swinton, three and a half miles, there is no trace on the ground, nor other indication.

From the north of Swinton, a parish boundary runs nearly due north to the river Dearne, and the course of Riknild Street is marked on Warburton's map as visible onwards in that line for several miles to beyond Thurnscoe, and on by broken lines, which seem to follow parish boundaries for some miles, to Nostell and Normanton, and to the river Aire at Woodlesford (Swillington bridge), four miles above Castleford. On the north of the Aire, the road is marked on Warburton's map as being visible for eight miles; Street Lane follows it, and in about a mile is joined by a parish boundary. On the east of Temple Newsham the ridge, which the boundary follows, is still visible on the west of the lane, and is again to be seen on the east of Austhorpe, and in places nearly as far on as to Scholes. For four and a half miles the course of the road is still plain, parallel to, and less than three and a half miles from Erming Street. Warburton's map shows it as being visible

on as far as the Roman road from York to Adel and the
west, which it probably crossed near Bardsey, and by
broken lines on by the west of Stockeld Park and Golds-
borough to Arkendale, from which place onwards it is
marked as visible. The course is by Minskip, where there
is a well-defined rectangular camp about 100 yards by 75
yards, apparently a military post on Riknild Street rather
than an outpost of *Isurium*, as it has been supposed to
be. Riknild Street is shown on Warburton's map passing
about half-a-mile west of Boroughbridge, and joining
Leeming Lane at Kirby Hill.

If this be taken to be the continuation of Riknild Street
the difficulty presents itself of two Roman roads running
parallel to one another and only a few miles apart. The
explanation, as regards the southern part, appears to be
that the original road to the north was Riknild Street, and
that when York rose to such importance that access from
the south without crossing the wide Humber was necessary,
the road by Littleborough, Doncaster, and Aberford was
made, and was kept inland to avoid the lower courses of
the Trent, Don, Calder, and other rivers falling into the
Humber. With regard to the road shown on Warburton's
map further north, no traces of it appear to be known,
and modern maps afford no indications of it, but both it,
and Rudgate, four or five miles to the east of it, were
mapped by Warburton, his journal showing, as in other
cases, that his map is the result of personal observation.

CHAPTER IX

ROMAN ROADS FROM LONDON TO SILCHESTER AND THE SOUTH-WEST

(1) *General Course.*—The Roman road from London, which branching at Silchester communicated with the west of England and South Wales, is not referred to in the Laws of Edward, though it was as important as any of the Four Ways. The road takes a direct course from London to cross the Thames at Staines, beyond which it bends slightly towards the south, and then turns due west, straight to Silchester, the Roman *Calleva Atrebatum*. From Silchester a road of which little trace remains led to the north. To the south a road went to Winchester, and on to Porchester and Chichester, to beyond Southampton, and to Old Sarum. To the south-west the Portway led direct to Old Sarum, from which one road went to Dorchester and Exeter, and another westward, perhaps on to the Mendips. From Silchester to the west was a road to

235

Speen, where it divided, one branch going to Bath and across the Severn to Caerleon and South Wales, and the other to Cirencester, Gloucester, Brecon, and to beyond Carmarthen. Crossing these roads was a road from Winchester by Marlborough to near Wanborough, which formed a part of Higden's Erming Street from St. David's to Southampton.

(2) *London to Silchester.*—The course of the road from Roman London towards Silchester has been noticed as far as the south end of Edgware Road (p. 59). The course continues on to Notting Hill along the line of the Bayswater Road, which a parish boundary follows nearly all the way to the Westbourne stream. There is then a slight change of direction, and thence to Staines, $14\frac{1}{2}$ miles, the course of the road is so direct that it is nowhere more than a quarter of a mile out of a straight line. It would seem that from Notting Hill, on the edge of a terrace 95 feet above the sea and overlooking the Thames valley, some landmark or beacon, on ground (175') near Upper Bakeham to the south-west of Egham, was the point to which the course of the road was directed. From Upper Bakeham the towers of South Kensington and Westminster can be plainly seen, and the high ground at Upper Bakeham must have been equally visible from Notting Hill before houses obscured the outlook. From Notting Hill the Roman road followed this line, which is the general course of the present high road, until the latter turns southwards towards Chiswick. Stukeley rode on by a narrow straight way to Turnham Green, where to a discerning eye the trace of the road was manifest.[1] A footway followed the line until streets were set out for building, and parish boundaries, which have followed the present road all along, continue straight on in the same line by Stamford Brook Road to Stamford Brook, through Bedford Park, across Acton (Turnham) Green, and south of Acton Green railway-station, to near Gunnersbury station, and then along the high road again; and indicate the course of the Roman road to near Kew Bridge railway-station. The straight line appears then to have been departed from to keep clear of the Thames, and through Brentford, and on nearly to Hounslow, the course of the road is uncertain. It is probably followed

[1] *Itinerarium Curiosum*, p. 205.

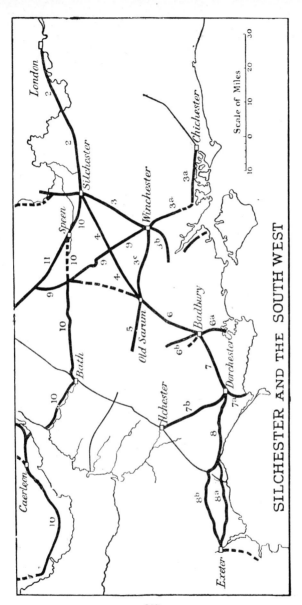

London

Chichester

Silchester

Winchester

Speen

Old Sarum

Badbury

Dorchester

Bath

Ilchester

Caerleon

Exeter

Scale of Miles

SILCHESTER AND THE SOUTH WEST

by the present road, again curving northwards from the
straight line near Spring Grove to avoid a stream.   From
the east end of Hounslow lengths of straight road, almost
in the same line, followed almost continuously by parish
boundaries, indicate that the present road follows the
course of the Roman road to Baber's Bridge.   The Roman
road itself was uncovered by General Roy at the end of the
eighteenth century on Hounslow Heath, at the side of the
modern road.   For two miles on to East Bedfont a parish
boundary runs straight a little on the south of the modern
high road, and then the latter, with a slight turn, goes
straight to Staines with parish boundaries along it for the
last mile and a quarter.   The straight line crosses the
Thames to Hythe a little to the south of the present bridge,
and near the site of the old bridge, to the west of which
Stukeley [1] saw the old road very evidently go through the
fields, the ridge being then visible ; but no sign of it now
appears.   He traced it along a lane and a footpath towards
Thorpe Lea.

    In 1835 the officers studying at Sandhurst made a
survey of the Roman road onwards to Silchester, and
a memoir was furnished to the *United Service Journal*.[2]
At Bakeham House, now called Upper Bakeham House,
the substratum of the road, and also the foundation of a
building, and other Roman remains, had then lately been
discovered, proving apparently that the straight course
of the road had continued from Notting Hill to that point.
In the valley, nearly half-a-mile to the south of this line,
a stone pillar erected near Great Fosters in 1850 records
that it marks the site of a Roman road to Silchester, a
portion of which remains in the adjoining meadow.   If so
the road did not continue straight on, but bent to the south
after crossing the Thames ; the pillar may, however, mark
the site of a branch road.   Beyond Bakeham the memoir
referred to states that the course was through the yard
of the inn at Virginia Water, where according to a tradition
a foundation of gravel, supposed to be the Roman road,
had formerly been discovered; and also that the line cuts
Virginia Water, and that the ridge could be distinguished
for 300 yards, where one of the drives in Windsor Forest

[1] *Itinerarium Curiosum*, p. 205.
[2] *Gent. Mag.*, 1836, part i. p. 535.

ran along it.   The yard of the inn seems to be out of a line across any part of Virginia Water, and no trace of the ridge is now distinguishable on to Belvedere, and the course of the road is uncertain.

It is likely that the hill on which the Belvedere Tower stands (260′) was the point made for from Bakeham Hill, though it was perhaps avoided by the road.   Beyond, the course of the road lies in a straight line between it and Duke's Hill, Bagshot (300′), the direction changing slightly, but the road from Notting Hill to Duke's Hill, so far as it is known, is so nearly straight for 23½ miles that no part is as much as three-quarters of a mile away from a straight line between those places.   At Sunningdale the road is found in digging in the allotments near the church, and it was until lately visible on by Chater's Pond, and south of King's Beeches to the back of Windlesham Hall, where the county boundary marks the line of it for a mile and a half. Enclosing, planting, and laying out the grounds of new houses have now however almost effaced all trace of it. About a mile east of Duke's Hill it is described in 1835 as being raised to a considerable height where it crossed a marsh.

From near Duke's Hill a Roman road has been supposed to have gone southward to Frimley, Farnborough and Farnham, and the change in the direction of the Silchester road has been thought to confirm the supposition, but without much reason.   Stukeley tells us [1] that he traced a Roman road from Winchester to Farnham and Farnborough, and which he supposed went on to Staines.   He says that between Farnham and Alton the bank was visible, and in several places between Alton and Alresford.   There appears to be no evidence of this road.

At Duke's Hill (300′) there is a change of 27° in direction, and the road goes nearly due west for 16 miles to Silchester. Under the local name of the Devil's Highway, it passes over Easthampstead Plain in a straight line to Crowthorn (311′), and then in nearly the same line to Ridge Farm, Finchampstead (331′), and, with a slight turn southwards, on by St. James' and West Court.   On Easthampstead Plain it passes a mile south of a large intrenchment called Cæsar's Camp, between which and the road, at Wickham

[1] *Itinerarium Curiosum*, p. 203.

Bushes, Roman coins and pottery are found. The Devil's Highway is said by Bishop Bennet [1] to have been raised, with a trench on each side, and to have been 90 feet wide, which probably included the trenches. It was levelled at the beginning of the last century when the ridings were cut. In 1835 portions were still existing to the north of Finchampstead Church and it was visible in a small meadow to the east of Jouldins Ford, where, or at Thatchers Ford, it crossed the Blackwater. The county boundary follows it over Riseley Common, where it was formerly visible. It crossed the river Loddon at Stanford, near the north of Stratfieldsaye Park, and beyond that, Park Lane, also called the Devil's Highway, with the county boundary along it for two miles, runs in a straight line to within half-a-mile of the east gate of Silchester (*Calleva*).

From Duke's Hill, Bagshot, to Silchester, 16 miles, no part of the road is a quarter of a mile out of a straight line joining those places.

Silchester, on ground 300 to 320 feet above the sea, is in shape an irregular polygon 860 yards from the east to the west gates, and 833 yards from the north to the south gates. Outside the Roman walls are earthworks of uncertain age. Five Roman roads converge to *Calleva*, approaching it in different directions, and it cannot be doubted that it owed much of its importance to its being the place from which the road from London branched.

The excavations carried on in recent years show that the street in continuation of the road from Staines ran straight from the east gate to the Forum, and a parallel street about 93 yards to the north of it led to the west gate. A street at right angles to these led from the north to the south gate. The east and west gates consisted of two covered passages, 13 feet wide, separated by a middle pier, while the north and south gates had only one passage of 13 feet.

There was, no doubt, a road from *Calleva* northward. Faint traces appear to have been observed in 1837 in a line between the north gate and Ufton Church, and 25 or 30 years before that the road is said to have been traced by excavations in that line for 800 yards.[2] It is said to be still traceable beyond Ufton Church, a hard concrete-like track being well known to old ploughmen, in a line with

[1] Lysons, vol. i. p. 201.   [2] *Gent. Mag.*, 1838, part i. p. 192.

Sulhampstead Rectory, crossing the garden of Cottage
Farm nearly a mile north of Ufton Church. According to
Mr. O. G. S. Crawford, the road lies a quarter of a mile
to the west of Ufton Church, and is plainly marked by a
causeway on the south and the north of Kiln Farm. The
modern road by Englefield to the ancient ford across the
Thames between Pangbourne and Whitchurch is a continuation of the line. The indications of a Roman road
in this direction on the west of the Thames through Streatley
from Dorchester have already been noticed (p. 202).

(3) *Silchester to Winchester.*—This road left *Calleva* by
the south gate, and its course is marked by the road by
Three Ashes and Hall-in-the-Hole to Latchmere Green.
Sir R. Colt Hoare says [1] that the ridge was " seen very
fine " behind a barn on the side of the road from Three
Ashes to Scotchman's Green, but he appears to refer to an
earthwork a quarter of a mile away from the line of the
Roman road, and the pitching of the latter was afterwards
opened on Latchmere Green.[2] In 1905 a trench was cut
in a garden to the west of the road at Latchmere Green.
At a depth of between five and six feet the road was found,
20 feet wide, of flints set in a bed of blue clay, one foot deep,
resting on gravel. The eastward edge was 88 feet 6 inches
from the centre of the modern road.[3] For three miles
from Latchmere Green the course is obscure, but on mounting the chalk at Sherbourne St. John the line is taken up
by the present road, and by a track over Rook's Down, on
the highest point of which (440′) a short bit of the ridge
remains supporting two old fir-trees. From this point
Silchester is visible, and a lane, followed by a parish
boundary, takes up the line for a mile and a half to Worting
Cross. The parish boundary continues on in the same
straight line for four miles from Rook's Down, and no doubt
marks the course of the Roman road, of which there is
now no trace on the ground. Near Southwood Farm the
parish boundary bends, and is soon joined by the Basing-
stoke and Winchester road, along which it runs to the
Wheatsheaf Inn. It would seem that the Roman road was
laid out in a straight line between Rook's Down (440′)

[1] *Ancient Wilts, Roman Æra.*
[2] Maclauchlan, *Archæol. Journ.*, vol. viii.
[3] *Archæologia*, vol 60, p. 168.

and high ground (552′) between Southwood Farm and Kempshott House, and that there a turn more to the south in the direction of Winchester was made. The course of the Roman road continues on in the same straight line from the Wheatsheaf to about a mile south of Popham, the present road lying a little to the west of it; there is then a slight turn, and the modern road, followed by a parish boundary for three miles, occupies the line of the old road along the west side of Stratton Park, and on in a straight line to King's Worthy. The road there turned away from the river and passed through Headbourne Worthy in a course not very plain, and then followed the line of the present road in a straight line as far as Abbot's Barton, through the grounds of which the same straight line is continued, and where some remains of the ridge can still be traced. The course onwards to the site of the north gate of *Venta Belgarum* (Winchester) is now covered with buildings.

The Roman city, on the west of the river Itchen, was a rectangle with rounded corners, measuring about 860 yards from the east gate near the river bank to the west gate at the other end of High Street, and about 780 yards from the north gate to the south gate; the principal cross street of the Roman city being marked by Southgate Street and Jewry Street at right angles with High Street.

(a) *Winchester to Porchester and Chichester.*—A Roman road left *Venta Belgarum* by the east gate, and after crossing the Itchen and turning south, curved round between St. Catherine's Hill and Deacon Hill, and then bent nearly at right angles towards the south. A parish boundary along the road for three miles and a quarter round the curve and on to Morestead, shows that the present Bishops Waltham road follows the same line. A straight line is then entered upon which ranges with high ground (471′) on Deacon Hill, and can be traced for about six miles. There are remains of the ridge in the wood a little south of the turn, and in the belt of trees on the west of the present road. South of Morestead a parish boundary runs alongside the road for half-a-mile, and in Jackman's Copse there are remains of the ridge. The old Ordnance map shows it for a mile and a quarter near Owslebury, where it was very conspicuous, and it is still to be traced through

Anstice's Copse, and on through Rowhay Wood for more than half-a-mile. Traces of the ridge are to be seen beyond, and the line is taken up by a lane a mile and a quarter further on, and the ridge is to be traced for half-a-mile on to Wintershill Farm, a mile and a quarter west of Bishops Waltham. Beyond that, on the tertiary beds, there is no trace except perhaps the name Cold Harbour, a mile north-west of Wickham. Stukeley says that upon Portsdown Hill, along which a parish boundary runs for three miles, he found some of the Roman way, which he supposed to go by Fareham and Havant to Chichester. Another course to Chichester has now been traced by Mr. O. G. S. Crawford, from the east of Wickham along the north side of Ports-down to Bedhampton. He found it visible as a causeway on Wickham Common, a mile east-south-east of Wickham, and in the fields beyond, in a line with the road from Wine Cross towards Havant. It was plain a mile east of Wine Cross as a hard track across marshy ground, and was traceable onwards in the same straight line to Belmont. It is continued by the present Chichester road to Havant, which with a slight turn, goes straight on to within three miles of Chichester.

Iter VII. of Antonine from *Regnum* to *Londinium* passes by *Clausentum, Venta Belgarum, Calleva,* and *Pontes.* Between London and *Clausentum* at Bitterne, where it is usually placed, the Itinerary distances agree fairly well with measurements on the map, bringing *Pontes* a mile or more to the west of Staines, a more likely situation than on the low ground by the Thames, but between *Clausentum* at Bitterne and *Regnum* (Chichester) the distance is 28 miles, compared with 20 M. P. in the Itinerary. If *Clausentum* be put near Wickham, where the course traced by Mr. Crawford joins the Roman road from Winchester, the distances would agree fairly well with those in Iter VII., but no remains are known there.

The road to Porchester, one of the most perfect Roman walled fortresses remaining, is unknown. It stands on a low point of land jutting into Portsmouth Harbour, the east wall, with a water-gate, being washed by the tide. It is a square of about two hundred and ten yards, with corner towers and mural bastions. It appears to be of a late Roman period.

(*b*) A Roman road left the south gate of *Venta Belgarum* and followed the course of the present road through St. Cross to Compton. Between the latter place and Otterbourne the old Ordnance map shows the ridge of the road for half-a-mile close alongside the present road and on the east of it, where it is still traceable. It can be traced in Otterbourne Hill Wood, but no further towards Bitterne, on the east bank of the Itchen, near Northam Bridge, where a *vallum* 460 yards long cuts off a promontory, supposed to be the site of *Clausentum*. There seems to be no trace of a Roman road from Bitterne in the direction of Chichester.

The Roman road from Winchester has been traced from Otterbourne Hill onwards to Nutshalling by Mr. O. G. S. Crawford.[1] He found it distinctly visible for 100 yards on the common on the east of the main road, formed of tertiary pebbles, and he traced it onwards. It is plain in Fryern Hill Wood, and to the south of that a section was exposed in a boggy peat-covered field, showing a thick band of pebbles upon clay. It crosses the road and railway near Chandlers' Ford at the railway bridge, and appears on the west of Titlark Farm. It can be traced on to near Chilworth Court, the ridge being well preserved in Hut Wood, and it crossed the high road near the inn. On the south of Chilworth House the ridge is shown for half-a-mile on the old Ordnance map, and can still be seen there, and in Dymore Wood, and beyond. There are no certain traces after crossing the Southampton and Romsey road, but the river Test is supposed to have been crossed at Nutshalling Mill.

The Roman road of which traces remain on Beaulieu Heath was presumably connected with this road. It is described in 1797,[2] as bearing for two or three miles straight towards the enclosure of Little Holbury, very high, 26 feet wide, and covered with ling. It appeared again, high-ridged and paved, in a meadow a little beyond Great Holbury, pointing into Warren Wood, and was very visible, two miles further on, on Langley Green. It was traced on to the Solent near Lepe, whence it is supposed was the crossing to the Isle of Wight. Rew Street, running south-ward from Gurnard Bay, has been thought to show the

1 *Proc. Hants. Field Club and Archæol. Soc.*, vol. vii. part i. p. 35.
2 Leman MS., *Wilts. Archæol. and Nat. Hist. Society.*

point of landing in the island, but there is no evidence for that or any other Roman road in the Isle of Wight.

Another supposed Roman road to Nutshalling, said to come from Bitterne, has been described [1] as passing along Burgess Street and the north of Southampton Common, where the road is a parish boundary for a mile, and on over Shirley Heath.

(c) *Winchester to Old Sarum.*—The Romsey road is nearly on the course of the Roman road from Winchester to Old Sarum for three-quarters of a mile from the west gate. It then leaves the line of it, which is followed straight on by a highway to high ground (484') at the south-west corner of Teg Down, where there is a turn, and a straight course begins, followed for six miles to the east side of the Test valley. The ridge of the road is shown on the old Ordnance map for nearly the whole distance. It is still observable beneath the present road between Teg Down and Crab Wood; it can be followed through West Wood, and it is plain on the west of the wood. Beyond Garlick Farm the straight line is now taken up by a hedge-row about half-a-mile south of Kings Sombourne, and on the edge of the Test valley (200') the hedgerow and a lane bend slightly towards the north, and descend to Horse-bridge Mill. In the beginning of the nineteenth century the pebbles of which the upper crust of the road was formed were still apparent on the east side of the Test valley, and the piles of a Roman bridge are said to have been found in cutting the canal near Horsebridge lock. [2] A bank somewhat resembling the ridge of a Roman road in the meadow on the north side of the road from Kings Sombourne, was the boundary fence of John of Gaunt's Deer Park.

On the west of the river a piece of the ridge is shown on the old Ordnance map in the same line, and again towards Pittlewood, on the north of which it is still visible. [3] The present road then joins the course of the Roman road,

[1] *Journ. Archæol. Assoc.*, 1891, p. 182.

[2] Sir R. C. Hoare, *Ancient Wilts, Roman Æra.*

[3] A pig of lead, found at Bossington on the west of the river in 1783, now in the British Museum, bears a stamp showing the date of it to be A.D. 60. (*Gent. Mag.*, 1783, part ii. p. 935.) It apparently is evidence of traffic along the road from the Mendip mines at an early period.

which lies in a straight line between Farley Monument (587'), erected on a barrow four miles east of the Test valley, and Middle Winterslow (500' +), seven miles west of the valley.   The old Ordnance map shows the ridge for the greater part of the way; and traces remain beyond Buckholt Farm and towards Winterslow, where the present road leaves the line.   A parish boundary follows the road for a quarter of a mile near Noad's Coppice.   From Middle Winterslow the ridge of the old road is shown on the old Ordnance map winding down the steep hill and then running straight for three miles across the lower ground, over Winterbourne Gunner Down, and through Stock Bottom on Winterbourne Down, half-a-mile south of Figsbury Rings.   The traces of the ridge are now effaced in the low ground, and a good deal of the down has been ploughed up, but on Winterbourne Down it is still to be seen for a mile and a half.   There is a bend on leaving the down, and the road makes straight for the south side of the inner mound of Old Sarum.   It crosses the Bourne at Winterbourne Ford, and the lane which now marks the course may be seen from the railway, running straight up to Winterbourne Down.   A lane continues on westward straight to Old Sarum, followed for one mile by a parish boundary.

The 19 M. P. between *Venta Belgarum* and *Sorbiodunum* in Antonine's Itinerary measure 21½ miles.   The inter-mediate station, *Brige*, was placed by Sir R. Colt Hoare at half-a-mile east of Buckholt Farm, about 12 miles from Winchester.

(4) *Silchester to Old Sarum*.—This road, called the Portway, was supposed by Sir R. Colt Hoare to branch off from the Winchester road outside the south gate of Silchester, in the wood below the wall, where he says it was visible.   A comparison of his map with that of Maclauchlan (1850) shows that the Roman roads of the former are ancient intrenchments in the latter.   The new Ordnance map, as it seems rightly, shows the road by a dotted line from the West Gate, through Pamber Forest, and by Tadley Place Farm to Foscot.   Sir R. Colt Hoare failed to trace it, and Maclauchlan, in 1851,[1] found not the least vestige of the road eastward of Foscot.   There the tertiary beds are

[1] *Journ. Archæol. Inst.*, vol. viii.

quitted, and on the chalk escarpment, six miles from
Silchester, the ridge of the road is shown on the old Ordnance
map for one and a half miles pointing towards the south
side of Silchester, and in the opposite direction to high
ground (700') at Freemantle Park Farm, but it is now
hardly traceable. At Freemantle Park Farm (700') there
is a very slight change in direction, and the road appears
to have been directed to the high ground (450') on the south
side of Quarley Hill, nearly 19 miles off. The ridge was
formerly traceable by Walkridge Farm and over Ridgeway
Heath for four and a half miles, but it has been effaced by
planting a belt of trees along it. The line is fortunately
preserved by parish boundaries for three and a half miles
to Bradley Wood, where it was lately visible. Beyond,
traces of the road are lost for two miles and a half. About
half-a-mile on the west of St. Mary Bourne, the paving of
the road was removed in 1879 for a length of a quarter of
a mile on account of its interference with farming operations.
It was found at from four to eight inches below the surface,
and was about eight yards wide.[1] The outline of the road
is traceable in the wood to the eastward, and the course
of the Portway onwards is taken up by the present road
to Andover by Finkley. At Finkley, 18 miles from *Calleva*,
Sir R. Colt Hoare placed *Vindomis*, a station named in
Iter XV., but the distances from *Calleva* and from *Venta
Belgarum* would place the station to the east of St. Mary
Bourne. The Roman road from Winchester to *Cunetio* and
Cirencester (p. 261) crosses the Portway about one mile to
the west of Finkley.

The Portway was formerly visible on the south of East
Anton, but there are now few traces of it for two and
a half miles across arable land until the Andover and
Weyhill road is reached. There, in a straight line with
the course of the Portway, which can be seen by Finkley
and towards St. Mary Bourne, is a road to the south-west
followed by a parish boundary, and the same line is continued by the road onwards through Monkston and the
park of Amport House to the south side of Quarley Hill.
From this, looking eastward, the course of the road can be
traced in a straight line to Freemantle Park, more than 18
miles distant. There is then a turn, and the line of the road

[1] *Journ. Brit. Archæol. Assoc.*, vol. xxxv. p. 92.

lies straight between the south side of Quarley Hill and the south side of the central mound of Old Sarum, 10 miles off. From the top of Quarley Hill Old Sarum is visible, as it would doubtless be from the line of the Roman road on the south slope of it if a plantation of trees did not intervene. The present road occupies the course for about half-a-mile, and then there is a track over the downs, generally a slightly raised grass-covered ridge, but in places worn down to the flint surface of the old road.   In about a mile the railway approaches it on the south and runs close alongside it for three and a half miles to near Idmiston.   On down land the appearance continues the same, but where the land has been ploughed up the road is no longer traceable.   On the down on the east of Idmiston the ridge of the road remained inside the railway fence until the railway was lately widened.   At the descent into the Idmiston valley the track of the Roman road leaves the railway and diverges somewhat from the straight course in crossing the valley.   It is shown on the old Ordnance map resuming the same straight line and passing round a barrow, but all traces of road and barrow are now effaced by ploughing.   Through Porton and Gumbleton the course of the road is uncertain, but on the other side of the Bourne valley it is shown by a line of highways and tracks pointing straight to the south side of the central mound of Old Sarum, and continuing to within half-a-mile of it.

A straight line from Silchester to Old Sarum (*Sorbiodunum*) passes a mile to the south of the Roman road at Quarley Hill, where the road lies farthest away from a straight line in the 36 miles between those places.

It is to be noticed that this road, the Roman road from Winchester, and that on to the west, all three point to the inner of the two immense concentric ramparts of Old Sarum. The outer ring, which is supposed to have been strengthened by Alfred, has a mean diameter of about 520 yards.

(5) *Old Sarum to the West.*—The course of this road for the first three and a half miles across the valleys of the Avon and the Wily is uncertain.   A ford and causeway across the Wily about a quarter of a mile below South Newton Mill may possibly mark the crossing of that river.   Sir R. Colt Hoare described this road, and gave a map of it,[1] which is

[1] *Ancient Wilts, Roman Æra.*

based on the old Ordnance survey, with additions and slight alterations. Then, as now, the first traces of the Roman road appear as a ridge issuing from the north-east side of Grovely Wood, pointing to the ramparts of Old Sarum, and according to Sir R. Colt Hoare it continued an uninterrupted course through thick copse wood for several miles until it made its exit near Dinton Beeches, and he speaks of its well-known course. The old Ordnance map and Sir R. C. Hoare's map both show the ridge through Grovely Wood in a straight line between the south side of the inner rampart of Old Sarum, and high ground (648′) near Dinton Beeches, and then on in nearly the same straight line through Stockton Wood and Great Ridge Wood to a quarter of a mile north of Lower Pertwood Farm, sixteen and a half miles from Old Sarum. The new Ordnance map marks the course through Grovely Wood, where it is now very difficult to follow it, by a dotted line not straight, but changing its direction at Grovely Lodge, and bending in the wood to get to Dinton Beeches; and beyond, what is a very crooked ditch and bank on the south of Stockton Wood and Great Ridge Wood, is marked Roman road, Sir R. Colt Hoare carefully mapped and described both the ditch and the road, and he found the latter beyond Dinton Beeches distinguishable across arable fields by a line of large flints, and passing into Stockton Wood, where he shows it on his map of the Stockton earthworks.[1] It is not now traceable, but there is little doubt that the true line of the Roman road is that laid down on the old Ordnance map, straight through Stockton Wood and Great Ridge Wood, to the north of Lower Pertwood Farm, where it is shown, as described by R. C. Hoare, passing round a tumulus in its course. Beyond that traces of the road are lost; Sir R. Colt Hoare conjectured that the course was along a road north of Kingston Deverill, and then confesses himself at fault for a very considerable distance; and the course he gives by Maiden Bradley and East Cranmore to the Mendip Hills appears to have little evidence on the ground, or from parish boundaries. The old Ordnance map shows a piece of ridge nearly in the line of the ridge at Lower Pertwood, on Long Knoll, one mile south of Maiden Bradley. A parish boundary follows the ridge, which points to a barrow on the west end of the knoll. It is six miles

[1] *Ancient Wilts.*

from the ridge near Lower Pertwood, and there are no traces
of the road beyond. The continuation of Sir R. Colt
Hoare's road over the Mendips has already been noticed in
connexion with the Foss road (p. 218).

(6) *Old Sarum to Badbury.*—This road quitted Old Sarum
on a line straight from the south side of it to the crossing
of Bokerly Dyke (410'), 10 miles distant. A lane called
Portlane leads to a ford south of Stratford-sub-Castle,
where the Roman road crossed the Avon near Coldharbour
Farm, and a track, and Folly Lane, mark the course on
in the same line to Bemerton, where Stukeley tells us [1] a
stony ford over the Nadder was still very perfect. Leman
records that the vicar's barn stood upon the road, which was
visible over the meadows,[2] pointing to a lane leading up to
Wilton racecourse. A parish boundary follows the lane,
and beyond, a green track through ploughed land, a track
and a ridge across the down, and a lane, mark the course to
near Toney Stratford, where the river Ebble was crossed.
A track, now a good deal effaced, leads on to high ground
(500'), one mile south-south-west of Bishopstone, where
a remarkable diversion from the straight line begins. The
latter was no doubt laid out from points on the high ground
(500') intermediate between Old Sarum and Bokerly Dyke,
but if it had been followed it would have crossed in the space
of a mile and a half three steep-sided coombes 150 to 250
feet deep, separated by two spurs of similiar height, before
regaining the 500 feet level. The straight line was therefore
departed from, and the road was kept on the high ground
to the south of the coombes. The ridge of the road is
shown on the old Ordnance map for nearly the whole
length of the diversion. Sir R. Colt Hoare described it
some few years later as in very perfect form on the down,
and traces still remain. A narrow lane, and a track beside
a hedge where the land has been ploughed up, now mark
the course. Stukeley, who described this *diverticulum*,
says that the ridge was very perfect to the west of it, butting
full upon the end of a vast valley very deep and of steep
descent. The course of the road where it resumes the same
straight line as before is now marked by a track along a
hedgerow north-west of Knighton Woods, where traces of a

[1] *Itinerarium Curiosum*, p. 187.
[2] MS. notes to *Britannia Romano* at Bath Library.

paving are marked on the new six-inch Ordnance map, and by Vernditch Woods to the down, where the embankment is very conspicuous, and the ditches at the side remain, including which the total width is about 20 yards. A parish boundary follows the ridge here for a mile and a half. Where the embankment is away from the modern road it remains almost perfect, about five and a half yards wide at top, and as much as six or seven feet high, and where a drove-way has been cut through, it shows a coating of tertiary gravel, two feet six inches to three feet thick. This must have been brought some four or five miles from the south. A little further on the ridge has been has entirely cleared away, the materials having been taken to make the embankment of the modern road where it crosses a hollow. There are no traces of side ditches on the surface, but sections cut by General Pitt Rivers [1] revealed them, and showed the ridge to consist of a layer of nodules of flint on the old surface, upon which were six inches of rammed chalk, ten inches of tertiary gravel, six inches of rammed chalk rubble, six inches of gravel with rounded (tertiary) pebbles, with five inches of surface mould over, making a total height of three feet from the orginal surface to the top. The gravel top must have been entirely removed where this section was made. Towards Woodyates, where the old and the modern roads approach, the gravel top has been dug out from the middle of the embankment to a depth of more than two feet. Bokerly Dyke, a rampart and ditch which for some miles constitutes the county boundary, here crosses the Roman road, and the excavations made by General Pitt Rivers throw light on both. He cut a section through Bokerly in the line of the Roman road, which proved that the dyke was raised upon and across the road. A flint pitching mentioned in connexion with the latter would seem to have been the lowest stratum, not the surface of the road. Coins found in the rampart proved it to be not earlier than A.D. 394-423, and General Pitt Rivers [2] considered it might possibly have been thrown up by the Romanized Britons, and he supposed that the Romano-British settlement excavated by him here was *Vindogladia*, a station in Antonine's Itinerary 12 M. P. from *Sorbiodunum*, but also eight M. P. from *Durnonovaria*. Sir R. Colt Hoare placed *Vindogladia*

---

[1] *Excavations in Bokerly Dyke,* pl. clxiii.　　　[2] *Ibid.,* p. 20.

at another settlement found by him on Gussage Down, some five miles further on ; and he altered the Itinerary distances accordingly.

Immediately on the west of Bokerly the Roman road makes a turn through about 25° towards Badbury Rings, a conspicuous British camp 11 miles off. The first point made for was, however, on Harley Down (360'), five miles distant. For half-a-mile from the turn the line of the old road is in enclosed land on the west of the present road, and nothing remains visible but an undulation of the surface. Woodyates, in coaching days Woodyates Inn, is on the course of the Roman road, and then for a mile the present road occupies the site of it, the ridge having been destroyed, but a parish boundary running along the road. The present road then turns towards the west, and the Roman road, here called Achling or Ackling Ditch, or Dyke, goes straight on, and is very perfect for four miles across the downs, a parish boundary following it for three miles. It is five yards wide across the top, and four, five, or six feet or more high. The gravel top has been dug away in places to a depth of two or three feet for the sake of the material. Traces of the side ditches remain, and in several places they cut the annular bank and ditch surrounding a barrow. This is perhaps the most striking example of the embankment of a Roman road remaining in the country. It runs for miles in a straight line in bold and sharp relief over the open down, and the magnitude of the work and its situation are alike imposing.

At the highest point on Harley Down (360') there is a slight turn more to the south in the direction of the east side of Badbury Rings. When the down is left the ridge appears as a hedgerow at the side of a lane, worn away on the other side by the plough, and with a parish boundary along it. After crossing the Gussage brook the lane ends in an old chalk-pit, but the parish boundary continues on for a quarter of a mile to a lane, beyond which a footpath and a fence along the east side of the enclosed Holly Down carry on the line. In a mile the grounds of Crichel Park are entered, and the ridge is traceable through the rookery. The school on the small common to the south of the park appears to be on, or close to, the line of the road, which is no longer traceable across the fields beyond. Witchampton

Common, where Sir R. Colt Hoare saw the ridge entire in parts, has been enclosed, and a road has been made along the course of it, which is then followed by a lane for two miles to near Badbury Rings, except at one place where it cuts across the corner of an arable field which the lane goes round. From near Broadford, where a small stream is crossed, a parish boundary follows the lane for half-a-mile.

(a) *Badbury to Poole Harbour.*—On the north of Badbury Rings the Roman road divides, one branch continuing on with a slight turn to the south, and the other branching off at an angle of 40° to the south-west. The ridge of the road is plain a quarter of a mile north of King's Down Farm, and can be followed through a wood, on emerging from which it is again plain, first with the upper surface hollowed by digging out the coating of pebble gravel, and further on as a turfed ridge three yards wide and about two feet high. The direction is here a few degrees west of south, pointing between Badbury Rings and High Wood.

The great earthwork called Badbury Rings consists of three concentric ramparts and ditches crowning a detached hill of chalk (327'). It is rather larger than Old Sarum, the mean diameter of the outer defence being about 533 yards.

It is to be observed that for six miles north of Badbury the direction of the Roman road from Old Sarum is straight towards the east side of that earthwork, and with a slight turn, passes more to the east of it, as if in the first place the road was laid out to communicate with the south rather than the west, and the road branching off towards the west was afterwards laid out.

Between Badbury Rings and High Wood the road bends to the south-east, and arable ground is entered upon, across which the course could be traced in 1847 [1] but it is no longer so, and the course through Kingston Park is not known. Beyond, the ridge was discovered in Abbot Street Copse by the Rev. G. Herbert, and when the undergrowth was cut in 1907 it was very distinct. Less than half-a-mile farther on, on the slope of the Stour valley, is what appears to be the remains of a square camp about 87 yards by 72 yards, enclosing a mound. On the south side of the river the ridge

[1] Dr. Wake Smart, *Proc. Dorset Nat. Hist. and Antiq. Field Club,* vol. xv. p. 22.

can be followed across Eye Mead along the track marked on the Ordnance map, the gravel surface of the road being found a few inches beneath the turf. After the Stour valley had been crossed the road seems to have turned toward the west of south, and on the high ground on the south of the river, a section of the road was formerly to be seen in Corfe Mullen gravel-pit. The position in the pit, which covers several acres, is now unknown, and there is nothing to indicate the course of the road from the river. On the south of the gravel-pit a parish boundary marks the line, along which the ridge can be traced on to a lane about a mile west of Merley House, and then it is plain, a cart-track running sometimes alongside, and sometimes on the top of it, and on the heath it is almost perfect, four yards wide across the top, and three feet high. On the descent into a valley the ridge disappears, but on the ascent of the opposite hill it is again seen, and is very plain on the heath at Corfe Hills, of the same dimensions as before. After again disappearing where the line crosses a hollow, the ridge reappears on the brow of the next hill, and a section exposed in a gravel-pit in 1900 showed one foot six inches of gravel on the old heath soil, with a bottom width of six yards. The ridge is higher on the top of the hill, and is again visible on the high ground to the south of the road to Broadstone. From that, down the hill, and across the railway to Upton House on Poole Harbour, the course of the road is marked by a track alongside a straight fence. Parish boundaries follow the straight road continuously for three miles from Corfe Mullen gravel-pit to Upton. The same straight line is continued on the south of Upton, and a piece of the ridge remains between Hamworthy Junction and Holes Bay. Traces also exist on the higher ground of Hamworthy Heath. The remains of the ridge there show a turn to the south-east, and in cultivated ground a little further on the road was taken up not many years ago. It was also dug through about 70 yards west of Hamworthy Churchyard. According to Warne [1] it crossed the Poole road, and after passing to the east of the old Manor House (now the Rectory), it terminated on the shore of the Poole estuary.

(b) A Roman road leaving Badbury at or near the point

[1] *Ancient Dorset*, p. 183.

where the road from Old Sarum divides has been traced northward to Donhead, by Hemsworth Down, to the east of Tarrant Monkton and Tarrant Hinton, through the grounds of Eastbury Park, and over Main Down, where the ridge is visible, to the high ground (850') on the north of Ashmore overlooking the vale of Wardour, into which it descends by Donhead Hollow.[1] It preserves a straight course for 11 miles, which if continued would, in another 10 miles, join the Roman road from Old Sarum to the west at the last point to which it is traceable, near Pertwood.

There are indications of another road from Badbury to Hod Hill, where there is a Roman camp within earlier intrenchments. A parish boundary in a straight line along a belt of trees for a mile and a quarter, points to Hod Hill eight miles off, and there are tracks onwards in the same line.

(7) *Badbury to Dorchester.*—The course of the Roman road in the direction of Dorchester, branching off on the north side of Badbury, where the ridge is plain, appears to be through Shapwick, nearly parallel to and on the north of the street, crossing the river Stour a little below the church. At the beginning of the last century the road was visible over the parish marsh on the south of the church. It continued on through Little Coll Wood to high ground (240') on the south of Coll Wood near Mapperton, where a hedgebank is in the line. Warne [2] describes the ridge a little farther on as highly raised for 300 yards. A slight turn brings the line in the direction of the road through Winterbourne Kingston, and also pointing to the north side of the hill crowned by Maiden Castle (400') 15 miles distant, beyond Dorchester. A bit of the ridge remains in this line in Bagwood, half-a-mile west of Winterbourne Kingston, and there are several other traces between that and Tolpuddle, and fences and footways and bits of parish boundaries follow the line. From half-a-mile west of Tolpuddle a parish boundary marks the course for a quarter of a mile, and then there is no trace for several miles. The new Ordnance map shows remains of the ridge on Puddleton Heath, not in the same line, and where it is entirely hidden by the thick heath and furze. A piece of the ridge remains

[1] *Proc. Dorset Nat. Hist. and Antiq. Field Club,* vol. ix. p. 147.
[2] *Ancient Dorset,* p. 174.

along the north side of the road through Kingston Park. The present road from Grays Bridge to Dorchester appears to be on the line of the Roman road.

Dorchester, generally considered to be *Durnonovaria*, is bounded irregularly on the north side by the river Frome. Along the High Street the Roman city from the east to the west is 660 yards, and from the north to the south it measures from 360 yards at the east to 730 yards at the west. Though rectangular towards the south the general form approaches a quadrant of a circle.

The Itinerary of Antonine (Iter XV.) makes it 20 M. P. from *Sorbiodunum* to *Durnonovaria*, which is less than half the distance between Old Sarum and Dorchester. If the latter be *Durnonovaria*, as it almost certainly is, 21 miles must be left out, with a station, probably Badbury, in the same way as a station and distance must have dropped out of Iter XIII. between Cirencester and Speen.

(*a*) *Dorchester to the South.*—A Roman road from Dorchester to the south was very perfect between Maumbury and Winterbourne Monkton before the present turnpike road was made, " a high, broad ridge paved with stone." [1] Near the latter place it passes within half-a-mile of Maiden Castle, a camp of oval form 1200 yards from east to west, and 550 yards from north to south, crowning a chalk hill (400') with vast triple ramparts, enclosing 43 acres of ground. There are evidences of Roman occupation, and some traces of the ridge of a road on the Dorchester side of the earthworks. The present Weymouth road is straight for three miles to Ridgeway Hill (440'); and at the beginning of the last century the elevated ridge, pitched with stone and nearly covered with turf, was still visible for half-a-mile beyond,[2] and the course of the road was traceable on the south side of the hill to the west of the modern road. A parish boundary follows the course for three-quarters of a mile. On the south of Upway the Roman road appears to be on the east of the present Weymouth road, and the ridge, 10 yards wide, was lately visible in the lane leading to Thornhill Farm, and could be traced in a meadow opposite Broadway Church.[3] On the south of Broadway a parish boundary

---

[1] Hutchins' *Dorsetshire* (1796), p. viii. of 3rd edition, 1861.
[2] Hatcher, quoted by Warne, *Ancient Dorset*, p. 186.
[3] Warne, 1872, p. 186.

follows the straight road for half-a-mile to Redlands, and traces of the Roman road are said to have been found at the foot of the hill in Radipole parish. A parish boundary follows the present road for a quarter of a mile to the mouth of the Wey, near Radipole church.

(b) *Dorchester to Ilchester.*—The road from Dorchester to Ilchester, which has been already mentioned (p. 220), appears to have left by the west gate, passing to the south of Poundbury, following the course of a straight road for a mile and a quarter to Bradford Peverel, and crossing the river Frome to Stratton in a straight line to the high ground (611') north of Frampton. It is described in 1796 as a " *dorsum* broad and high and paved with flints," and as being visible in the meadows near the Frome.[1] It is still plain in the fields beyond Stratton, and at Grimston Common Field it was described as an elevated ridge paved with flints.[2] The present road takes the line beyond Grimston, and then there is a turn (611'), and Long Ash Lane, with a parish boundary along it, continues the course for four miles to high ground (800'), half-a-mile east of Frome St. Quintin. Between this point and a point (400') near Vagg, two miles north-west of Yeovil, and 11 miles distant, the course of the road seems to have been laid out. Roads and lanes here and there, sometimes with parish boundaries along them, lie in the line, which passes one mile west of Yeovil. From Vagg to Ilchester the present road follows the course for three miles in a straight line.

(8) *Dorchester to Exeter.*—To the west of Dorchester the modern road occupies the site of the Roman road for three and a half miles as far as Knowle Hill. From about half-a-mile from the town it appears to be directed straight for two and a half miles to a tumulus on Bradford Down. A parish boundary follows it for a mile and a half along the straight road, and continues to follow the winding road for seven miles to Eggardun Hill (828'). When Stukeley saw the road between Dorchester and Bridport, then called the Ridgeway, the original ridge remained, made of flints laid in a fine bank and covered with turf.[3] He noticed that it frequently made great curves to avoid valleys, and

---

[1] Hutchins' *Dorsetshire.*   [2] Warne.
[3] *Itinerarium Curiosum*, p. 161.

R

kept on the highest ground; there are, however, pieces of straight road as well as curves. The ridge is still plain nearly all along, and in many places it is conspicuous.

To the north of the road, on Eggardun Hill, is an oval camp, triple-trenched on the west, about half the size of Maiden Castle, which it somewhat resembles. It would seem that the Roman road took the course of an older road to this stronghold, and the Roman manner of setting out is not characteristic of the road onwards.

From near Eggardun the road turns towards the south-west and slants down the hill by Spyway Green, and is traceable through the arable land. When the old road was broken up it was seen to be "composed of a bed of large flints laid on the substratum of chalk, with a thick layer of smaller stones on the top, the whole almost as compact as a wall." [1] According to Davidson, the course of the road is joined by the present road to Bridport about a mile and a quarter west of Askerwell; but there is a good deal in favour of the course given by Warne on the authority of a local antiquary, through Up Loders and Yondover and along the road from Yondover to the main road one mile east of Bridport. From that point parish boundaries follow the present road to Bridport, and it appears to be on the line of the Roman road through Bridport, and on to half-a-mile beyond Chideock. Then the Roman road mounted Chardown Hill, and passed over Stonebarrow Hill, the course being by Cold Harbour and along a lane followed by a parish boundary for two miles on to the river Char. At Charmouth the Roman road is supposed to have divided, one branch continuing along the coast, and the other going by Axminster and Honiton.

(a) The former road seems to have passed north of Lyme Regis to Heathfield Cross in the course of the present road, which parish boundaries follow for three-quarters of a mile, a quarter of a mile, and half-a-mile; and on by Axbridge, Colyford, and Elverway, to Sidford, parish boundaries following the road for three miles on the east of Salcombe Regis, and for half-a-mile on the east of the river Sid. At Stowford the modern road leaves the line of the old road, which is represented by a lane with a parish boundary along

[1] Davidson, *British and Roman Remains in the Vicinity of Axminster*, 1833.

it over the shoulder of a hill, and is rejoined by the present road in three-quarters of a mile. The parish boundary follows the present road on to the river Otter, and then runs at the back of the houses on the north of the street at Poppleford, and again joins the present road, along which it runs to Windmill Hill, having apparently followed the course of the Roman road continuously for six and a half miles from Stowford. Then, after an interval of one mile, there is a quarter of a mile of parish boundary, and after another interval of three-quarters of a mile, parish boundaries follow the present road continuously for two and a half miles to the junction with the Roman road through Axminster and Honiton.

(b) This latter road goes over Charmouth Hill by Penn Cross and Hunter's Lodge to Axminster, county and parish boundaries following the present road for two and a half miles from Penn Cross. Just before reaching Axminster a road called Stony Lane, turning off to the north to Millbrook, appears to mark the junction or crossing of the Foss Way (p. 221). On the west of Axminster, after the valley of the Axe and the Yarty has been crossed, a straight road a mile and three-quarters long begins, pointing to high ground (700') on the east of Axminster and continuing to Shute Hill (455'). Then the road winds, with a parish boundary following it for two miles, and descends Moorcox Hill, close to the railway four miles east of Honiton, where in 1828 the structure of the old road was seen, 18 inches thick with large stones at the bottom and smaller at the top, closely cemented as with mortar.[1] The present road occupies the line of the old road through Wilmington, parish boundaries following it for two miles, and then for one and a half miles on to Honiton the course is not clear. Through Honiton the present road is straight for three miles, and it continues in nearly the same line to Patteson's Cross, and on to the river Otter at Fairmile, on the west of which a parish boundary follows the road for a mile and a half. From near Whimple the road, straight for two and a quarter miles, is followed by parish boundaries for nearly a mile and a half, and they continue along the road for another mile and a quarter through Rockbere ; and again after an interval of a mile, parish boundaries follow the road from

[1] Davidson, *loc. cit.*

the river Clyst to the fork roads near East Wonford, where the Roman road along the coast joins. The road continues on through Heavitree to Exeter (*Isca Dumnuniorum*).

The Itinerary of Antonine (Iter XII., Iter XV.) makes it 51 M. P. from *Durnonovaria* to *Isca Dumnuniorum*, which agrees fairly well with the actual distance between Dorchester and Exeter by either route. The intermediate station, *Muridunum*, 36 M. P. from the former and 15 M. P. from the latter, is placed by Camden and others at Seaton, which is seven miles too far to the east. On the inland line the distances would place it near Honiton, a site which agrees better with the inland position of *Ridunum*, as it seems to be shown in the *Tabula Peutingeriana*.

Iter XII. of Antonine has occasioned much discussion. Wesseling gives the heading *Per Muridunum Viroconium*, and it was made a *Calleva per Muridunum Viroconium* by Gale to suit the Iter as it stands. Parthey and Pinder give it *a Muriduno Viroconium*, and while printing the Iter continuously as it stands in all MSS., they suggest in a note that the first eight lines, enclosed within brackets, were by mistake transferred from Iter XV. On this supposition the first station after *Muridunum* would be *Leucarum*, and the length of the Iter by addition of the distances would be 166 compared with the 186 in the heading. The position of the three stations between *Muridunum* and *Isca Leg. II. Augusta* (Caerleon) are unknown. Bishop Clifford [1] continued Iter XII. from Exeter by Hembury, putting *Nidum* near Taunton and *Bomium* near the mouth of the river Parrett, 27 miles by water from Caerleon. No trace of either road or stations are known ; the country about the river Parrett must have been a swamp in Roman times, and a 20 mile passage across the Bristol Channel does not seem likely. The suggested removal of these stations to South Wales will be reverted to (p. 280).

There appear to be no roads set out in the characteristic Roman manner beyond Exeter. According to Bishop Bennet, an old road, converted by the Romans to their own use, went over Haldon to Teignbridge, and was quite plain at the beginning of the nineteenth century on the right of the turnpike road on the ascent to Haldon. It seems to have passed by Alphington, on the south of which

[1] *Somerset Archæol. Proc.*, vol. xxii., pp. 2, 22.

a parish boundary follows the present road for a quarter of a mile, and on by Red Cross and Kennford. On Haldon a parish boundary follows the road for half-a-mile, and then leaves it and joins the road branching to Teignmouth, which it follows for half-a-mile, and then follows Haldon Lane for two miles to the east end of Ugbrooke Park, where it rejoins the Exeter road, and follows it to Sandy Gate, a mile and a quarter north of Teignbridge. This line of parish boundaries, more than five miles long, seems to mark the course of the old road. Teignbridge is claimed to be of Roman origin, and it is certain that remains of a very ancient bridge were found in rebuilding the bridge in the latter part of the eighteenth century. Bishop Bennet continued the road by Totnes to St. Michael's Mount, led so far probably by the itinerary attributed to Richard of Cirencester.[1] Another old road over Little Haldon, now called Portway, and the boundary of Dawlish parish, is mentioned in a deed of 1044 as "Strœte" and "Port Strœte," and has been thought to be the line of a road which crossed the Teign below Newton Abbey.[2] Bishop Bennet mentions the crest of a Roman road visible for a mile near Uffculme on the road from Exeter to Taunton, and he says there was a road from Exeter in a north-easterly direction, but there seems to be no trace of these, and of a supposed Roman road from Exeter to Stratton, on the Cornish coast, there seems to be no evidence at all.

(9) *Winchester to Cunetio and Wanborough.*—This is a road crossing the Portway near Andover, passing by the Roman station *Cunetio* near Marlborough, and joining the road from Speen to Cirencester about half-way between those places. The road left the north gate of *Venta Belgarum*, and the present Andover road, followed by a parish boundary for five miles, is on the line of the Roman road from the suburbs of Winchester to Barton Down Farm, six and a half miles from Winchester. The course is straight to Worthy Down (400′), where there is a slight turn, and a straight line begins which continues for 15 miles to the north side of Conholt Park, a highway following it for nearly the whole distance. A plantation on the north side of the present road interferes with the view along the line of the road,

[1] Lysons, vol. vi. p. cccxiv.
[2] Davidson, *Trans. Devon. Ass.*, xiii. p. 106.

but from Worthy Down Conholt is plainly visible in clear weather, and it is quite possible that the long straight line was laid out between Deacon Hill (471') two miles south-east of Winchester, which the line cuts, and Conholt (790'). From Chute Heath, close to the latter, the high downs beyond Winchester can be plainly seen in clear weather.

The ridge of the road has been destroyed in making the modern road, but it is visible between Barton Down Farm and the Test valley, and again on the north side of the valley through Harewood Forest, where a parish boundary follows it for a mile and a half. The line of the road is crossed by the railway a mile and a half east of Andover station, and the straight lines which follow it can be seen from the train. Near East Anton the line of the Portway is crossed, but there is no sign of it. On approaching Charlton Woodlands Farm the course is across fields for half-a-mile, and then it is again followed by a lane, along which the ridge is visible in places. At the south-east of Conholt Park the road bisects a circular earthwork, and through Conholt Park the embankment is very plain. It was described as long ago as 1760,[1] and it was cut into by Mr. G. Knowles, the owner of Conholt Park, in December 1898. In one place, where the old road is a terrace on sloping ground, some six feet high on the lower side, and four or more yards wide, it was found that beneath a foot or 15 inches of soil there are five and a half inches of white chalk compacted together, then three or four inches of clay, under which was found a layer, 18 inches thick, of large flints, apparently set by hand, the upper four or five inches of which appeared as if they had been burnt and were mixed with a black powder. We learn from the old account of 1760 that the upper stratum was a beautiful gravel, no parts of the country near producing any such material. That has since been removed, probably to make garden-paths. In other places the black powder appears immediately under the turf, the upper layers having probably been removed. Near the north side of the park the layer of large flints is 12 inches thick, the flints closely packed together and the upper surface apparently burnt. Under the flint layer a bed of stiff clay with small flints embedded was found, but was not dug into for more than a few inches.

[1] *Archæologia*, vol. i. and vol. viii.

The appearance of black ash or cinder over the layer of flints apparently burnt is remarkable, and attracted the notice of R. Willis in 1760, who likened them to the cinder and ashes of a blacksmith's forge, but found that they washed white. They must date from the making of the road, as they are covered by the upper layers, and the supposition may be hazarded that we have here traces of fire lighted on the flint foundation of the road, perhaps to make a smoke as a beacon for the laying out of the 16 miles of straight road from the south.

In the north of the park the long straight line ends; if continued, it would lead into Hippenscombe, a steep-sided valley more than 200 feet deep, commanded by high ground on all sides, and by Fosbury camp on the east. To keep on the high ground the Roman road, still well defined, bends westward through an angle of 60°, and skirts round the heads of the two branches of the coombe, by Chute Heath and Scots Poor, bending round to the north and north-east until a prolongation of the original line is reached, more than two miles from where it was quitted. This remarkable bend is roughly a half-circle of a mile and a quarter radius, and is followed for a mile by the county boundary between Wilts and Berks. The ridge of the road is still very plain over Chute Heath, raised three or four feet above the surface, and six or seven yards wide. The semicircle ends near Tidcombe, and another straight line is entered upon which lies between Haydown Hill (850'), near Fosbury camp on the north of Hippenscombe, and Barbury Castle (871'), 16 miles distant, and visible from Haydown. Highways having parish boundaries along them for a mile and a half, and traces of the ridge, mark the course of the road from near Tidcombe by Marten and Crofton to Savernake Forest, and the ridge is shown on the old Ordnance map nearly on to Savernake House, close to which Sir R. Colt Hoare found it visible. The course continues through the forest, on the north-east of the avenue and nearly parallel with it, and it is shown on the Ordnance map for nearly 300 yards near the boundary of the forest pointing towards the east side of the Roman camp *Cunetio* at Folly Farm, on a commanding position (644') overlooking the valley of the Kennet, and some 200 feet above it. The Roman camp, so far as it can now be traced, seems to have been about 300 yards by 250 yards. Roman coins, pottery, and other objects have been found within it from time to time, and a Roman well was opened to a considerable depth about 30 years ago.   The Roman road onwards, leaving the camp on the east, seems to have followed the course of Cock-a-trip Lane towards Werg, and there are indications of a road slanting down from the camp in that direction.   Hereabouts the road from Speen to Bath, which will be presently followed (p. 268), crossed.

A Roman road is shown on Sir R. C. Hoare's map of *Cunetio* (1819) coming from the direction of Old Sarum, and joining the road from Winchester on the south of Folly Farm.   It cannot now be traced there, but across the enclosures at Braden Oak, half-a-mile distant, the ridge is just observable on the same line.   From Old Sarum, a road with parish boundaries along it runs in this direction for four miles to Porton Firs, and the road continues on, pointing to Sidbury (735′), a doubly-intrenched earthwork rivalling Old Sarum in magnitude.   From the north entrance of it what Sir R. Colt Hoare calls a bold, broad, and straight raised causeway, resembling a Roman road, runs for more than a mile to Everley, intersecting a barrow in its course.[1]   There is nothing definite beyond to indicate the course of a Roman road.

From the south side of the Kennet valley the Roman road may be seen rising up to Poulton Down, and the course is almost straight onwards for six and a half miles to the edge of the chalk escarpment between Badbury and Chisledon.   It is marked by a line of highways up to Poulton Down, across which is a green track with the ridge almost entirely effaced.   At the highest point on Poulton Down (700′) one can see Folly Farm, and northward, through the notch in the escarpment near Badbury, into the vale beyond, and there can be little doubt that the road was laid out straight between this notch and the high ground near *Cunetio* from intermediate points.   A lane follows the line to Ogbourne, from which onwards the Roman road was evident when Sir R. C. Hoare saw the turnpike road being made on it in 1818.   There is a very slight turn at a high point (560′) near Whitefield Farm, and beyond a

[1] *Ancient Wilts*, p. 180.

parish boundary runs along the road for a mile. Near Badbury the road bends to the east and descends into the valley; and it then lies straight between a high point (556′) on the edge of the chalk escarpment and the point of junction with the Roman road from Speen. At the time of Sir R. Colt Hoare's survey the workmen making the new road described the old road at Badbury Wick, then called High Street, as having been composed of flint, 10 or 12 feet wide, with large sarsen stones for a foundation in wet and marshy places.[1] In the fields beyond the Liddington road the Roman road then appeared " very broad and high crested," and could easily be seen and traced. A parish boundary runs along the present road for three-quarters of a mile towards the junction of the Roman roads. Here, three miles due east of Swindon station, where foundations of buildings and many remains of Roman pottery and coins have been found, Sir R. Colt Hoare fixed a station to which he gave the name of *Nidum*. In Iter XIII. of Antonine *Spinæ* figures as 15 M. P. from *Durocornovium*, whereas Speen is really 34 miles from Cirencester. Fifteen miles brings us to the junction of the roads, and adding 19 miles, the distance on to Speen, makes up the total at the head of the Iter. It is a reasonable supposition that a station has dropped out, but on Wanborough Plain, 15 miles from Speen, there are also Roman remains. A Latin name given to a supposed station is misleading, and *Nidum* is the more unfortunate as it is the name of a station in Iter XII. of the Itinerary of Antonine, the site of which is uncertain, but which cannot be here. Unfortunately, too, the name has been perpetuated on the new Ordnance map.

[1] *Ancient Wilts, Roman Æra,* p. 94.

CHAPTER X

(10) *Silchester to Speen, Bath, and South Wales.*—A road from Silchester to Speen (*Spinæ*) appears in Iter XIII. and in Iter XIV. of Antonine. It issued from the west gate, and its course is indicated by a highway with a parish and county boundary for three and a half miles, beyond which there is little or no trace to Speen. It is natural to suppose that the Kennet was crossed at Newbury, and in the streets on both sides of the bridge the lowest layers of ancient road metal, some three feet thick, has yielded remains believed to be of Romano-British date. A Romano-British cemetery was also found near the goods-station in excavating gravel for ballast.[1] At Speen, a mile to the north-west of Newbury, on the higher ground between the Kennet and the Lambourne, is the site of *Spinæ;* and beyond that there is little or no trace of the road nearly as far as *Cunetio.* It probably followed roughly the line of the Bath road from Newbury towards Hungerford,

---

[1] *Trans. Newbury Field Club*, vol. ii. p. 126.

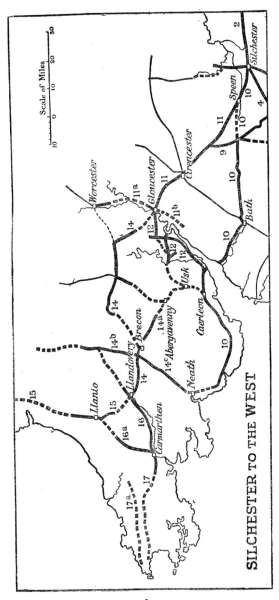

SILCHESTER TO THE WEST

Scale of Miles

Silchester
Speen
2
10
10
4
11
10
9
Cirencester
Bath
Worcester
11
11a
Gloucester
11b
14
12
10
12
12
Usk
14
Caerleon
Brecon
14a
Abergavenny
14b
10
Llandovery
14c
14
Neath
Llanio
15
16a
Carmarthen
16
15
17
17a

and continued on by Rudge [1] to the north of Hill Barn, on the south side of the Kennet valley, about three-quarters of a mile to the east of Mildenhall, where the ridge remains on the down. Sir R. Colt Hoare, in his map of *Cunetio*, shows the Roman road onwards from this to the lane at Cockatrip Cottage, along the south of a field in which many coins and fragments of pottery, etc., have been found. It would seem that the road from *Spinæ* slanted down into the valley from near Hill Barn, passing, about a quarter of a mile to the south of the camp at Folly Farm, *Cunetio* on a commanding position 200 feet above the valley. Sir R. Colt Hoare shows on his map, and mentions "an earthwork of a square form by which the parish church was surrounded," [2] which he supposed to be a Roman camp, and called Lower Cunetio. Traces are visible, but there is good reason to think that they are not Roman. There are undoubted evidences of a Roman settlement in the more sheltered valley, and it may have succeeded the camp above after the country became more peaceful. This is confirmed by the coins found in a well opened to a depth of 25 feet by the Rev. C. Soames. With much pottery, including fine "Samian" ware, the coins dated from Augustus to Honorius and Arcadius, a period of 400 years, but those in greatest quantities date from the middle of the third century to the middle of the fourth. [3]

There are no traces of the Roman road onwards, but Sir R. Colt Hoare records the finding of many skeletons, with Roman coins, black and red glazed pottery, about half a mile to the west, in a field on the north of the London road, near where it is crossed by the railway. There may have been here a cemetery by the side of the Roman road. Stukeley supposed that there were remains of a camp near the river in what is now the garden of the Master of the College. R. Gale found that he was mistaken, but it seems likely that the Roman road crossed the Kennet thereabouts. The first trace of the road is three miles further on, near West Overton, where a short length of the ridge is

---

[1] In a well at Rudge was found the curious brass vessel bearing the names of five Roman stations on and near the Wall of Hadrian. A Roman pavement was also discovered there in 1723.

[2] *Ancient Wilts*, p. 34.

[3] *Wilts Archæol. and Nat. Hist.*, May, 1821, p. xix, p. 36.

shown on the old Ordnance map on the north side of the
Bath road, and it is still traceable. A little further on,
near West Kennet, Sir R. Colt Hoare observed the causeway five feet high and 18 or 20 feet wide, and the line of it
seemed to be nearly certain from the top of the hill overlooking Fifield.[1] The ditches were distinct in 1884. The
road passed round Silbury Hill on the south side, and
although it has been ploughed up it is now sometimes
traceable by the eye. In 1867, to test Mr. James Fergus-
son's contention that Silbury was upon the Roman road,
some sections were cut across the road, and the trenches
on each side of the road were found at a distance of 18 feet
apart, and were traced round the hill to the straight portion
of the road on the west of it. The road there ranges with
the south side of the mound, and it can be traced in dry
summers. From Silbury the course is straight for two
miles and a half to a point (665′) on a spur of Calston Hill.
A slight curve brings the road in a mile and a half to the
700 feet contour line on the north side of Morgan's Hill,
along which it is carried on a terrace about five yards wide,
cut into, and embanked upon, the slope of the hill. Where
it passes round the head of a coombe at Horse Coombe
Bottom Wood, the banking up is considerable. To this
point parish boundaries follow the road for three miles,
and after a break of half a mile follow it again for three
miles. On the west of Morgan's Hill the Roman road is
joined by Wansdyke, an intrenchment which crosses the
Wiltshire Downs for many miles, and is plainly traceable
from the borders of Hampshire to this point. It follows
a devious course, and varies a good deal in size ; over
Morgan's Hill it is unusually crooked, and consists there
of a ditch with a rampart on the south side, and a slight
counterscarp on the north. The crest of the rampart is
nine or ten feet above the down, and 18 to 20 feet above
the bottom of the ditch, as they now exist, and rampart
and ditch together measure 80 to 90 feet across. Coming
over the downs it joins the Roman road at an acute angle,
and Stukeley thought that there was " incontestable
proof that it was in being before Roman times," and that
the Roman road followed the course of Wansdyke.[2] Local
antiquaries have generally insisted on the pre-historic, or

[1] Hoare's note-book.   [2] *Itinerarium Curiosum*, p. 142.

at least pre-Roman age of the great intrenchment, and that the Roman road took the line of it. If so, as Sir R. Colt Hoare pointed out,[1] we must suppose that Wansdyke, which winds about through all the rest of its course, takes an absolutely straight line for three miles to Wans, and then again for 10 miles on to Ashley Wood, making together 13 miles of straight course along which a Roman road follows it. The excavations made by General Pitt Rivers in Wansdyke close by[2] plainly proved that the work is Roman or post-Roman in date, and the earthworks themselves show the manner in which the pre-existing Roman road was made use of by the makers of Wansdyke. The road, which is on a terrace five or six yards wide along the steep northward slope of the down, is joined from the south by Wansdyke—here a deep ditch with a high rampart on the south of it, together some 27 or 30 yards wide —at the head of a coombe about a quarter of a mile east of the Calne road; and there the whole character of the intrenchment changes. There is no longer a rampart on the south of the ditch, but the edge of the embanked terrace has been raised by material excavated from a ditch along the road, and thrown up as a counterscarp, some four feet high, on the north of the ditch, the steep slope of the down rendering any other defence unnecessary, and the whole is not more than 17 yards wide. It is probable that the rampart crossed the road and joined the counter-scarp, but that is now obliterated by a cart-track. As the slope of the hillside gets less steep going westward, a rampart appears on the south side and increases in height, and near Smallgrain plantation, to the east of the Calne and Devizes road, there is a considerable bank on either side of a hollow way.

From the junction of Wansdyke the course of the Roman road is in a straight line between the top of Morgan's Hill (847′) and the south end of Lansdown (760′), 18 miles distant; and it may be seen from the former to continue in that direction for three miles to near Wans. Beyond

---

[1] *Ancient Wilts*, p. 27 (1819). A few years later he considered that the Roman road was probably formed on a Belgic boundary bank (*Roman Æra*, p. 106).

[2] Samian ware was found on the original surface beneath the rampart (*Excavations, etc.*, iii. p. 243).

the Calne and Devizes road the ground falls, and cultivated land is entered upon, and a hedgerow followed by a parish boundary marks the line, and there is little other trace of road or dyke for one and a quarter miles, when it appears more plainly for half-a-mile to the south of Stockley. The old Ordnance map shows the ridge all along, and Sir R. Colt Hoare mentions hereabouts traces of a ridge with a bank and ditch on the north side. Hedges followed by parish boundaries continue the line, and looking back from near Wans a straight line of hedges can be seen rising out of the lower ground towards Morgan's Hill. On nearing Wans the hedgerow and parish boundary bend towards the north, and soon the latter is the only trace now left of the Roman road, though Sir R. Colt Hoare's map (1819) shows the ridge to within one-eighth of a mile of the lane which the parish boundary joins about 60 yards south of the cross roads, and follows across the Calne road. Then the ridge of the Roman road is plain in the belt of trees on the east of the grounds of Wans House, with the remains of a ditch on the north-east side, along which the parish boundary runs. The ridge bends round to the house, and there it is effaced for 200 yards; but the parish boundary marks the line of it on to the Chippenham road (475'). Then another straight line is entered upon pointing to high ground (600'), south of Ashley Wood, 10 miles distant, overlooking the Avon valley near Bathford. This line is nearly parallel with that from Morgan's Hill, and a quarter of a mile to the north of it, and is joined by a rough reversed curve. Sir R. Colt Hoare placed *Verlucio* at Wans, where much Roman pottery and other objects have been found, and thought that the road entered the station at the south-east angle and left it at the north-west angle. There are no remains of a camp, and there is no reason to suppose that the course of the road was affected by the station, which there is some reason to think lay to the north of Wans House. It would rather seem that, as at Elstree on Watling Street, two high points were made use of in laying out the road, the second being perhaps Calston Down (800'), near Oldbury, a mile north-east of Morgan's Hill, to which the straight line from Ashley Wood points.

At the Chippenham road Spye Park is entered, and for about 300 yards, where the ground was formerly ploughed,

a low undulation of the surface is all that remains of the
ridge.   It then appears plain for a quarter of a mile ; five
or six yards across the top and four or five feet high, having
on the north side traces of a ditch with a ramp or counter-
scarp outside, showing the modification of the road by
the makers of Wansdyke.   According to a section made
here by Sir R. C. Hoare's surveyor in 1820, " the *agger* was
20 feet broad and six feet high, and the smaller one rising
on the outer side of the ditch nine feet wide." [1]   A steep-
sided valley appears to have been crossed by winding up
stream and back again to the same line, as in many other
instances, and on the west side of the valley the banking
up of the road on the low side is plain, and there seem to
be remains of the road surface on both sides of the valley.
The ridge continues for a quarter of a mile on to another
valley, beyond which there are now no further traces within
the park, though the ridge is shown on the old Ordnance
map, and on Sir R. Colt Hoare's map (1819).   There are
some indications of the ridge outside the park, and in less
than a mile a line of hedgerows, with remains of the ridge
here and there, and followed by parish boundaries, takes
up the same straight line for upwards of eight miles.   From
Bowden Hill (500′) the entire course of the road to Ashley
Wood, eight miles, is in sight.   Sir R. Colt Hoare noticed
that a cottage built upon the Roman road at Forest Gate
was a free tenement,[2] a similar case to that already mentioned on the Foss road near Radstock (p. 216).   On the
east of the canal near Lacock he describes the ridge as being
20 feet wide and four feet high with a regular trench on the
north side.   Where the Roman road is crossed by the railway, one and a half miles north of Melksham, the parish
boundary leaves the line of the road and no trace appears
for a quarter of a mile ; and then the course of the road,
followed by a parish boundary, curves round a low hill as
if to avoid the highest part, and resumes the same straight
line.   Near Neston Park Sir R. Colt Hoare noticed the
agger six feet high with a ditch on the north side, and in
the park he described a section as being four paces wide
and six and a half feet high, at top a layer of loose stones,
then one of earth, lower down a stratum of stone grouted

[1] *Ancient Wilts, Roman Æra,* p. 83.
[2] *Ibid.*, 1819, p. 82.

or pounded,[1] the lowest foundation being concealed. It would seem from a note on the authority of Mr. Leman that " the bank and ditch of Wansdyke were there plainly visible, as made on the foundation of the previous Roman road." [2] At Wraxall Wood, about two miles further on, the remains of the road are described by Sir R. Colt Hoare as 30 feet wide and nearly 12 feet high,[3] and he says that the flat stones which formed the foundation of the road, with a concrete layer over them, were still to be seen. The old Ordnance map shows the ridge in a straight line for two and a half miles between Neston Park and Ashley Wood. There is now to be seen a somewhat dilapidated fence wall of rough local stone, of which there is plenty about, upon what appears to be the bank of Wansdyke on the north of the track of the Roman road. Through the arable land beyond, an undulation of the surface is all that remains, which would hardly be noticed if it were not in the line of the road marked by a parish boundary. There seem to be some traces of the Roman road with Wansdyke alongside it towards Ashley Wood, in which Sir R. C. Hoare found the ridge visible at the beginning of the nineteenth century.

A supposed Roman road branching from the Foss on the south of Bath, and joining this road hereabouts has been already noticed (p. 216).

On the high ground above Bathford, Wansdyke leaves the Roman road and turns south-west, and the course of the latter through Bathford is probably along the line of Chapel Row, and round the bend of the Avon to Batheaston, where it is joined by the Foss road (p. 215), and thence with a sharp turn straight for two miles to Walcot, where the road into the Roman city of *Aquæ Solis* (or *Sulis*) probably turned off. The road followed by Iter XIV. went on through Weston and by North Stoke to Bitton. The grass lane over the hill from Weston towards Bitton is on the line of the Roman road. For 200 yards westward of the lane to Keston digging in places revealed a layer of stones not more than eight inches thick beneath the turf, and a trench cut across showed the width of it to be about 12 feet. A similar layer of stone was found where a foot-

[1] *Ancient Wilts, Roman Æra,* 1819, p. 79.
[2] *Ibid.,* 1812, p. 27.   [3] *Ibid.,* 1812, p. 77.

S

path continues the line down the hill towards Weston.[1] Near North Stoke the Bristol road takes up the straight line on to Bitton.

The Itinerary distances agree fairly well with the positions of the stations from Silchester to Bath, but the course of the road from Bath westward has been the subject of much difference of opinion. Iter XIV. of Antonine's Itinerary gives the distances of the stations, beginning from *Aquæ Solis*, thus—

To Trajectus	vi.	M.P.
,, Abone	ix.	,
,, Venta Silurum	xiv.	,,
,, Isca	ix.	,,

At six miles from Bath is Bitton, where there are traces of a Roman camp and evidences of a station, but only an insignificant stream, the Boyd, to be forded, and to give the name *Trajectus* to the station; and there has been a disposition to assume that *Trajectus* is connected with a ferry across the Severn. Harris,[2] and others following him, placed *Trajectus* at Aust, 20 miles from Bath, deriving that name from Augustus, and Gale put it at Oldbury, three miles still higher up the Severn. Bishop Clifford[3] declined to throw over the Itinerary, and supposed that the name *Trajectus* has reference to a passage across the Avon near Bitton, by a British road going north and south. Coxe,[4] writing in 1801, continued the road from Bitton to St. George's Church, by the south of Redland Down, and over Durdham Down, where he says it was still high and visible to Sea Mills near the confluence of the river Trim with the Avon, three and a half miles from the mouth of the latter; and there he places *Abone*. Thence he says that paved remains of the road still existed, joining the turnpike road, and so on to the Severn. On Durdham Down, the ridge still appears as a low undulation on the surface. It was opened on the west of the Stoke road, near Durdham Lodge, in 1900.[5] Under three inches of turf a paving of large

---

[1] *Proc. Soc. Antiq.*, xx. 249.   [2] *Archæologia*, vol. ii. 1763.
[3] *Somerset Archæol. Soc.*, 1876.
[4] *Tour in Monmouthshire*, p. 13*.
[5] Martin, *Trans. Bristol and Gloucs. Archæol. Soc.*, vol. xxiii p. 309.

stones was found, bedded on a layer of about six inches of earth, under which was about a foot of calcareous earth and limestone. Traces of the side ditches were found, about 16 yards apart, and one foot two inches to one foot nine inches below the crown of the paving of the road, which appears to have been about 20 feet wide. The distance from Sea Mills to *Venta Silurum* across the Severn is rather more than thirteen miles, compared with the 14 M. P. of the Itinerary.

Bishop Clifford objected that vessels going down the Avon from Sea Mills with the tide would have the ebb against them in the Severn going up to Southbrook, and places *Abone* near King's Weston Park, with a landing-place on the Severn. There is no doubt that in former times the tide flowed up to the foot of the high ground on which he places *Abone*. It would do so now if it were not banked out, the land for a width of one and a half miles bordering on the Severn being several feet below high-water level. The Bishop suggests a causeway,[1] and mentions Chittening Street, which is three miles from the mouth of the Avon, as probably representing it. Another way to the Severn is marked " Roman road " on the new Ordnance map. But such a causeway appears an insufficient provision for crossing an estuary four miles wide with a 40 feet tide without a sheltered port at hand such as *Abone* at Sea Mills would have afforded. From the mouth of the Avon there is a straight run of about five miles in a slanting direction across the Severn to Caldicot Pill, below " The Shoots " and clear of rocks, and by choosing the ebb or flow a favourable tide in either direction could be secured for the passage. Waiting for a change of tide would not have been a serious matter, and a causeway may have been available at favourable times.

On the Welsh side of the Severn a landing-place may have existed near the supposed Roman camp at Sudbrook, of which now only half remains on the cliff near the Severn Tunnel pumping station. Shelter was certainly afforded by St. Pierre Pill and Caldicot Pill on either side of the camp, and about two and a half miles apart. The former is the outfall of the Meyric stream, and Caldicot Pill is the estuary of a stream originally the Twrch, Latinized as

[1] *Bristol and Gloucester Archæol. Assoc.*, vol. iii.

Tarocus, and now called the Troggy. Both pills were used by shipping until the construction of the railway, and they were so used from very early times. A grant, preserved in the *Liber Llandavensis,* of the land lying to the west of St. Pierre Pill, then called Pwll Meyric, includes the free right to bring ships to land in the mouth of the pill, and another grant of land includes the free right of bringing ships to land in the mouth of the Troggy (*in hostio Taroci*), *i. e.* in Caldicot Pill. The grants probably date from the seventh century, and the conclusion is that at that time both were old-established harbours.[1]

For the passage to and from the Avon, Caldicot Pill would be the more convenient harbour, and a paved causeway has been traced from Caldicot to Caerwent, less than two miles distant. It enters Caldicot common field, where it is soon lost under the soil, it is marked for a short length as " track of Portway " on the Ordnance map, and is joined by the present hauling way for about half-a-mile, and is then lost as far as the Nedern brook.[2] Coxe in 1801 found vestiges of an ancient paved causeway between the brook and the eastern gate of Caerwent, which, within the memory of man, had been more perfect.[3]

The Roman station *Venta Silurum* at Caerwent measures about 527 yards from east to west, and 440 yards from north to south. The road runs through the middle from the east to the west gate. It is 20 feet wide, paved with cobble stones. The road to the south gate was found to be 13 feet to 27 feet wide, one foot six inches thick in one place, and six inches in another, and to be roughly pitched in places.[4] From Caerwent the road runs on straight for upwards of a mile, followed for three-quarters of a mile by a parish boundary, to Five Lanes, where there were vestiges of a causeway in a field close to the present road in 1801.[5] The present road then turns to the north, but in a mile and a half resumes the same line near Penhow. Two miles further on, at Catash, the course of the Roman road appears to follow a parish boundary on the north of the present road.

[1] This information from the *Liber Llandavensis* has been courteously furnished by Mr. James G. Wood, F.S.A.

[2] Ormerod, *Strigulensia,* 1861, p. 20.

[3] Coxe, *Tour in Monmouthshire,* p. 17*.

[4] *Archæologia,* vol. v. part 2, p. 204.   [5] Coxe, p. 29.

It leaves the latter again near Woodville, and passing by Summerhill, crosses the Usk and enters Caerleon in the line of High Street.

The rectangle enclosed by the walls of the Roman *Isca leg. II. Augusta*, which can still be traced, measures about 530 yards by 450 yards. It is thus of the same dimensions as *Venta Silurum* and rather larger than *Clevum*. It is situated on the north-west bank of the Usk just above the confluence of the Afon Llwyd, and on a navigable river. Leland writes of Caerleon in 1536–9 that " very great shippes might wel come now to the towne as they did in Romayne tyme, but that Newport bridge is a lett." [1] It is the starting point of Iter XIV., which has now been followed in the reverse direction from Silchester, and also of Iter XIII. by *Burrium* to Gloucester, Speen, and Silchester. *Burrium* is placed near Usk, the distances from Caerleon, and from Abergavenny, *Gobannium* in Iter XII., corresponding. There appears to be no trace of the road from Caerleon to Usk, nor of a Roman road onwards in the direction of Gloucester. The indications of a Roman road on to Abergavenny are only a few short lengths of boundary along the present road, and no Roman remains are now to be seen at Abergavenny. Horsley, however, mentions bricks found about the old castle with the stamp of *Leg. II. Aug.*, and says that the military way was still visible.[2]

Camden [3] cites a passage quoted by Leland from a poem by Necham (1215–1225), in which *Julia Strata* is mentioned in connexion with the Usk, entering the Severn.[4] On this hint the author of the spurious Itinerary of Richard of Cirencester gave the name *Via Julia* to his Iter from Bath to St. Davids. Sir R. Colt Hoare made it *Via Julia Maritima*, and Scarth extended it eastwards to Marlborough, Speen, and Silchester. The only authority for this name is the reference above mentioned.

On the west of Caerleon " traces of an ancient road " are marked on the old Ordnance map on the south of the road

---

[1] *Itin.*, part vi.   [2] *Britannia Romana*, p. 319.
[3] *Britannia*, iii. 109.
[4] *Intrat et auget aquas Sabrini fluminis Osca*
   Præceps ; testis erit Iulia Strata mihi.
It is now said that *Iulia* should properly read *vilia*.

to Pilmaur, which may be those mentioned by Coxe. The old Ordnance map also marks as Roman the road onwards from Bassaleg, and at about a mile from that place traces of the ridge remain, and the road is laid out in a straight line for a mile and a half. A little further on is a square camp by the side of the road, one mile beyond which the modern road turns south to St. Mellon's, Rumney, and Cardiff.

Cardiff Castle has generally been assumed to have been where the Roman road crossed the river Taff; but it is probable that the old road continued straight on where the modern road turns south to St. Mellon, and crossed the Rhymney river near Julian's Farm, whence a line of roads and parish boundaries for a mile and a half to the Taff at Gabalva, and for a quarter of a mile in the same line between Llandaff and Ely Bridge may indicate the line of the Roman road.

There is no doubt, however, that a Roman fortress guarded the mouth of the river Taff two miles lower down, at Cardiff Castle. The Roman walls have of late years been discovered beneath the mediæval ramparts along the eastern and northern and part of the western sides; the Castle buildings covering the rest of the latter, and the southern side. The rectangle of the Roman walls, which are 10 feet thick, measures 190 yards from east to west, and 204 yards from north to south. There is a gateway in the northern face, but none on the east, and nothing is known as to gates on the south and west. The walls have round bastions on the outside, suggesting a late date, and coins found in excavating the walls show that the fort was occupied down to A.D. 363.[1]

It may be assumed that there was a Roman road north-wards to the outlying fort at Gellygaer, 13 miles distant, a walled fort, 134 yards by 128 yards, with rounded corners. The road may have gone over Craig Llanishen at Mor Graig, and by Caerphilly, and along a line of old road, leading to Heol Fawr, but the course is not ascertained. From Gellygaer, Heol Adam may represent a Roman road on to another fort at Penc-y-arran nine miles further north, where Roman remains have been found.

Beyond Ely Bridge the modern road to Cowbridge is fol-

[1] *Archæologia*, lvii. 335.

lowed by parish boundaries for half-a-mile near Caerau, where there are remains of a Roman camp about half-a-mile to the south of the road, and after a break, again for a mile and a quarter, where the boundary follows the old road up the hill to St. Lythan's Down, while the modern road goes round it. On the west of the down the parish boundary again follows the road over the hill, and continues along the modern road for a quarter of a mile along Coedriglan Park. There are other indications which seem to show that the present road follows the line of the Roman road through Bonvilston and onwards, deviating from it at Llantrythid Park, between Old Post and Three Ashes, and again at Stalling Down, to avoid hills. Here the characteristic features of the setting out of a Roman road appear. From Stalling Down (400′) one mile east of Cowbridge, westward to Stormy Down (310′) $11\frac{1}{4}$ miles distant, there lie in a straight line half-a-mile of highway, half-a-mile of Cowbridge street, and then three and a half miles of the main road as far as Brocastle. The same line is continued by a lane in the direction of Ewenny Abbey for a mile, and then there is no trace for two and a half miles across the Ewenny and Ogmore valley. A lane with a parish boundary along it for a quarter of a mile then takes up the same line for three-quarters of a mile on the south of Laleston. After an interval of a mile the straight line is joined by the main road, which follows it for a mile, with a parish boundary along it from Park Isaf to Twmpath-y-ddaiar, where there is a Roman camp (331′) and a clear view along the straight line back to Stalling Down 11 miles distant. The main road and the parish boundary turn off northward to Pyle, but the line of the Roman road continues on with visible traces in nearly the same line by Heol-y-sheel, and Heol-las, to Kenfig. From Kenfig the road seems to have turned north along Water Street, past what is marked as a Roman monument on the old Ordnance map, to Beggarsbush on the main road near Margam. It possibly continued over the Margam mountain, and by the east of Mynydd-y-gaer crowned by a camp, to join Sarn Helen near Neath. This would be more in accordance with Roman practice than a course along the shore of the Neath estuary, commanded on the land side by high and steep hills. The difficulties of the way across the sands from

Margam to Neath at the end of the twelfth century are described by Giraldus Cambrensis. The finding of two milliaries, near Port Talbot and near Aberavon, may be thought to show that the road passed those places, but the original positions of the stones are unknown.[1] No traces of the road are known, nor are there any vestiges of a Roman station, nor of Roman remains of any sort at or near Neath.

Iter XII. of Antonine has been thought to pass over the road which has now been followed. Camden, who supposed that transcribers had " strangely confounded the two Iters from *Calleva* to *Isca*, and from *Maridunum* to *Viriconium*," placed *Bomium* near Cowbridge, *Nidum* at Neath, *Leucarum* at Loughor (Llwchwr), and *Muridunum* (*Maridunum*) at Carmarthen. In this he was followed by the writers of the spurious Itinerary of Richard of Cirencester, and by Bishop Bennet and others. If Parthey and Pinder are right in supposing that the first eight lines of Iter XII. were transferred by mistake from Iter XV., the next station to *Muridunum* would be *Leucarum*, XV. M.P. distant, compared with 19 miles from Carmarthen to Loughor; the XV. M.P. on to *Nidum* would compare with 13 miles on to Neath; and the XV. M.P. on to *Bomium*, with 22 miles to a point near Cowbridge, 27 miles (the Itinerary distance) from Caerleon. Neither the total nor the intermediate distances agree; no traces of Roman stations are known at Loughor, Neath, or near Cowbridge, although an altar, coins and pottery have been found at Loughor; and there are no evidences of a Roman road between Carmarthen and Neath. *Muridunum* appears in Iter XV., and *Ridunum* in the *Tabula Peutingeriana*, in both XV. M.P. from *Isca Dumnuniorum ;* while *Maridunum* of Ptolemy is stated by him to be in the country of the Dimetæ, that is to say in South Wales. Whether the latter is the *Muridunum* mentioned in Iter XII. must remain uncertain.

(11) *Speen to Gloucester.*—There is no trace of this road until the tertiary beds are quitted near Wickham, four and a half miles from Speen. There a road is entered upon which is straight in general direction for nine miles to Baydon Hill (786′), and points in the reverse direction to

[1] One of them had made voyages as ballast in a pilot boat.

Speen. For some miles from Wickham the present road
is not straight, being sometimes on the line of the Roman
road, but generally winding from one side of it to the other.
There is little trace of the ridge until beyond Poughley,
where a piece of it remains on the north of the present
road, which then takes the line of the Roman road, and
by its elevation between hedges wide apart shows traces
of the ridge. The road is soon narrowed to 12 or 15 feet
between the fences, and the Hare and Hounds Inn stands
on the line of the Roman road. At Woodlands Farm the
present road turns south at a right angle, and the course
of the Roman road can be traced straight on across a meadow
by an undulation of the surface, with browner herbage.
In the arable field beyond the stones of the road were
ploughed up 30 to 35 years ago. In three-quarters of a
mile the present road rejoins the Roman road and follows
it through Baydon. In the beginning of the nineteenth
century the Roman road hereabouts is described by Bishop
Bennet [1] as presenting an elevated crest raised many feet
above the downs in various parts. Beyond Baydon a
parish boundary follows the present road for a mile, and
continues on in the same straight line for three-quarters
of a mile further to Peaks Down, and then the Roman
road is traceable across the down in the direction of Wanborough Plain Farm. Near this place remains have been
found, which may mark the site of the Roman station
already mentioned (p. 265) as having dropped out of Iter
XIII. between *Durocornovium* and *Spinæ*. The road
thence turns due north-west, and runs straight for Callas
Hill on the escarpment of the chalk half-a-mile to the
east of Wanborough, and a straight road is entered upon
which passes through Stratton St. Margaret's to Blunsdon
Hill (494′), seven miles distant. On this length of road,
a mile and a half from Stratton St. Margaret's, and three
miles due east of Swindon station, is the junction of the
Roman road from Winchester, where Sir R. C. Hoare placed
a Roman station to which he gave the name of *Nidum*,
which has already been referred to (p. 265). There the
Roman road lies on the west side of the present road, and
the ridge is so shown on Sir R. Colt Hoare's map. Looking
back from Blunsdon Hill the road can be seen to the south-

[1] Lysons, vol. i. p. 200.

east mounting up Callas Hill, the chalk downs beyond being
visible; and towards the north-west Cricklade and Cirencester, the latter ten miles off, with the Cotswold hills
beyond, are in sight. The road, where it has not been encroached upon, is 50 or 60 feet between the fences, but it
has generally been narrowed on one side or the other,
and in consequence the straightness is not so apparent.
On Blunsdon Hill there is a slight turn, and a straight road
runs to Calcott Bridge, near Cricklade. There is now an
interval of nearly a mile at Cricklade, in which, however,
portions of a causeway across the meadows were dug up
at the end of the eighteenth century.[1] Parish boundaries
run along the road from Blunsdon to Seven Bridges, Water
Eaton.

From the north-west of Cricklade a straight road runs
for three and a half miles to Driffield Cross (320'); looking
back from which Blunsdon Hill is plain, and the road up
the chalk escarpment at Callas Hill can be seen in clear
weather. Near Driffield Cross there is a round turn and
then another straight road leads to Cirencester. This
straight line points from Driffield Cross, to the south-
east gate of Cirencester, and to high ground (700') near
Duntisbourne House, four miles beyond Cirencester. If it
were not for the elm trees along the road Driffield Cross
would be visible from the entrance of Cirencester. Parish
boundaries follow the road for two miles and three-quarters
through Driffield Cross to Siddington. The road is not
much raised above the surface until Preston is reached, and
then for about half-a-mile it is carried across the meadows
to Cirencester, on a causeway on the south side of the river
Churn.

From Wanborough Plain Farm, where there is a decided
change in the general direction, to Cirencester, no part of
the road is as much as half-a-mile away from an absolutely
straight line 19 miles long. The road here bears the name
of the Ermin Way, as it is called by Higden, the monk of
Chester, and under that name it goes on through Cirencester
to Gloucester. It constituted the main street of the Roman
Corinium, or *Durocornovium,* and between the south-east
gate and the church is now represented for 150 yards by
Tower Street, the rest being built over. North of the

[1] Sir R. C. Hoare, *Ancient Wilts, Roman Æra,* p. 97.

church, Dollar Street and Gloucester Street occupy the site
of the same Roman street, which measures seven furlongs
from gate to gate. About midway it was crossed at right
angles by the principal street about half-a-mile long from
gate to gate, now represented by Lewis Lane and Queen's
Lane, and the other Roman streets and buildings so far as
they are known appear to be laid out parallel to, and at
right angles with Ermin Way. The enclosing walls, which
are still traceable, do not suggest the rectangular plan of a
Roman camp; and they enclose an area far larger than the
largest Roman camps such as *Glevum, Venta Silurum*, or
Isca. In these respects Cirencester resembles Verulam,
Colchester, Chichester, and Silchester; British towns rebuilt
and afterwards walled by the Romans.

From Cirencester the course of the Roman road, followed
by the present road, is straight for eight miles to Gloucester
Beeches (900′), with a slight turn on high ground (500′)
at Daglingworth Down, and with some twisting up the hill
by Stratton, due in part at any rate to modern improvement
of the gradient. The ridge of the Roman road makes its
appearance soon after leaving Cirencester, and on the high
ground it is now seven yards wide and four to five feet high,
and near the third milestone as much as six feet high.
There are ditches at the sides in places which may be in part
Roman, or may be more recent quarries for road materials.
Looking back from this high ground the chalk downs, which
are crossed by the Roman road, 20 to 22 miles off, to the
south-east, are visible. Beyond Gloucester Beeches the
road passes round the head of the Side valley at Nettle-
combe to Birdlip, and winds down the hill, followed by
parish boundaries. Near Little Witcombe, five miles from
Gloucester, a straight line is entered upon which, as one
looks back from Wootton Cross one mile east of the
cathedral, points to high ground (900′) above Birdlip Hill.
Stukeley says that from Cirencester the Roman road appeared with a very high ridge and very straight for eight
miles to Birdlip Hill,[1] and Camden says that on Birdlip
Hill it showed a very bold ridge and appeared to have been
paved with stone.[2] Where the road is crossed by the railway to Cheltenham the Roman paving was found entire 18
inches beneath the surface. The road turned to the south

[1] *Itinerarium Curiosum*, p. 67.   [2] *Britannia*, i. 384.

at Wootton Cross and entered *Clevum* (or *Glevum*) by the north gate, together with the road from the north. In Northgate Street, Gloucester, the Roman road was found about ten feet six inches below the surface, composed of stones of irregular shape bedded in mortar on concrete.

The walls of the Roman *Clevum*, as traced by Bellows,[1] included a rectangle 510 yards by 435 yards. The north corner was in the Cathedral cloisters, the east corner at the junction of Aldgate Street and King Street, the south corner inside the turn from Brunswick Road into Parliament Street, and the west corner at the angle of the County Prison facing Commercial Road.

(*a*) The road from Gloucester to the north appears to have been on the line of the Tewkesbury road. At King-holme Roman burials occur on both sides of the road, and at Longford a closely-pitched pavement was found six feet below the surface of the road. To the north of Twig-worth, a parish boundary follows the present road for about a mile, and beyond that there seem to be no indications of the course for more than nine miles, and then Stratford, at the boundary of Gloucestershire, seems to mark the line. From about four miles north of Stratford, highways, tracks, footways, and a parish boundary continue in a line between Stratford and Worcester for more than six miles. A foot-way crosses Croome Park from Kinnersley to a highway in the same line for half-a-mile, and then a footway leads to and follows a belt of old trees in the same line for half-a-mile, followed for a quarter of a mile by a parish boundary. A narrow strip of enclosed land on the west of Kempsey Common, with the footway alongside, continues the line to a broad lane leading on to Napleton, where the straight course is lost for a quarter of a mile. A lane continues it for a mile, and then a footway takes up the line for a mile and a quarter, passing on the east of Timberdine Farm, to the Worcester road. After crossing the latter the course is across pasture fields, marked by a line of old trees, to a footbridge over Duck Pool, and then a highway takes up the line, pointing in the direction of High Street, Worcester.

There is no definite trace of a ridge along this line, but there are appearances which suggest that the Roman road materials have been removed, leaving a shallow hollow along

---

[1] *Proceedings of the Cotteswold Field Club*, vol. vi. p. 150.

the course of the road. The same thing is to be seen along
the course of Riknild Street through Hindlip Park, on the
north of Worcester (p. 222); and several other instances
where the ridge has been removed, and the materials have
been dug out, leaving a shallow trench, have been already
noticed.

(b) Parish boundaries along the present road from
Gloucester towards Bristol, at Hempsted, Quedgeley,
Moreton Valence, and on the south of Stroud Water, for
lengths of a quarter of a mile to a mile and a half, seem to
indicate the line of the Roman road in that direction.

(12) *Gloucester to Redbrook, and to Caerwent.*—From the
west gate of *Clevum* the Roman road proceeded in a
north-westerly direction straight to the Severn. The low
meadows between the two branches of the river are crossed
by a causeway which is noticed by Leland, and is now
called Over Causeway. It is raised some five feet above
the meadows, and an old man lately described it as having
been paved in the middle with cobble stones in his father's
time, the width of the road being then the same as it is
now, about 10 yards. The approach to Telford's bridge at
Over turns off to the north, and the causeway beyond
has been destroyed, but a bit of the old road with the
narrow bridge over the old course of the river Leadon, in
line with the causeway, is still to be seen on the west of the
river between the approach to Over bridge and the railway.
The Ordnance maps mark a road along the low eastern
bank of the Severn northward to Maisemore Bridge as a
Roman road, on what evidence is not apparent.

On the west of the Severn the course of a Roman road
is marked on the Ordnance map through the meadows by
Moorcot to Minsterworth, where it falls into the present
road to Newnham and Lydney. There are no traces of it,
and the road near Minsterworth is below the level of the
Severn floods. The road westward from Over points to high
ground (630') on the south of Mitcheldean, and is straight
for four miles except where, at Linton, it leaves the straight
line for half a mile. It is followed by parish boundaries
for a mile and a quarter, and with some improvements of
gradient appears to follow the course of the Roman road
to beyond Halfway Bridge. It there turns towards the
north-west, but the direct line is continued on by a lane,

a footway and parish boundaries for two and a half miles, and then the present road by Huntley rejoins, and follows the direct line onwards for a mile.   Ogilby [1] in 1675 followed the road by Huntley, but shows the direct road on his map, marking it " the worst way."   The course of the Roman road on towards Mitcheldean is uncertain.   The post road on the old maps continues on from Mitcheldean by Drybrook to Monmouth, and " traces of Roman paving " are marked on the Ordnance map at many points on the road onwards between Mitcheldean and Drybrook, and it is marked as a Roman road on to Ruardean; and beyond " traces of Roman paving " are marked along a narrow road at Lower Lydbrook, near the Wye.

" Traces of Roman paving " are marked in many places on the new Ordnance maps on the roads of this part of the country.   They are marked on roads which were improved as turnpike roads in the latter part of the eighteenth and the early part of the nineteenth century, and which were in some cases afterwards improved as mail roads.   The traces are marked where the roads have been diverted or lowered to improve the gradients, and also where the roads are sunk in the ground as if from the effects of long wear previous to the laying of the paving.   Paving was no doubt to be seen where it is marked, and traces of it, or more frequently of a line of kerbing, are still visible here and there, but it by no means follows that it was always Roman.   In the Forest of Dean, paved Roman roads still remain, and on old roads and tracks which have lately been modernized, the traces may in some cases have been of Roman paving.[2]   But when roads were improved in the early part of the last century, a paved foundation was not unfrequently laid, and if

---

[1] *Britannia*, pl. 15.

[2] A belief has arisen that the use of wheeled vehicles was forbidden in the Forest, and that consequently all roads except those made in recent years must be Roman.   In a summary of the " Laws and Customs of the Miners of the Forest of Dean," supposed to date from the time of Edward I., as given by Rev. H. G. Nicholls (*Iron-making in the Olden Time*), it is stated that " carts and waynes are prohibited; " but what really was prohibited was to " make carriage " of the mine otherwise than by the measure called Bellis, so that the King might have his rights.   That is, the quantity of ore was not to be measured by cart or wain load in assessing the royalty, and proves that carts and wains were in use, and that a load was then, as now, a variable quantity.

repairs were afterwards neglected, the road wore away, and the paving-stones became exposed on the surface. This was the case in 1881 on the Shrewsbury and Holyhead road, constructed with a paved foundation in 1823, and may well have been the case in the neighbourhood now under notice, where the roads were much worse cared for.

At or near Mitcheldean a Roman road turned to the south, but the course is uncertain for a mile and a half. At three-quarters of a mile south of Mitcheldean, the Ordnance map marks " traces of Roman paving " for half-a-mile beyond the turn in the present road near Abinghall, but it seems likely that a lane along the higher ground from the Folly to near Gun's Mill may be the course of the Roman road. To the south of Gun's Mill, the paving, consisting of squared blocks, and apparently Roman, was entire not many years ago. The Ordnance maps mark " traces of Roman paving " in six places in the mile and a half onwards by Tibbs Cross to Littledean, and the kerb bordering is still to be seen here and there in the improved road.

At Littledean two roads from the east converge. They are for the most part narrow, sunk, crooked roads, with little to suggest a Roman origin, but both are marked all along on the Ordnance map with " traces of Roman paving." On the road which passes from the Severn side through Newnham to the south of Littledean, a paving of squared blocks is said to have been entire not many years ago, but some of the " traces of Roman paving " are marked on the maps in places where the road must have been worn into a deep hollow before the paving was laid. Westward from Littledean, in continuation of this road, " traces of Roman paving " are marked on the Ordnance maps in eight places in the mile and a quarter to Cinderford Bridge, and in eight other places onwards to the Speech House, but with the recent improvement of the road, all have now gone. On the hill between the Speech House and the railway-station, a strip of bordering kerbstones and some of the paving, said to be Roman, remained not long ago. A paved Roman road in the same direction still remains in the Forest to the west of the railway, and to the north of the present road, and it can be traced for some distance pointing towards Worcester Lodge. It is of squared stones bordered with kerbing, and about eight feet wide. It may have joined a Roman road along the course of the old post road from Mitcheldean, which seems to be that of a road mentioned in a perambulation of the bailiwicks of the Forest in the tenth year of Edward I. (1283), as *altam viam tendens apud Monmouth*.[1]   The course onwards is by Coleford Meend and Lower Berry Hill to Cherry Orchard near Newland railway-station, where a road from Clearwell through Scatterford and Newland joins.   Traces of Roman paving are marked along the latter on the Ordnance maps, and Mr. J. G. Wood describes it and the kerbing as being still visible after rain, and plainly Roman.   This road is in continuation of a straight road to Bream Cross in the direction of Lydney Park, two and a half miles distant.

A parish boundary, and then a county boundary, follows the road from Cherry Orchard down to the Wye at Redbrook, where probably the river was crossed to reach *Blestium*.   The old post road turns off to the Wye bridge at Monmouth, passing by Duffield Lane on the south-west of the Kymin.

The Ordnance map marks as a Roman road a track in the wood on the north side of the road from Staunton to Monmouth, which a county boundary follows for half-a-mile from Staunton.   The track is crossed twice by the modern road, and can then be followed as a narrow, hollow way northwards to the river Wye at Hadnock, a mile and three-quarters above Monmouth.   It has the appearance of an old packhorse road, which, however, may have been in use in Roman times, and even earlier.   Roman coins have been found in the workings of the iron mines near Clearwell, and coins, fibulæ, and other Roman objects have been met with deep in the cinder-heaps of the old bloomeries, especially at Whitchurch, on the west of the Wye, two miles to the north of Hadnock; showing that the conveyance of the hæmatite ore for reduction to bloomeries, situated where wood fuel was plentiful, went on at least as early as the Roman occupation.

Continuing southward from Littledean, traces of paving are still to be seen in the sunk road near Grange; and along the present modernized road in Sutton Bottom " traces of Roman paving " are marked in six places on the Ordnance map.   At about half-a-mile from Soudley the present road

---

[1] *Trans. Bristol and Glouces. Antiq. Soc.*, vol. xiv. p. 362.

diverges from the old track, and along the latter traces
of paving can still be seen. It soon divides—one track
going straight to Soudley Camp, and the other through
Soudley Plantation to the Dean road at the ford. Soudley
Camp occupies the end of a ridge between two brooks;
it is triangular in shape, each side measuring about 60 yards.
From Soudley Ford the paving of the Roman road is plain,
and onwards traces and remains of a paved road distinctly
Roman are almost continuous along the forest track called
Dean Road. Towards Blackpool Bridge the pavement
remains almost perfect for 150 yards. It consists of blocks,
about eight inches square, between kerbstones five or six
inches wide, and 10 to 18 inches long. In some places the
kerbstones are held in place by blocks of stone outside,
breaking joint with them, and this seems to be the case
where a less massive kerbstone has been used. Towards
Soudley the width is as much as nine feet, but the more
perfect length towards Blackpool is eight feet wide. It can
be traced on both sides of the stream at Blackpool to
a ford on the west of the bridge. The bridge is not 100
years old, but it may be noticed that there are plain traces
of paving leading to it, as well as to the ford. The Roman
paving is again plainly visible on the Dean road for 40 or
50 yards about 100 yards south of the Blakeney road, where
it is nine feet wide. Neither this nor the Roman paved
road to the west of the railway, near Speech House station,
is noticed on the Ordnance maps. The Dean road continues
on as a green track through the forest for another mile and
a half to Old Croft, and on to Allaston, and then, following
a track and footway, it falls into the main road from
Gloucester on the north of Newerne.

In the perambulation of the bailiwicks already referred
to, Dean Road is called *via Regia*.

From Newnham southwards to beyond Blakeney many
" traces of Roman paving," now no longer visible, are
marked along the road on the Ordnance maps, but there is
nothing characteristic of a Roman road. About a mile
south of Blakeney, the road takes a more direct course, and
follows the same general direction from The Purlieu past the
point of junction of the Dean road, and through Newerne and
Lydney, and then a footway by Lydney House follows the
same line to Aylburton, where the present road takes it up.

T

In Lydney Park many Roman remains, the foundation of a temple, and of a large villa, with baths, pavements, statues and objects in bronze and iron, show it to have been a place of some importance.

The Ordnance maps mark " traces of Roman paving " in the present road on the south of Aylburton, but the road seems to have been altered by modern improvements, and it may be doubted if the paving, now no longer visible, was Roman. It appears probable that the old road continued straight on by Sandford Bridge to Alvington. On the south of Alvington, after crossing the brook, the present road turns to the eastward, but a track and a footway straight on up the hill continues the line to join the present road near Brookend, and seems to be the old course. The road follows the same line onwards for a mile, except at a twist where the stream at Wyeford is crossed, and then there is a slight turn on high ground, and a parish boundary follows the road for three-quarters of a mile to Stroat, where a slight deviation seems to have been made. The present road continues straight in general direction to Tidenham, and then bends towards the west, and about a mile beyond Tidenham the course of the Roman road leaves the present road, and is followed by a footway to the north of Tutshill. In 1861 the road showed its line through the turf, and was found as a rude pavement in sinking foundations for buildings.[1] It could be traced down to the Wye at the site of the ancient bridge across the river at the south end of Piercefield Park, where remains of piles were clearly to be seen at low water. The structure was visible when the condition of the river was favourable until some five or six years ago, when the remains were explored and destroyed in a search connected with the supposed authorship of Shakespeare by Bacon. They seem to have been the framing of the foundation of the pier of a timber bridge. The track can still be traced on the Monmouthshire shore, ascending through Castle Wood to The Mount, Chepstow, from which a parish boundary and a road mark the line to Hardwick Hill. The parish boundary turns along the Newport road for more than a quarter of a mile, and then the Ordnance map marks " traces of Roman paving " on it. In about half-a-mile the road passes through Pwll Meyric,

[1] Ormerod's *Strigulensia*, p. 3.

and straight on to New Inn Smithy, where it bends to the south, and the course of the Roman road continues on in the same straight line to a highway leading to Crick and Caerwent.   In 1732 Horsley described it on the east of Caerwent as a military way large and remarkable.[1]

(13) *Iter XIII. of Antonine.*—The present road from Gloucester, which turns from the line of the old post road towards the north-west at about five miles from Gloucester and passes through Huntley, is marked as a Roman road on the Ordnance maps with " traces of Roman paving " along it.   The road was improved by Telford as the mail road to Ireland by way of Milford Haven in the earlier part of the last century, and it has no appearance of Roman laying out.   It is crossed by the road from Mitcheldean to Newent, also marked as a Roman road on the Ordnance map, and with " traces of Roman paving " for some little distance. Another road northwards from Mitcheldean, by Mitcheldean Road railway-station to Brooms Ash, seems to have quite as much claim to be considered a Roman road   From it the Ordnance map marks a Roman road branching to Bury Hill near Bollitree, where Roman remains have been found. They consist mainly of coins and fibulæ; and it has been thought that there are traces of hardware manufacture.[2] It has been supposed to be the site of *Ariconium*, a station in Iter XIII. of Antonine's Itinerary, xv. M. P. from *Clevum ; Blestium*, the next station westward, xi. M. P. distant, being placed at or near Monmouth   Bollitree is 13 miles from Gloucester, and 13 miles from Monmouth by way of Goodrich Ferry, and there is little evidence of a Roman road either from Gloucester or on to Monmouth, where no Roman remains are known.   At Usk, where *Burrium*, the next station in the Iter, has been fixed, Roman pottery, bricks and coins were formerly found.   *Burrium* occurs also in Iter XII., and the distances from *Gobannium* at Abergavenny in that Iter, and from *Isca* at Caerleon in Iter XIII., accord in fixing *Burrium* at or near Usk.

A route for Iter XIII. by Mitcheldean and Redbrook suggests itself as an alternative.   *Ariconium* would then be near Littledean, and *Blestium* near the Wye.

(14) *Gloucester to Llandovery.*—The Roman road appears

---

[1] *Brit. Rom.*, ii. p. 469.
[2] Rev. H. G. Nicholls, *Iron-making in the Olden Times.*

to have turned off to the north-west after the Severn was crossed, but there is little trace of it.   In a perambulation of the Forest of Dean, A.D. 1228, the road from Leadon bridge at Over to beyond Newent is called *"Magna Strata"*; and in a perambulation A.D. 1300 it is called " *regalis via* " :[1] names which furnish a presumption that it was a Roman road, though it is doubtful how far the present road follows the same course.   Beyond Dymoke there is more of the character of Roman setting out, the course of the present road lying in straight lines from point to point in very nearly the same direction for nine miles and a half to Stretton Grandison.   The road must have fallen into the continuation of Riknild Street coming from Worcester, of which there are unfortunately no traces.   From Stretton Grandison the course is perhaps straight to the present Hereford road near Shucknall, then following the old road to Lugg Bridge, and thence along a highway followed by the boundary of the city of Hereford for three and a half miles ; and on very nearly in the same straight line to the station *Magnæ* at Kenchester, parish boundaries runing along the present road for most of the way.   At *Magnæ*, the road coming southward from Wroxeter, which has already been noticed (p. 70), crossed.   Westward from *Magnæ* the course appears to be followed by the present road as far as Garnons, and a parish boundary across the Lawns in the same general direction probably represents the line on to the Hay road to the west of Garnons.   From Maddle Brook a parish boundary follows the straight road for nearly two miles to Staunton-on-the-Wye.   A mile and a half further on the straight road ends on a high point, and turns to avoid the Wye.   The course onwards is uncertain.   A parish boundary again follows the road for half-a-mile between Winforton and Whitney, where the modern road crosses the Wye ; but the Roman road seems to have continued on the north side of the river, and is probably represented by a lane turning south at Bronydd to the square camp near the bank of the Wye, which must have been crossed near Hay. Between Hay and Brecon there are but few indications of the course of the road.   At about a mile from Hay a piece of straight road begins, pointing for two miles straight to a conical hill near Three Cocks, and on it are two places called

[1] J. G. Wood, *Woolhope Field Club*, 1901.

Ffordd fawr (great road).   The course is perhaps followed roughly by the modern road to beyond Bronllys.   From near Pont-y-bat-fach, one and three-quarter miles west of Bronllys, a line of highways crossing the main road at Pen-isaf-waun, and continuing on in the same line to within one mile of Brecon, on which the name of Ffordd fawr again occurs, may probably represent the Roman road.

(a) This was joined near Brecon by a Roman road from Abergavenny, of which however there is little trace.   To the west of Crickhowell the course seems to have been followed generally by the present road as far as Glanusk, where perhaps the latter may turn more to the south.   Two miles on, near Pen-y-ffordd there are remains of a Roman camp, and thence it perhaps made direct for the Bwlch between Mynydd Buckland and Cefn Moel, on the east of which remains of the Roman road were formerly to be seen. A parish boundary then joins the present road, and after following it for half-a-mile, continues along a lane for a mile in the same direction to the south end of Allt-yr-ys-grin. The same line prolonged joins the present road in a mile.   A stone pillar, probably a milliary, dedicated to Victorinus (A.D. 265–7), which formerly stood by the side of the road at Scethrog,[1] seems to show that the present road follows the course of the Roman road on the west of the Brecon and Merthyr railway.

West of Brecon the road called Hen-heol (old street) is no doubt the Roman road leading to the walled fort at Aberyscir on the north bank of the river Usk, on the east of the confluence of the Yscir.   The fort called the Gaer, of which some of the masonry foundations remain, measures 207 yards by 140 yards.   From it Roman roads went in four directions.   Of Hen-heol to the east some traces remain, but the course of the others is not so plain.

(b) The road northwards appears to have joined a road branching at Brecon, and passing over the hill to the east of Pen-y-crug and by Sarnau and Cefn Sarnau.   It is supposed to have crossed the Honddu at Castell Madoc, from which a parish boundary follows the present road for a mile and a half, and it then mounted the high ground, on which from Post-y-pabell for two miles a parish boundary

[1] It was removed and in use as a garden roller for some time and again set up on the roadside.

runs along the track. The course is then uncertain. It is supposed to cross the Wye near Castell Llechryd, a camp 200 yards square close to Builth Road railway-station, and to have gone over Llandrindod Common, where traces are still visible on the west of the railway between Howey and Llandrindod. The ridge has been robbed of the stone, and the broken-up surface is overgrown with gorse, which when in blossom marks the line of the road. It is shown on the new Ordnance map continuing in nearly the same direction on the north of Llandrindod, over Cefn Llys pointing to Caibach on the east bank of the river Ithon. The remains of a raised causeway made of large pebbles and gravel and overgrown with grass,[1] visible in 1786, no doubt was part of this road. The river must have been crossed to reach the Roman camp, about 141 yards by 132 yards, known as Castell Collen. The road is supposed to have continued on to Caersws near Newton (p. 71), Montgomery, by Caerfagu, over Camllo Hill and up the Clywedog valley, and over Bwlch-y-Carnau, but the course is uncertain.

(c) *Sarn Helen to Neath.*—The Roman road to the south from Aberyscir, called Sarn Helen, seems to have crossed the Usk about half-a-mile west of the camp, where a parish boundary runs at right angles from the river to the end of a ridge, and then along the top of the ridge and along a lane to Heol Fwt-y-drain. The parish boundary continues along a road to the south of Mynydd Illtyd, but the Roman road is shown on the new Ordnance map, and is said to be visible, about half a mile more to the north-west. The course onwards is uncertain as far as the upper end of the Senni valley. It seems to have crossed the ridge between that valley and the Llia valley near Maen-llia and to join the present road from Brecon to Merthyr, and to have followed it for a mile, the pitching being lately visible in many places at the side of the road.[2] It then turns south-west over the mountain by Maen Madoc, crossing the valley of the river Neath near its source. The old Ordnance map shows it onwards over the steep escarpment on the west of the valley and descending into Nant-hir, but Col. Morgan traces it down the Neath valley by Cefn-ucheldref, where it remains well defined, to Gwaun-y-maerdy and over the moun-

[1] *Archæologia*, iv. p. 4.
[2] Col. W. K. Morgan, *Archæol. Camb.*, 1907, p. 130.

tain in a well-defined course into Nant-hir.   Near Cefn-gwen-
y-nawg this course joins that marked on the old Ordnance
map, and the old road is visible.[1]   Onwards towards Ton-
y-ffildre traces of the paving appear in the morass wherever
the water has washed away accumulations of soil, and at
Ton-y-ffildre the paving is 14 feet wide between the kerbs,
and both pavement and kerbs are in good condition on the
open ground between that and the camp at Ton-y-castell.[2]
Hereabouts in 1760 the causeway was described as being
uninterrupted for a mile, a raised road 40 feet wide with a
ditch on each side.[3]   The camp, now usually called Colbren
Camp, was excavated by Col. Morgan in 1904; it measures
about 145 yards square inside the ramparts, which were
found to be of turves upon a foundation of timber, and is
supposed to date from the first century.   From the south
gate of the camp Sarn Helen runs straight to Clwydall-
banwen, a parish boundary following it for a mile and a
quarter, and the pitching and kerbing remaining visible.[4]
It then mounts the high ground of Cefn-hir-Fynydd, and
for six miles a track followed by a parish boundary marks
the line of the road.   The pitching can be traced all along,
showing through the soil at intervals, and in places the kerbs
are to be seen.[5]   From Lledrafel, where the old road is visible,
the parish boundary marking the course slants down into
the vale of Neath along the high ground above Ynis-y-
geryn, about two and a half miles from Neath, where it may
have crossed the river, or may have followed the course of
an old road between the present main road and the river
and crossed further down.   It is said to have been visible
in the marsh there at the beginning of the last century.[6]

From Aberyscir the Roman road westward has been supposed to have crossed the Usk with Sarn Helen and continued along the south bank of the river, but it seems more
likely that it kept on the north bank, generally in the course
now followed by highways, to one mile beyond Rhyd-y-
Brew, where the modern main road joins it.   Hereabouts the
causeway was visible in 1774.[7]   At Trecastle the narrow
Cwm Dwr, through which the modern road passes, was

[1] loc. cit.   [2] loc. cit.
[3] Strange, Archæol., vol. i. p. 290.   [4] Archæol. Camb., 1907.
[5] loc. cit.   [6] Hoare's Giraldus Cambrensis, clvi.
[7] Strange, Archæol., vol. i. p. 292.

avoided, and the Roman road ascended the Trecastle mountain to the south of it. A rough track now represents what, until about 1785, was the coach road between Brecon and Llandovery. Near it in 1769 a stone supposed to be a milliary, inscribed to Postumus, A.D. 258, was found. On the edge of the west escarpment of the mountain (1267') the road passes close to the remains of a large camp called Pigwn, now a good deal obliterated. The Ordnance map shows a rectangle 466 yards by 400 yards, with another 366 yards by 300 yards placed diagonally within it, and not far off a small camp 46 yards square. The road then winds down by Black-cock (where oxen used to be kept to help the coaches up the steep hill) to Hafod. The course of the road is then straight for a mile to the head of a deep valley, which it passes round, and again runs straight for a mile, and then winds down the hill by Fron. The road appears to have crossed the river Brân near Llandovery Castle. At Llanfair-ar-y-bryn, half a mile to the north of Llandovery, where Roman remains have been found and where traces of a fort, about 194 yards by 130 yards, were formerly visible, *Luentium* of Ptolemy has been placed, but with little reason. Four Roman roads meet there. In a north-easterly direction there was formerly " a very notable Roman way of gravel and small pebbles." [1] The present road, straight for two miles, follows it, and about three miles further on Sir R. C. Hoare observed a causeway upon Cefn Llwydlo, where it is now visible. The road is said to have crossed the river Yrfon at Glancamddwr, and to have joined the Roman road which has been described (p. 294) from Aberyscir to Castell Llechryd and Castell Collen. It is also said to have gone from Glancamddwr in a north-easterly direction to Castell Collen, crossing the Wye near Newbridge.

(15) *Llandovery to Llanio and Sarn Helen.*—The road onwards from Llandovery seems to have crossed the river Towy in the direction of the railway-station. On the north of the river the course appears to be shown by a highway leading over Bwlch Trebannan to Cynfil Cayo, and the Roman gold-mines at Gogofau, and on to a Roman road bearing the name of Sarn Helen running north. This Sarn Helen is parallel to, and 24 miles west of the continuation

[1] Gough's *Camden*, iii. 142.

northward of the Sarn Helen from Neath to Aberyscir.
It is followed by highways in a straight line for two and a
half miles south of Bwlch Blaen-y-corn, and crosses over
the mountains, where it is very plain, to Llanfair Clydogau,
and then it went on by a course which is obscure to Llanio,
where at Caer Castell, Roman pottery, coins, and inscribed
stones have been found, but no traces are now to be seen
on the surface. Llanio has been supposed to be the *Luentium*
of Ptolemy, but with perhaps less claim than Llandovery.
A Roman road bearing the name of Sarn Helen can be
plainly traced in a direct line due north from Llanio for
nine miles, and it is visible further on at Cwmllechwydd, and
again at Llwynrhyngell, a mile and a half to the north of
the river Ystwith. It is supposed to have crossed the river
Dovey at Penallt near Machynlleth, where Llywd noticed
a Roman fort, and a broad hard way of pitched stones from
it to the waterside in a straight line for 200 yards, and 10
or 12 feet in breadth.[1] This road is supposed to have joined
the Sarn Helen, which has been followed southwards from
Conovium (p. **77**).[2]

(16) *Llandovery to Carmarthen.*—Soon after the river
Towy was crossed at Llandovery, a Roman road branched
off at right angles to Carmarthen. It has been traced
in the grounds of Blaen-nos, and about a mile further
on, the present main road is supposed to take the line of it,
though as far as Llanwrda it lies under a steep hill in a
position not usual for a Roman road. At Abermalais the
modern road turns south, but the Roman road ascended
a ridge of high ground overlooking the Towy valley, and is
represented by a line of highways passing by Cefn-glas-fryn,
and a mile and a half north of Llandilo. The modern road
is crossed two miles west of Llandilo, and again a mile and
a half further on at Broad Oak. Two miles further on
the line of highways following the course of the Roman road
rejoins the modern road at Pontdulas, but the Roman
road may have crossed the Dulas rather higher up the
stream. There is little in the present road, narrow and

[1] Gibson's *Camden*, p. 652.
[2] There are three roads called Sarn Helen in South Wales and one
in North Wales. The Helen is supposed by some authorities to
represent *y lion*—the legion; Sarn Helen would be then " the
causeway of the legion." There is also Rhyd-y-Halen (p. 78).

crooked, though direct in its general course, to suggest a
Roman road; but paving here and there may be vestiges,
and it is locally known as the Roman road. It seems to
have passed over the hill by Pen-cae-gwyn to Halfway
House, where Ogilby,[1] who follows the old road all along,
marks (plate 84) and mentions (p. 168) "a paved causeway
continuing about 6 furlongs" along the road.   In less than
a mile an old highway on the south of the modern road takes
up the line by Llanegwad to Pen-yr-heol, from which the
main road follows the course of the Roman road through
Abergwili to Tanerdy near Carmarthen.   It seems probable
that it continued on in the same direction, skirting the north
of the town, and taking the line of Catherine Street to Picton
Terrace.   On the north-east of the town most of the Roman
remains have been found, but the site of the fort has generally been supposed to be on the south, including St. Peters
Church and the Parade.   Carmarthen, communicating with
the sea by the river Towy, is generally supposed to be
Maridunum of Ptolemy, one of two towns in the country
of the *Dimetæ* of which he gives the position, the other being
Luentium.   According to the degrees of latitude and longitude by which the positions are given, *Luentium* is about 25
miles south-east of *Maridunum*, so that if the latter be
Carmarthen, the former cannot be at Llanio, nor at Llandovery.

   (*a*) *Carmarthen to Llanio.*—At Tanerdy on the north-east
of Carmarthen a Roman road appears to have branched
northwards along the course now generally followed by the
main road to Llan-y-byther.   There is little characteristic
of a Roman road, but the names Sarnau and Ffordd occur
on it.   It is visible in places and is known as Sarn Helen.
It passed through Pencarreg, and at the beginning of the
last century it was visible in the bank of the river Teifi,
and in the meadows adjoining near Lampeter bridge.[2]
It no doubt joined the Roman road from Cynfil Cayo near
Llanfair Clydogau, and with it continued on to Llanio.

   (17) *Carmarthen to the West.*—Westwards from Carmarthen the course of the Roman road appears to be that
of the present main road for about three and a half miles.
It would seem then to have passed north of Castell-y-gaer,
a British earthwork with a Roman camp in the north-west

----

[1] *Britannia*, 1675.   [2] Hoare's *Giraldus Cambrensis*, p. clxiii.

corner of it, and to have followed the line of roads by Sarn-
y-bwla and Pen-yr-heol, through Mydrim, by Caerlleon, to
Post Gwynne. Fenton tells us that in 1811 [1] the road was
discernible in many places through the vale of Whitland
after drought, and that there was appearance of a ridge near
Post Gwynne; and that the peasants would track the road,
called Ffordd Helen, for miles, though except where it
formed the modern road there was little trace of it. Four
miles west of Post Gwynne is a road in the same direction,
called Park Sarnau, with a parish boundary along it for
half-a-mile, crossed by another road in a north-easterly
direction, with a parish boundary along it for three miles.
After an interval of six miles, a road followed by a parish
boundary for four miles runs westward from Castell Hendre,
past the remains of a camp a mile north-east of Ambleston,
supposed by Fenton to be the station *Ad vigesimum* of
the fictitious Itinerary of Richard. For about two miles
west from Ford, and from Brawdy to Whitchurch, the road
is marked Roman road on the Ordnance maps to within
about three miles of St. Davids.

(*a*) Parallel to, and about four miles north of this road,
is the road called Ffordd Fleming—Latinized into *Via
Flandrensica* or *Flandrica*. It passes along the top of
Prescelly mountain with a parish boundary following it for
six miles, and it continues on along the tops of the hills
eastwards to the borders of Carmarthenshire with the name
of Hên Ffordd (old road). It slants down the south side
of Foel Eryr, at the west of Prescelly, and can be followed
on to the north of Letterston. According to Fenton it
could be traced into the promontory of St. Davids, and
he correctly describes its appearance for the greater part of
its length as that of a hollow way, or old unfrequented lane;
though he says that on the south of Foel Eryr portions might
" be distinctly traced in various stages from an open foss
to the perfect raised pavement through soft ground." [2]
Fenton's accuracy has been questioned, and the raised
pavement cannot now be found. Many Roman coins have
however been found along its course, and it is probably
an older road, used, and perhaps improved in parts, by the
Romans.

[1] *Historic Tour in Pembrokeshire,* p. 479.
[2] *Historic Tour,* pp. 484, 566.

That is perhaps as much as can be said for the road from Carmarthen westward, but there is ground for supposing that the Romans occupied this part of the country at a comparatively early period.   A hoard of 200 Roman coins found enclosed in two leaden boxes, in a camp at Llanboidy, 14 miles west of Carmarthen, in 1692, were none of them of later date than A.D. 91.[1]

The Itinerary of Antonine does not appear to extend further than to the borders of South Wales, to Caerleon, Usk, Abergavenny, and Kenchester, but it is evident that Geoffrey of Monmouth's road from St. David's (*Menevia*) to Southampton, which Higden calls Erming Street, and Higden's Riknild Street from St. Davids to Worcester and Chesterfield, represent roads which can still be followed; though the Roman characteristics are not so plain as we go westward. The more noticeable Roman roads beyond the limits of the Itinerary are those which run across these roads from the south to the north, parallels as it were by which the mountain country was divided up and subdued.

---

[1] Llwyd in Gibson's *Camden—Gough*, iii. p. 135.

CHAPTER XI

CONCLUSION

In the foregoing pages the Roman roads have been grouped, for convenience of description, under the names by which they are now generally known, which have little relation to the original planning of them. It is interesting to try and follow the hints afforded by the roads themselves of the sequence in which they were laid out, and to see how far they agree with what is known of the Roman conquest and occupation of the country.

The systematic excavation of camps and forts in recent years has thrown light on the probable age of them and to some extent on that of the roads with which they are so closely connected. The method of determining the date of manufacture of the *terra sigillata* (Samian) pottery by the shape and ornamentation of the vessels has been applied also to date sites where fragments of such pottery have been found. Broken pieces of pottery to which a date of manufacture has been assigned corresponding to an early period of the Roman occupation are widely distributed in Britain; and, without questioning the conclusions that have been come to as to the periods of manufacture of pottery of certain forms and ornamentation, it may be felt that many years may have elapsed before Samian ware manufactured in Southern Gaul reached Britain and was broken and thrown away; and that such a method of dating is not more conclusive than that from coins. But while bearing this in mind it is addition to the evidence available.

It may be taken for granted that one of the first Roman roads laid out was from the landing places on the Kentish coast, perhaps, following generally an older track, and that the way across the tidal land to the ford at Stangate was

followed until the Thames was shut out by an embankment.
On the north of the Thames *Verulamium* would have been
made for, already at the time of the Claudian conquest
(A.D. 43) an important place; and from the higher ground
roads would have been soon laid out to *Camolodunum*,
taken about A.D. 44, and westward to Silchester. The
former, along the course of Oxford Street and Old Street
and on to Old Ford, must also have been the only access
by road to *Londinium* from the south until the Thames
was embanked, and a bridge was built. By A.D. 61 we
learn from Tacitus that *Londinium* was a place of considerable commercial importance,[1] and if because a bridge is
not mentioned it may be supposed that none then existed,
it is reasonable to think that one was built not long after.
A large proportion of the broken pottery found in Southwark in refuse deposited on the old marsh surface, far below
high-water level, is of the first century. It appears to have
been thrown away on the low ground embanked from the
river, and from the quantity of it, it must have come from
Londinium, and by a bridge, to land already embanked
from the river.

The road westward from Watling street to Silchester
(*Calleva Atrebatum*) must have been an early work. The
earliest dated Roman object, apart from coins, found at
Silchester is a fragment of brick, with a stamp bearing the
title of Nero, A.D. 54–68.[2] Following closely upon the occupation of *Calleva*, the roads radiating from it to Winchester,
to Old Sarum, and to Cirencester must have been laid out.
From Winchester it is likely that a road was continued
on to *Portus Magnus*, where, according to Geoffrey of
Monmouth, Porchester was one of the landing-places in the
invasion of Claudius A.D. 43.

The road from Silchester to Old Sarum was evidently
laid out with the object of reaching that British stronghold.
It was continued to the equally strong fortress at Badbury,
and thence it would seem in the first place to Poole Harbour.
When the road branching westward from Badbury was
continued, the object seems to have been to reach Maiden
Castle, the immense earthwork near Dorchester. From the

[1] " Copia negotiatorum et commeatuum maxime celebre."—
Tacitus, *Ann.*, xiv. 33.

[2] *Archæologia*, vol. 59, p. 366.

latter road access to the sea was again secured by a road to Weymouth.

The road from Silchester to *Corinium*, the capital of the *Dobuni*, was the original stem from which the road to Bath branched off at Speen. It was soon continued on to Gloucester, where the Roman *Clevum* or *Glevum* was planted about A.D. 50, if not earlier. The construction of the road from Speen to Bath, and on to the mouth of the Avon, must have followed not long after. The Silures, on the west of the Severn, were attacked by Ostorius A.D. 51 or 52, and the Roman camp at Sudbrook, on the west bank of the Severn, and the two walled stations *Venta Silurum* and *Isca leg. II. Augusta*, each as large as *Clevum*, and of similar proportions, perhaps originated with that campaign. They lie to the south of the high tract of country between the Wye and the Usk, *Venta* in communication with the passage across the Severn from the mouth of the Avon, and *Isca*, only eight miles further west, accessible by the navigable river Usk. Both these great camps must have soon been connected by a road with *Glevum*, and that may have been the beginning of Riknild Street. The road from *Isca* by Kenchester to Wroxeter completed the hold on that part of the country, which probably was not secured before the conquest of the Silures by Julius Frontinus A.D. 76.[1]

The road onwards from Caerleon as far as the river Taff, with the road leading northwards to the outlying fort at Gellygaer must have been made when that fort was built, which from the evidence of pottery and coins is supposed to be about A.D. 85. The latest coins found are of the time of Hadrian, and it is supposed that the fort was abandoned early in the third century.

Parallel with the road from Caerleon to Kenchester and Wroxeter, and apparently marking the successive steps in the subjugation of Wales, are other roads with a general direction from south to north. Sarn Helen, from Neath to Aberyscir, Castell Llechryd, Castell Collen and Caersws, and continued by Sarn Swsog, is communicated with at

---

[1] Frontinus, after he was succeeded by Agricola, became Curator Aquarum at Rome, and he has left us interesting information concerning the water-supply of the city in his work, *De Aquis Urbis Romæ*. A treatise of his on Stratagems, unfortunately, is without any reference to his campaign in Britain.

Aberyscir by roads from Abergavenny, and from Kenchester, and was doubtless also joined at Caersws by a road
from Wroxeter. From excavations made in forts on this
Sarn Helen it appears that the forts, and presumably the
road, date from the first century. Ton-y-Castell near
Colbren, excavated by Col. Morgan in 1904, furnished
objects of that date; the fort at Aberyscir is supposed to
date from before A.D. 85, Castell Collen from A.D. 85–90,
if not earlier, and Caersws from probably before A.D. 75–85.
Again, after the dividing ridge between the Usk and the
Towy has been passed over by the Roman road from
Aberyscir westward a road is crossed communicating with
the sea at Carmarthen, and with Sarn Helen at Castell
Llechryd. The more direct road from Llandovery onwards
crosses the hills to the valley of the Teifi, and communicates
with another Sarn Helen from Carmarthen, which passes
through Cardiganshire and North Wales, and joins the
Roman road from Chester to Carnarvon at Caerhûn on the
river Conwy. The fort at Tomen-y-mwr on this road,
20 miles south of Caerhûn, is supposed to date from as early
as A.D. 85. The early date at which forts were built and roads
were laid out through the heart of the Welsh hill country
is remarkable, and the abandonment of the former seems
to show that the country had become settled in the early
part of the third century.

It is to be observed that all four roads are in connexion
with the sea at their southern ends, and it may be that it
was by way of the sea that the country to the west of Carmarthen was occupied at the early date which seems indicated by the coins found near Llanboidy (p. 300), none of
which were later than A.D. 91.

The cross-roads from Winchester to Old Sarum, and
from Winchester by *Cunetio* to join the road from Speen
to Cirencester, are probably later than the roads radiating
from Silchester. The pig of lead found at Bossington on
the former road, dated A.D. 60, seems to show, however, that
at that date, or soon after, the road existed.

The twist in Watling Street on the high ground between
London and St. Albans suggests that the road may have
been set out from *Verulamium* as well as from the south.
From *Verulamium* to Wroxeter it was carefully laid out on
the high ground between rivers flowing north and south,

and probably following generally the course of an older track. From High Cross, where Watling Street crosses the Foss Way to Lincoln, the latter constituted part of the main road from the south to York and the north. York seems to have been approached in the first place by sea and the navigable Ouse, and afterwards from Lincoln by Humber Street and the Ouse, and even when a road northward from the Humber was made, York was cut off from it by marshes about the lower courses of the Derwent and its tributaries, so that it could only be reached by a road branching off six miles from the Humber. Later, when York rose into importance, early in the second century, a road without crossing the wide Humber was needed, and one was made branching four miles north of Lincoln and reaching York by Doncaster, Castleford, and Tadcaster, and that is the road to the north in Antonine's Itinerary. The way in which this road was laid out to avoid the lower courses of rivers draining into the Humber brought it within a few miles of the older Riknild Street. Causeway Lane connects them where they are less than four miles apart, and both roads are plainly traceable for four and a half miles more to the north. Traffic seems to have been diverted from Riknild Street to the newer Erming Street, other roads were made, and the older ones left, so that traces which remain are perplexing.

Riknild Street is crossed by Watling Street near Wall, and though it cannot be traced south of Worcester in the direction of Gloucester and Caerleon, there is no difficulty in following it northwards to near Chesterfield, and the junction with Watling Street made a connexion between Legion II at Caerleon and Legion XX at Chester along the Welsh borderland.

The Roman occupation of *Viroconium* is supposed to date from about A.D. 50, and the earliest houses, of wattle and daub, exposed in the excavations in 1912–1914, appear to date from A.D. 75 to 85. The road south from it to Kenchester could hardly have been made before the conquest of the Silures by Frontinus, A.D. 76, by which time it would have been joined by a road from Caerleon.

Watling Street seems to have been laid out first to Wroxeter, perhaps the lowest ford in the Severn, and the road on to Chester to have been made later, perhaps in the first place from Wroxeter.

U

Inscriptions at Chester are assigned by Dr. Haverfield to a date as early as A.D. 50–60, and it seems to have formed a base for the expedition of Suetonius Paulinus to Mona, A.D. 60, in which he was aided by a fleet. The road due north from Wroxeter went to Chester, though the route of Iter II. is not known. The road to Carnarvon (*Segontium*) branching from the road to Chester almost at right angles, several miles south of Chester, must have been made before A.D. 78, judging from the rapidity of Agricola's advance to *Mona* in the autumn of the year of his arrival in Britain in the middle of summer. Coins and pottery found at *Segontium* are supposed to show that it was occupied soon after A.D. 75, and the fort on Sarn Helen, at Tomen-y-mwr 20 miles south of the road, is supposed to date from as early as A.D. 85.

Cerealis' expedition against the Brigantes in A.D. 70 may have been on the west of the high ground between Lancashire and Yorkshire, but as a line of advance to the north it was barred by Morecambe Bay and the estuaries connected with it, and by the mountains and fells of Cumberland and Westmoreland. Agricola's advance ten years later, as described by Tacitus, must have been along the east flank of the high land, and Riknild Street, branching at right angles from Watling Street at Wall, probably represents the line of it. By A.D. 80 Lincoln and York were ready to co-operate in such an advance.

How far to the north the country of the Brigantes had been occupied by the Romans before Agricola's advance is uncertain. The lower parts, including the capital *Isurium*, were probably conquered without much difficulty, but the hill country to the west was not finally subjected until after the time of Hadrian. It must have been occupied partially, at any rate, before the advance northward was made, and it is uncertain how far the Roman roads and forts through the wild moors and fells had to do with this early occupation. Excavation of later forts on them has revealed earlier camps to which such a date has been assigned. The thorough excavation of the camp at Elslack, on the west of Skipton, afforded no clear evidence of its date, but the majority of a considerable number of fragments of *terra sigillata* ware found are assigned to the second half of the first century, and one of them to the first decade of that half-century; while of four coins deciphered, one is as early as B.C. 88, another A.D. 86, and the other two A.D. 333–337.[1]

The Roman road branching on the north of Catterick after skirting round the high country of the Brigantes crossed it from Greta Bridge to Brough, and in the nine miles there are the remain of five forts by which it was guarded. It is likely that at first it had to do with the subjugation of the hill country, but it seems that it was soon continued onwards, and before long reached Carlisle, which has afforded pottery of the earliest type found in the north, the date assigned to it being from A.D. 70 to 80. It may have been in this direction that Agricola, A.D. 80, opened up new tribes as far as the estuary called Taus, probably the Solway.

We learn from Tacitus that in A.D. 79 Agricola personally explored estuaries and forests and established forts in fresh districts, probably on and near the north-east coast, and that in the following year new tribes were explored as far as the estuary called Taus. The summer of A.D. 81 was employed in securing the country which had been overrun, and in defending the narrow space between Clota and Bodotria by forts. It thus appears that by A.D. 81 the country as far north as the Clyde and Forth was occupied by the Romans and protected by forts. It is likely that the country occupied comprised at first only that between the east coast and the high fells, afterwards crossed by the Roman road over the Cheviots; and to this the road through Chester-le-Street and Newcastle would have afforded access, with the advantage of communication with the sea. The abrupt change of direction in the Northumberland Watling Street at the river Dearness has been noticed (p. 164). After pointing to Newcastle for several miles the road turns through an angle of 65° towards Corbridge, for no apparent reason except a change in the objective point. A course avoiding the high moors, and giving access to a seaport seems to be one likely to be chosen for the first advance. But the early forts on the road over the Cheviots, attributed to Agricola, and the large quantity of pottery of the first century found at Newstead suggest that it was not long before the road by Corbridge and over the high fells was made.

[1] T. May, *Yorks. Archæol. Jour.*, vol. xxi. p. 147.

Stanegate seems to have been an early connexion between the roads on the east and Carlisle. It lies from half a mile to a mile south of Hadrian's Wall, and is nearly two miles south of it at Newbrough. It crossed the North Tyne by a narrow bridge of earlier date than the Wall, and it seems to have joined The Devil's Causeway near Bewclay, and probably to have communicated with Corbridge. Stanegate appears to have been a road along a frontier, protected by forts of an early date, afterwards superseded by the Wall of Hadrian.

In A.D. 82, Agricola, crossing over in the first ship, subdued by many battles tribes till then unknown, and planted troops in that part of Britain which looks towards Ireland [1] This seems to refer to crossing the Solway, and the occupation of the country to the north of it passed through by the Roman road from Carlisle, by Birrenswork near Middlebie, to the Wall of Antonine. In the following summer Agricola caused harbours to be explored by the fleet, and war was pushed forward on the north of the Forth by land and by sea.[2] The land advance, as the roads and forts show, was from Camelon by Stirling, and round the west of the Ochil hills to Ardoch and Strageath, one of which may have been the scene of the attack on the ninth Legion.[3]

The result seems to have been that the country on the north of the Forth, and Strathearn, was conquered, that the forts at Ardoch and Strageath were strengthened, and that the road was continued on to Gask with fortified posts at frequent intervals, and on to a large camp at Bertha on the Tay above Perth. In the following year, A.D. 84, Agricola fought his great battle of the Grampian Hills, and, summer being spent, led his army to the confines of the Horesti, and then slowly back to winter quarters. The Roman camps in Aberdeenshire and Forfar are probably relics of that campaign, and the absence of traces of roads in connection with them is not surprising under such circumstances.

If on a map of Roman roads those passed over by routes of the Itinerary of Antonine are marked, it will be found

---

[1] Tacitus, *Vit. Agric.*, c. 24.   [2] *Vit. Agric.*, c. 25.
[3] *loc. cit.*, c. 26.

that they are comparatively few, and generally constitute through communications which are often passed over by more than one Iter. Three Itinera, II., III., IV., pass over Watling Street from the Kentish ports to London, and from London three, II , VI., VIII., pass over it on to High Cross (*Venone*). Of these, II. follows Watling Street to Wroxeter, and on by an unknown and, unless the distances are wrong, an indirect course to Chester, while VI. and VIII. follow the Foss Way from High Cross to Lincoln. At Lincoln Iter V., coming from Colchester, joins and with VIII. from London follows Erming Street by Doncaster to York, being joined at Tadcaster by Iter II. from Chester. From York I., II. and V. go on together to Catterick, whence II. and V. continue to *Blatum Bulgium* and to Carlisle, and Iter I. to Corbridge and Riechester (*Bremenium*). It thus appears that a line of undoubted Roman roads from the Kentish coast to Carlisle is passed over twice, and in parts three times, by routes followed in the Itinerary; while the road from Catterick to Corbridge and Riechester beyond the Wall, and the road from High Cross to Wroxeter and Chester, are passed over once by Itinerary routes.

Iter VII. alone leads from London to Silchester, whence VII. and XV. go to the south coast and to Exeter, and XIII. and XIV. to Speen, where they part, the former going to Gloucester and Caerleon, and the latter to Bath and Caerleon. From Caerleon Iter XII. leads to Wroxeter, where it joins Iter II. leading to Chester, York, Carlisle, and *Blatum Bulgium*.

Iter V. and Iter IX. follow the same road from London to Colchester, but beyond that the courses of the Itinerary roads in East Anglia, and whether they pass over Erming Street south of Lincoln, are quite uncertain.

It would seem from the headings of Itinera I. II. and V. that the Itinerary dates from a time when the line of the Wall of Hadrian was roughly the Roman frontier, and *Bremenium* and *Blatum Bulgium* were outposts beyond it. But not only is all the country to the north of these stations beyond the scope of the Itinerary, but other considerable areas traversed by undoubted Roman roads have no Iter passing through them. All the hill country extending for 130 miles from Catterick and Carlisle to Watling Street, with a width of 40 to 70 miles, has only one Iter, II., through it, though it is crossed by many Roman roads, and Riknild Street passes through it from the south. The roads made for the subjugation of the country were apparently not required for anything more than local traffic after that had been effected. The same may be said of all Wales. Between the road from Chester to Carnarvon, and the possible course of Iter XII. along the south coast of Wales there is no Iter. Coins show that *Segontium* at Carnarvon, and Carmarthen (? *Muridunum* of Iter XII.) were occupied down to the beginning of the fourth century, while the forts on the Roman roads through the interior which no Iter enters seem to have been evacuated early in the second century.

Considerable areas in the south and east of England are entered by no Iter of Antonine. The country soon became settled, as the numerous Roman villas testify, and only such roads are found in the Itinerary as were required for through communication.

The relation of the Roman roads with older tracks has been touched upon in connexion with some of the roads. There is no doubt that the Romans made use of the older tracks, and that they sometimes improved them in places without laying them out afresh in the Roman manner. Lengths so treated occur on roads which are Roman in their general setting out, and detached bits of older roads seem to have been repaired or improved by the Romans, or under Roman influence.

The isolation of Roman roads from neighbouring villages has been noticed. It is rare to find an old village on a Roman road unless it happens to be the site of a Roman station, and many stations mentioned in the Itinerary of Antonine are not represented by any. Generally the old villages, representing Anglo-Saxon townships, near a Roman road, are on a water-course half-a-mile or more from it, and the site seems to have been determined by the presence of water, without regard to the Roman road, for which the new settlers had no other use than as a boundary to their township.

There may have been some provision for the care of the Four Roads mentioned as being under the King's Peace in the laws of Edward the Confessor, but generally with the Anglo-Saxon invasion a period of fourteen centuries of neglect and spoliation of the Roman roads began. English names were given them—a fabulous origin was attributed to them—they were robbed of their materials, and were destroyed wholesale in making the turnpike roads. To the last cause their destruction is chiefly due. Remains which have escaped damage by man's action appear to be little affected by centuries of neglect. They are generally found under an accumulation of soil, and it would seem that their future preservation would be best secured by leaving them as much as possible under such a protective covering.

INDEX